TRAIN WRECK

The End of the
Conservative Revolution

(and Not a Moment Too Soon)

BILL PRESS

WILEY

John Wiley & Sons, Inc.

Published by John Wiley & Sons, Inc., Hoboken, New Jersey
Published simultaneously in Canada

For general information about our other products and services, please contact our Customer Care Department within the United States at (800) 762-2974, outside the United States at (317) 572-3993 or fax (317) 572-4002.

Wiley also publishes its books in a variety of electronic formats. Some content that appears in print may not be available in electronic books. For more information about Wiley products, visit our web site at www.wiley.com.

Library of Congress Cataloging-in-Publication Data:

Press, Bill, date.
    Trainwreck : the end of the conservative revolution (and not a moment too soon) / Bill Press.
        p. cm.
    Includes bibliographical references and index.
    ISBN 978-0-470-18240-6 (cloth)
    1. Conservatism—United States. 2. United States—Politics and government—2001– I. Title.
    JC573.2.U6P76 2008
    320.520973—dc22

                                                                    2007044572

Printed in the United States of America

10 9 8 7 6 5 4 3 2 1

For Mark and Cari

Contents

Acknowledgments

As Hillary Clinton might say, and probably once did: it takes a village to write a book. And I'm grateful to the village people who helped with this one.

Once again, Ron Goldfarb, my literary agent and friend, hovered over this project from beginning to end. He helped create it and shape it. Thank you, Ron and Joanne.

For the fourth time, I've been blessed with the assistance of Kevin C. Murphy, a diligent researcher and keen editor. As a student of American history, Kevin provided many valuable insights into this overview of the conservative revolution. I haven't yet managed to write a book without him, and doubt I ever shall.

Eric Nelson is more than an editor: he's a good and demanding editor, I might add. For his enthusiasm, advice, and many contributions to the book, I am most grateful. As I am grateful to the entire, talented professional team at John Wiley & Sons, including Kitt Allan, Ellen Wright, Rachel Meyers, Laura Cusack, Mike Onorato, and Keira Kordowski. I'm proud to be associated with them.

And, as always, a special word of thanks to Carol, who bravely suffered through yet another ordeal of my being chained to the keyboard, while offering her own important suggestions along the way.

Introduction

The modern conservative movement is dead.

It began with Robert Taft and his opposition to the New Deal. It was fueled by the intellectual fervor of Russell Kirk and William F. Buckley Jr. It picked up steam and political power with Barry Goldwater. It peaked in influence with Ronald Reagan and Newt Gingrich. It crashed and burned with George W. Bush.

The Progressive Era lasted twenty years, from the election of Teddy Roosevelt to the end of World War I. The New Deal Era lasted thirty-six years, from the election of Franklin D. Roosevelt to that of Richard Nixon. And the Conservative Era lasted *more than fifty years*, from the rise of Robert Taft until the fall of George W. Bush.

Now the conservative revolution is finally over—and it was a total bust.

If the Republicans were a restaurant, they'd have been closed by the Board of Health. If they were a building, they'd have been condemned. If they were a Hollywood starlet, they'd be in rehab.

It's not just that they've failed by the standard I would have set for them. They've failed at everything they claimed to be really good at in the first place.

Once champions of fiscal responsibility, conservatives have instead delivered record-high federal spending and bloated budget deficits. Once leery of foreign entanglements, conservatives have instead launched us into an unprecedented age of imperial wars and conquests. Once apostles of honesty and integrity in government, conservatives have instead used their positions of power to enrich themselves or evade the rule of law. And that's just for starters.

By failing at every turn, in Congress and the White House, conservative politicians proved one thing above all others: conservatism is a fundamentally flawed governing philosophy. As the Boston College professor Alan Wolfe wrote in the July-August 2006 issue of the *Washington Monthly*: "Conservatives cannot govern well for the same reason that vegetarians cannot prepare a world-class boeuf bourguignon."

Why? Because when you start out hating government, you can't make government work. And you shouldn't even be given a chance to try.

But for more than fifty years, the United States has given conservatism a try. And we learned one abiding lesson: Conservatives can't govern. Consequently, they should never again be entrusted with power. Rather, their proper—and, hopefully, permanent—place is in the political minority, making sure that a liberal majority, whose governing philosophy remains fundamentally sound, still doesn't push government too far.

Recognizing the failure of their time at the plate, some conservatives have tried to blame all their problems on George W. Bush. And, indeed, he deserves a good share of the blame. But blaming him is like saying *Ishtar* was all Dustin Hoffman's fault. He may have had top billing, but you can't make a mess that big all by yourself.

When Bush leaves office, he will do so with a legacy that will include the biggest federal budget in history, the biggest federal workforce in history, the biggest federal deficits in history, and the most Orwellian executive branch in history. His legacy will also include an imperial foreign policy and, in the name of his self-proclaimed "war on terror," a direct assault on Americans' basic constitutional rights. Bush followed the game plan for a conservative heaven—and ended up creating a conservative hell.

Conservatives have been arguing for a long time that black is white and up is down. So maybe we shouldn't be surprised that when they said they'd bring us a smaller, more compassionate government, what they really meant was a larger, more invasive government. But that's certainly what we got.

Indeed, for Bush's first six years in office, conservatives rallied to support all of his misguided policies. And why? Because, in many ways, he was merely continuing the failed record of earlier conservatives, once they gained political power.

For decades, conservatives had struggled to topple liberals from the federal throne. In 1980, they finally won the White House. In 1994, they took control of the House of Representatives. In 2000, they won the House and the Senate. Because they controlled the Supreme Court, they were also awarded the White House. But, once in power, with total control of all three branches of government, they didn't deliver.

Given the chance to govern, conservatives tried and failed. Everything they touched, they trashed.

Here's how it started.

Guarding the Gates

When visitors to the U.S. Capitol hear the strains of patriotic music floating across the grounds, they predictably look up to the Capitol dome. But the sounds of "America, the Beautiful," and other familiar American hymns are coming from nowhere on the Capitol grounds. They ring out instead from the Robert Taft Memorial and Carillon, across Constitution Avenue.

It's fitting that the only monument in Washington erected in memory of a member of the U.S. Senate be dedicated to the Ohio senator Robert A. Taft. Few senators in history have exercised so much clout. The son of the former president and chief justice William Howard Taft, Robert Taft became known in the Senate as "Mr. Republican" and was the leading conservative politician throughout the 1940s and early 1950s.

The leading conservative scholar of the day was the political philosopher Russell Kirk. In fact, some historians date the beginning of the modern conservative movement to 1953, with the publication of Kirk's *The Conservative Mind*. And with good reason. Defining a conservative as "one who finds the permanent things more pleasing than Chaos and Old Night," Kirk celebrated the role of conservatives in guarding the gate against "sudden and slashing reforms." In all things, Kirk argued, they were to be guided by the "principle of prudence." Kirk's book soon became known as the "conservative Bible."

Kirk remains arguably the leading theologian of the conservative revolution. He outlined, in *The Conservative Mind*, what he called the six "canons," or basic principles, of conservatism:

- A divine intent, as well as personal conscience, rules society;
- Traditional life is filled with variety and mystery, while most radical systems are characterized by a narrowing uniformity;
- Civilized society requires orders and classes;
- Property and freedom are inseparably connected;
- Man must control his will and his appetite, knowing that he is governed more by emotion than by reason; and
- Society must alter slowly.

Kirk's six canons reflect the central tenets of an American conservative tradition that dates back to John Adams and remain the guiding principles of true conservatives today.

Yet long before Kirk published his manifesto, the conservative crusader Robert Taft had been elected to the U.S. Senate and immediately set out to slay what he perceived to be dragons, in the form of those "sudden and slashing reforms" pushed by President Franklin D. Roosevelt. Starting in 1938, Taft led a conservative coalition of Republicans and Southern Democrats in Congress against the New Deal, which he labeled as "socialistic." In its place, Taft advocated unfettered corporate enterprise, individual economic opportunity, a strong national defense, and noninvolvement in foreign wars.

As one indicator of how far today's conservatives have strayed from their roots, you need look no further than Taft's opposition to the United States' entry into World War II. (Isn't it amazing how conservatives are constantly evolving, yet remain constantly wrong?) As the leading conservative opponent of FDR's willingness to enlist the United States in a European war, Taft rejected the argument—repeated so shamelessly today by George Bush and Dick Cheney—that public criticism of a president's policies during wartime is unacceptable because it only serves to "aid and abet the enemy." Just the opposite, argued Taft. At no time, he insisted, is dissent more vital to a democracy than during wartime.

"As a matter of general principle," Taft declared, "I believe there can be no doubt that criticism in time of war is essential to the maintenance of any kind of democratic government. . . . Too many people desire to suppress criticism simply because they think that it will give some comfort to the enemy to know that there is such criticism. If that comfort makes the enemy feel better for a few moments, they are welcome to it as far as I am concerned, because the maintenance of the right of criticism in the long run will do the country maintaining it a great deal more good than it will do the enemy, and will prevent mistakes which might otherwise occur."

Those words of wisdom notwithstanding, Taft was marginalized, even within his own party. He sought but failed to secure the Republican nomination for president in 1940, 1948, and again in 1952. In short, Taft was still too conservative for most Republicans of his day. At the Republican Convention in 1952, he lost the nomination to General Dwight D. Eisenhower—who, just days before the GOP convention, considered running as a Democrat.

Taft died in 1953, just as Russell Kirk, writing in *The Conservative Mind*, linked Taft's political philosophy to a conservative tradition dating all the way back to Edmund Burke. Into the intellectual and political arena next stepped the young William F. Buckley Jr. A Yale graduate and a member of the secret Skull and Bones fraternity, the young Buckley had earlier, in his book *God and Man at Yale*, skewered his alma mater for having abandoned its conservative founding principles. In launching the *National Review*, still arguably the most influential conservative publication in America, he determined to take on the entire country for the same liberal transgression.

Conservatives would no longer simply stand by and let liberals introduce radical changes without challenge, Buckley announced. Instead, now newly motivated, they would stand "athwart history, yelling Stop!" In the first issue of *National Review*, November 19, 1955—and in a tone similar not only to that used by student radicals of the day, but also used by radical abolitionists some 120 years earlier—Buckley sounded the clarion call:

> Middle-of-the-Road, qua Middle of the Road, is politically, intellectually, and morally repugnant. We shall recommend policies for the simple reason that we consider them right (rather than "non-controversial"); and we consider them right because they are based on principles we deem right (rather than on popularity polls).

Note: Already we see, when considering "accomplishments" of the conservative movement, that this was a movement created to tear things down, not build them up. And Buckley made no apology for that. The role of *National Review*, he admitted, was to help undo the New Deal and other Democratic, liberal reforms—just as leftist, political publications had helped to create them. "The New Deal revolution, for instance, could hardly have happened save for the cumulative impact of *The Nation* and *The New Republic*, and a few other publications, on several American college generations during the twenties and thirties."

And so the battle was joined.

Fighting the Good Fight

With their intellectual foundation in place, conservatives again turned to gaining political power—first, within the Republican Party and, later, across the nation. The first to take up the challenge was Arizona's colorful maverick Barry Goldwater and conservatives who rallied to his standard.

In many ways, Barry Goldwater was ahead of his time. He warned Americans to change their wasteful ways or reap a whirlwind of huge federal deficits. Like a modern-day Moses, he led the Republican Party out of the barren East and into the fruitful Southern and Western states, where milk and honey and political success awaited them. He was, in the words of admiring conservative commentator George Will, "a man who lost forty-four states but won the future."

In his 1964 campaign, Goldwater defined the conservative take on issues that still dominate national political debate, now over four decades later. They include:

Social Security: which Goldwater argued was actuarially unsound but could be strengthened by allowing young people to opt out of the system and set up private accounts, instead.

Privatization: government services should be contracted out to private companies.

Law and Order: the rights of victims are more important than the rights of criminals.

Ethics: public officials should avoid scandal and not use their public office for private gain.

Judges: the president should appoint to the federal bench judges who will respect the Constitution, but not rewrite it.

Sound familiar? It should. In many ways, politics today is simply a continuation of the political debate started by Barry Goldwater. Even many Democrats today would agree that we need smaller government, lower taxes and spending, tougher anticrime measures, and less Washington meddling in our daily lives. Every one of those ideas— plus criticism of "big guv'mint"—was a plank of the Goldwater campaign of 1964.

Goldwater was also ahead of his time when it came to dealing with some of the social issues that so many conservatives are obsessed with today. He was greatly troubled by the growing influence in the Republican Party of so-called religious conservatives. In his later years, he grew to distrust people like the Reverend Jerry Falwell, the Reverend Pat Robertson, or Dr. James Dobson, and he considered their political influence a dangerous intrusion on the separation of church and state. He warned his fellow Republicans:

> When you say "radical right" today, I think of these money-making ventures by fellows like Pat Robertson and others who are trying to take the Republican Party away from the Republican Party, and make a religious organization out of it. If that ever happens, kiss politics goodbye.

No doubt about it, were Goldwater alive today, he would never have tolerated the de facto merger between the Republican Party and religious conservatives that was engineered, for purely political purposes, by Karl Rove and George W. Bush. Goldwater distrusted godly conservatism as much as he distrusted godless communism.

> I'm frankly sick and tired of the political preachers across this country telling me as a citizen that if I want to be a moral person, I must believe in "A," "B," "C" and "D." Just who do they think they are? And from where do they presume to claim the right to dictate their moral beliefs to me?

In July 1981, when the Reverend Jerry Falwell suggested that "every good Christian should be concerned" about President Reagan's nomination of the Arizonan Sandra Day O'Connor to the Supreme Court—because of her perceived softness on the question of abortion—Goldwater famously shot back, "I think every good Christian should kick Falwell right in the ass."

And when religious conservatives first made a big issue about banning gays and lesbians from serving in the military, Goldwater urged fellow Republicans not to endorse discrimination in any form. "You don't have to be straight to be in the military," he insisted, "you just have to be able to shoot straight."

How times have changed! In 1964, most Americans came to consider Goldwater a dangerous reactionary. When his supporters chanted, "In your heart, you know he's right," Democrats responded with "In your guts, you know he's nuts." Yet compared to conservatives today, Goldwater looks downright sane. He was even able to poke fun at his own chosen profession. "Sex and politics are a lot alike," he once said. "You don't have to be good at them to enjoy them."

In the wake of Goldwater's defeat, the editors of *Human Events* magazine, a conservative companion to Buckley's *National Review*, insisted that not all was lost. There was a silver lining to the cloud of Republican doom. Despite the Republican Party's historic loss, conservatives argued that Goldwater's 1964 campaign had accomplished three critical things: "The Republican Party is essentially conservative; the South is developing into a major pivot of its power; and a candidate who possesses Goldwater's virtues but lacks some of his handicaps can win the presidency."

They were correct on every point. In fact, the Goldwater campaign had already introduced that future winning candidate to the nation: a handsome, articulate new conservative spokesman from California named Ronald Reagan.

An actor and a former president of the Screen Actors Guild who grew up a fond believer in FDR's New Deal, Reagan had only recently switched his party affiliation from Democrat to Republican in 1962. Yet as a recent and photogenic convert to conservatism, he played a major role in Goldwater's 1964 campaign, which included nominating him at the convention. But it was his nationally televised address on October 27, 1964, sponsored by the Goldwater-Miller campaign, that really made Reagan a hot political commodity. Reagan titled his remarks "A Time for Choosing."

More than forty years later, presidential historians still refer to Reagan's televised remarks as "The Speech." And, indeed, it remains a remarkable document.

In it, Reagan first laid out the distrust of big government that became the centerpiece of his presidency. He ridiculed a statement by Senator William Fulbright that the "full power of centralized government" was essential in order to lift Americans out of poverty. Countered Reagan,

> [T]he full power of centralized government—this was the very thing the Founding Fathers sought to minimize. They knew that governments don't control things. A government can't control the economy without controlling people. And they knew when a government sets out to do that, it must use force and coercion to achieve its purposes. They also knew, those Founding Fathers, that outside of its legitimate functions, government does nothing as well or as economically as the private sector of the economy.

By the time Reagan himself was sworn in as president, seventeen years later, he had boiled that antigovernment philosophy down to a bumper-sticker. He declared in his Inaugural Address:

> Government is not a solution to our problem; government is the problem.

In the meantime, having failed to catapult Barry Goldwater into the White House, Ronald Reagan hunkered down and charted his own course. Slowly.

Taking the Helm

In politics, even twelve months is a long time. Ronald Reagan took an eternity, from 1964 to 1980, before winning the White House. In the meantime, he perfected his signature speech, served two terms as governor of California, and practiced running for president the very best way: by running for president and losing, twice.

A lackluster governor, Reagan entered the White House to low expectations—and proceeded to meet them. He was popular. He was genial. He was good at reading a script or following his cues before the cameras. But he governed as a "hands-off" president, generally leaving the ship of state to drift aimlessly and eventually, in the Iran-Contra scandal, to crash upon the rocks.

Ironically, the Reagan presidency will be remembered both for providing some of the finest hours of the conservative revolution and, at the same time, sowing the seeds of its demise.

The movement's finest hours came in honing and articulating, for popular consumption, the basic tenets of conservatism. Not for nothing was Reagan called the Great Communicator. He took conservatism from the textbook to the playbook. By the time he got to the White House, he left no doubt what the conservative revolution was all about.

When you heard Ronald Reagan speak, you could easily believe that he, like Moses, had been to the mountaintop and brought down with him, on stone tablets, the ten commandments that all conservatives should live by.

Government is always the last resort.

The smaller the government, the better.

The private sector can do anything cheaper and more efficiently than government.

Change must come slowly, if at all.

Taxes are excessive and should be reduced to the bare minimum.

Government spending must never exceed government revenues.

Government should stay out of people's personal lives.

Private property is sacred and untouchable.

The Constitution, like the Bible, must be taken and applied literally.

American foreign policy should be restrained and noninterventionist.

No one before or since has articulated the conservative creed to the American people better than Reagan. He summed it up in one sentence:

The federal government has taken too much tax money from the people, too much authority from the states, and too much liberty with the Constitution.

Reagan then went on to cut government spending and grant a historic level of new rights to all Americans. Gotcha! He did nothing of the kind. As we shall document in the coming chapters, he and subsequent conservative leaders, seduced by the promise of power, proceeded to destroy those principles they claimed to hold dear—each and every one of them.

Inadvertently, Reagan himself also greatly undermined the conservative movement by helping to eliminate what was once its very raison d'être: the ever-present threat of godless communism. From the days of Robert Taft, conservatives were particularly motivated by their fierce opposition to communism. They were the guardians of the flame, protecting the nation against socialistic change advocated by liberals like Franklin Roosevelt—changes in government policies they perceived to be nothing less than the American equivalent of Marxism.

Life before Reagan was simple. Everything was black and white. Communists were the bad guys, we were the good guys. The Evil Empire was the enemy. Fighting communism was the single, most powerful force uniting all Americans, but especially conservatives. In fact, that's why God made conservatives: to man the barricades against godless communism abroad, not to mention anything here at home that smacked of communism.

With the collapse of the Soviet Union, that urgency disappeared— and so did the primary focus of the conservative movement. Without it, looking for new meaning, conservatives began to drift from economic issues to cultural issues, from nonintervention to nation-building, and even from smaller government to big government.

To keep their often disparate coalition glued together, many conservatives later transformed themselves from rabid anticommunists to rabid anti-Clintonistas, seeing and invoking in the centrism of Bill Clinton the same threat they formerly perceived in communism.

They might still call it conservatism, but it wasn't the same animal.

In any event, as Reagan prepared to leave the national scene, a younger generation of conservatives was waiting in the wings.

Upsetting the Applecart

Two years before Ronald Reagan reached the White House, the man who would continue the conservative revolution's rise to power arrived in the House of Representatives.

The college professor Newt Gingrich ran unsuccessfully for Congress twice before being elected in 1978 to represent Georgia's Sixth District. He ended up serving ten terms in the House and ascending to the leadership of the House, but even as a freshman backbencher he had started to shake things up. He railed against alleged ethical violations of Speaker Jim Wright and other Democrats. He led the fight for Bill Clinton's impeachment during the Lewinsky imbroglio (while simultaneously enjoying his own affair with a congressional staffer). He became the leader of the young conservatives' "Gang of Seven" that engineered the Republican takeover of the House in 1994, and he then served as speaker from 1995 to 1999.

The key to the success of Gingrich and fellow conservatives in 1994 was their Contract with America, a ten-point campaign platform that Gingrich himself authored. Standing on the steps of the U.S. Capitol, Gingrich led Republican members of Congress in promising that if entrusted with control of the House of Representatives in November 1994, they would introduce ten major policy initiatives within the first hundred days of the new 104th Congress, ranging from a balanced-budget amendment to term limits for members of Congress.

Buoyed by Republican success at the polls, Gingrich became Speaker of the House in January 1995 and, as promised, immediately introduced legislation to turn the Contract with America into the law of the land.

When Gingrich resigned as Speaker, four years later, not one of the ten planks of the Contract with America had become law—even though polls showed that 64 percent of Americans agreed with its provisions. Today, the Contract remains nothing but a list of unfulfilled promises.

The failure of the Contract with America served as an unmistakable warning that conservatives just can't be counted on to deliver. Despite what the media says, knowing how to run a campaign doesn't mean you'd know how to run a country. Rhetoric is not reality. Getting elected is not the same as governing. And running against government is no guarantee you can make it work. Gingrich and company clearly could not.

But at least Gingrich had a good excuse: in his day, conservatives held power in only one house of Congress. George W. Bush had no such excuse.

Attempting to Govern

Whatever his shortcomings in the exercise of government, Gingrich was skilled in articulating the theory of government. By the time he resigned as Speaker, building on the earlier contributions of Taft, Kirk, Goldwater, and Reagan, Gingrich left behind a relatively clear understanding of the principle ideas driving conservatism—on paper, if not in office.

In 2000, conservatives once again got the chance to translate those principles into action. They not only retained control of the House, they won control of the Senate. And, thanks to the Supreme Court's conservative majority, they were handed control of the White House.

And yet, when George W. Bush and Dick Cheney did everything "right," it all came out wrong.

On federal spending, they promised to balance the budget. Instead, they racked up the biggest budget deficits in history, effectively burying America's children in a mountain of debt. They also repudiated the conservative fiscal philosophy inherited from Ronald Reagan, by claiming that budget deficits don't really matter, after all.

On personal liberty, they promised to get Big Government off our backs. Yet today—with the federal government rifling through our phone, bank, and library records at will; holding detainees without benefit of trial; torturing prisoners; controlling women's bodies; and prying into the bedrooms of gays and lesbians—there is less personal privacy than ever before. Conservatives, who once derided the Nanny State, brought us the age of Big Brother instead.

On morality, they promised to restore honesty and integrity to public life. Yet from the moment they assumed power, they began selling their services to the highest bidder. The result: from Duke Cunningham to Scooter Libby, from Bob Ney to Mark Foley, from Tom Delay to Jack Abramoff, David Safavian, Claude Allen, and

Ralph Reed—conservatives have mired themselves and official Washington in the most widespread morass of sleaze and corruption since the days of Teapot Dome.

On international diplomacy, they promised to conduct a "humble" foreign policy, while leading the world in a quest for peace among nations. Yet they have delivered the most arrogant and bellicose foreign policy of modern times. Treaties have been broken, old alliances have been destroyed, preemptive war has been adopted as the new way of doing business, acts of terror have multiplied, and nuclear bombs have spread into dangerous hands. Under Bush and Cheney's so-called conservative rule, America has gone from being the world's most respected nation to the most despised.

In short, the conservative legacy is a government that is inefficient, inept, incompetent—and broke.

Again, some conservatives try to lay all the blame on George W. Bush, accusing him of abandoning true, traditional conservative values. But if that were true, where were DeLay, McCain, Frist, Gingrich, Giuliani, Lott, Boehner, Hastert, and all other conservatives the last six years? Standing alongside Bush!

The reality is not that simple. From Katrina to Iraq to No Child Left Behind, President Bush not only proved to be incompetent, he proved to be an incompetent conservative. Of course, he's not the first conservative to fail to govern well, he's just the latest—and the worst.

An examination of the record proves that it's not just George Bush or Newt Gingrich or Ronald Reagan who failed, it's the entire conservative governing strategy.

The fact is, conservatives are philosophically, and perhaps genetically, incapable of governing well. As long as they believe government is intrinsically evil, they will never do a good job. Conservatives can't make government work because they hate government in the first place. Indeed, ideologically they were never meant to govern, but rather to act as a permanent check against the excesses of the majority—nothing less, and nothing more.

In this book, we will see how Republican presidents from Reagan to Bush 43 have either failed to deliver on conservative ideas or, in some cases, actually contradicted them. Either way, as a governing philosophy, conservatism has failed.

Let the examination begin.

CHAPTER 1

Loving the Great Outdoors

I mean, if you've looked at a hundred thousand
acres or so of trees—you know, a tree is a tree,
how many more do you need to look at?
Ronald Reagan

Trees cause more pollution than automobiles.
Ronald Reagan

We will mine more, drill more, cut more timber to use
our resources rather than simply keep them locked up.
Reagan interior secretary James Watt

Conservation may be a sign of personal virtue,
but it is not a sufficient basis for a sound,
comprehensive energy strategy.
Dick Cheney

I know the human being and fish can
coexist peacefully.
George W. Bush

Natural gas is hemispheric. I like to call it
hemispheric in nature because it is a product
that we can find in our neighborhoods.
George W. Bush

E very politician needs a role model. Once selected president, George W. Bush chose as his role model Ronald Reagan.

Like Reagan, he bought a ranch. Like Reagan, he spent his spare time on the ranch clearing brush. Like Reagan, he took long rides on ranch trails—Reagan, on horseback; Bush, on mountain bike. And, like Reagan, he exuded the great outdoors: a man close to nature, a friend of wildlife, and the protector of all living things.

But, of course, like Reagan, it was all phony. While both Reagan and Bush pretended to be champions of the environment, the only outdoors they cared about protecting was their own private property. The rest of the environment, be damned. One after the other, they racked up the two worst environmental protection records of any presidents— which is not really what we should expect from conservatives.

In fact, I believe that one of the stranger contradictions about contemporary politics is how saving the environment came to be known as a liberal issue—embraced by Democrats, but ridiculed by Republicans.

It shouldn't be that way, and it wasn't always. In fact, when I got my start in politics, Republicans were the stronger advocates of saving the environment.

In 1969, in San Francisco, two years out of the seminary, I joined a new campaign management firm headed by Sandy Weiner, who was then the hottest political property in California. I was a committed Democrat, but my first assignment was working for a Republican. The attorney and environmental pioneer Peter Behr was running for state senator from the counties of Marin, Napa, and Solano. After helping Peter win his Senate seat and discovering him to be such an outstanding public servant, I eagerly accepted his invitation to accompany him to Sacramento as his chief of staff.

As a Marin County supervisor, Behr had previously led the successful campaign to establish the majestic Point Reyes National Seashore. Elected to the State Senate in 1970, he quickly established himself as the leading environmentalist in the State Legislature and helped to organize California's participation in the nation's first "Earth Day," the brainchild of a Democrat from Wisconsin, Senator Gaylord Nelson.

Behr's signature accomplishment was the passage of the California Wild and Scenic Rivers Act in 1972. Designed to protect the Eel, the Trinity, and the Klamath—California's last three "free-flowing" rivers—from dams and other man-made obstructions, the Wild Rivers bill was hotly contested by all of the powerful interests that then ruled California: the timber industry, Central Valley agribusinesses, and thirsty Southern California cities. It was also strongly opposed by the dam-happy Bill Gianelli, Governor Ronald Reagan's director of water resources, whom Behr once accused of having a bad case of "beaver fever."

Against all odds—and with the help of fishermen, organized as "The California Committee of Two Million," and the state's nascent conservation organizations—Behr won approval of the controversial Wild Rivers bill in just two legislative sessions. I remember standing with him as Governor Reagan, remembering his own experience as a lifeguard on the Rock River in his hometown of Dixon, Illinois, signed the measure into law. Behr's bill became the template for the Federal Wild and Scenic Rivers Act, enacted into law by Congress just a few years later.

Yes, Peter Behr was both a Republican and an environmentalist. But among members of his party in the 1970s and 1980s, he was hardly alone. At that time, Republicans led most environmental battles in California, and, as Behr's right-hand man, I was lucky enough to work with all of them.

In Northern California, for example, efforts to "Save Lake Tahoe" were led by the attorney Dwight Steele, a Republican. In the Bay Area, the great campaign to "Save the Bay" was organized by the Berkeley activist Sylvia McLaughlin, a Republican. In Santa Barbara, Get Oil Out, or GOO—the citizens' crusade to prevent future oil spills by blocking offshore drilling—was launched by the civic activist Lois Sidenberg, a Republican. Proposition 20, the successful 1972 initiative campaign to protect the entire California coastline from development, was led by Woodside's Janet Adams, a Republican. Sacramento's most effective environmental lobby, the Planning and Conservation League, was headed by the Mendocino rancher Richard Wilson, also a Republican. And it was Norman "Ike" Livermore, Reagan's Republican resources secretary, who convinced his boss to sign the Wild Rivers legislation.

Similarly, across the nation, Republicans were leading efforts to save the New York Adirondacks, the Delaware coastline, the Florida Everglades, and the Texas barrier islands, among other environmental campaigns. At the time, it seemed a perfect fit. Because conservation was seen, correctly, as a conservative issue. And because preserving the environment was considered part of a proud Republican tradition, inherited from a man who is still honored as one of the greatest conservationists of all time.

It All Started with Teddy

To this day, Teddy Roosevelt remains our one true environmental president. He did more to protect the environment than did all of his predecessors combined—and arguably more than any president since.

Despite his record, however, Roosevelt does not get the credit he deserves from environmental purists, which is understandable but unfortunate. True, Roosevelt's brand of conservation does not square with today's preservationist ethos. But in his appreciation for, and actions to protect, the environment, he was a man far ahead of his time.

Roosevelt was an outdoorsman and a hunter, and his first interest in the environment was limited to preserving wildlife habitat so that there'd be more wildlife for him and fellow hunters to shoot. From there, however, Roosevelt soon developed the ethic of long-range management. He thought that the aim of conservation was not to protect natural resources by setting them aside, but to assure their survival through wise, efficient, and limited use. And Roosevelt held to that theory, despite some extraordinary personal lobbying by John Muir, the founder of the Sierra Club and the father of the modern environmental movement.

Life was simpler for presidents in those days. When Muir and President Roosevelt took off on a three-day camping trip in Yosemite Valley, there was no presidential motorcade, no army of assistants, no swarm of reporters and photographers. It was just the two of them, with a couple of aides, for three nights under the stars. Imagine their conversation, as Muir unveiled to Roosevelt the grandeur of Yosemite and stressed the urgent need to preserve it and other special places for future generations.

Later, Muir expressed his displeasure with Roosevelt and his forestry chief, Gifford Pinchot, for allowing continued logging, mining, and drilling on public lands. But Teddy Roosevelt stuck to his "wise-use" brand of conservation, which reflected his concept of democracy. The United States' abundant natural resources were the strength of our economy, he believed. Therefore, they should be used wisely in order to produce the greatest good, for the greatest number, over the greatest period of time. That meant careful management and long-term planning. It was undemocratic, Roosevelt argued, to allow corporations to exploit and squander natural resources for short-term profit. While disappointing to John Muir, because it did not ban all logging in national forests, even that sentiment was considered radical for its time. Indeed, there are many who would find the environmental philosophy of the Roosevelt administration, as expressed by Pinchot, radical for today:

> The noblest task that confronts us all today is to leave this country unspotted in honor and unexhausted in resources, to our descendants who will be, not less than we, the children of the founders of the Republic.

So, in a very real sense, Roosevelt's approach to the environment was not so much antipreservation as it was a first step toward preservation. He recognized the importance of conserving our natural resources enough to brand it "the fundamental problem which underlies almost every other problem of our national life." And, more than anyone else, he understood the urgency of the task: "We are prone to speak of the resources of this country as inexhaustible; this is not so."

Roosevelt was no strict preservationist, but he did not hesitate to act like one when he saw the need. While in the White House, this president, criticized then and now for not being willing to do more, nevertheless created the National Park Service and five national parks, including the first, Oregon's Crater Lake; eighteen national monuments; four big game refuges; fifty-one national bird sanctuaries; and dozens of national monuments. He established the National Forest Service, placing 230 million acres of national forests under its protective umbrella. And in 1908 he hosted the first ever White House conference on the environment.

Just how deeply Teddy Roosevelt had caught the preservationist fever by the end of his presidency is evident in remarks made on his first visit to the Grand Canyon.

I hope you will not have a building of any kind, not a summer cottage, a hotel or anything else, to mar the wonderful grandeur, sublimity, the great loneliness and beauty of the canyon. Leave it as it is. You cannot improve on it; not a bit. . . . What you can do is to keep it for your children, your children's children and for all who come after you, as one of the great sights which every American, if he can travel at all, should see.

John Muir himself could not have said it any better.

Teddy Roosevelt made his mark on the environment. Several leaders who followed him promised to be the "environmental president," but none really came close—until, believe it or not, Richard Nixon.

From Watergate to the Clean Air Act

Unlike Teddy Roosevelt, Richard M. Nixon was neither an outdoorsman nor a conservationist. Before he became president in 1968, the environment wasn't an issue he talked about at all. Which is not surprising. Gallup and other national pollsters didn't even add the environment to the list of issues on which they sought public opinion until 1965.

But Nixon, for all his faults, was a brilliant political tactician. Soon after reaching the Oval Office, he saw the angry public response to the 1969 oil spill on the beaches of Santa Barbara and the enthusiastic response to the nation's first Earth Day in 1970. Nixon didn't become an environmentalist, but he eagerly embraced the environment—perhaps cynically, but no less effectively—as part of his own political agenda.

To this end, he was assisted by none other than his disgraced top aide John Ehrlichman, who had graduated with a degree in environmental land-use law, was a committed environmentalist himself, and convinced Nixon that the environment was a winning political issue.

On this issue, like all others, Nixon remains a contradictory figure. He hired but soon fired the antienvironment Alaska governor Walter Hickel as his first interior secretary. He vetoed the Federal Water Pollution Control Act Amendments of 1972 because, he complained, they appropriated too much money to water cleanup. Congress overrode his veto. He repeatedly refused to pressure Detroit to increase fuel-efficiency standards. And, in private, Nixon railed against environmentalists as "enemies of the system" whose policies would mean "going back and living like a bunch of damned animals."

Yet in public, thanks to Ehrlichman's prodding, Nixon racked up an impressive environmental record.

His contributions include:

- The Endangered Species Act: signed by Nixon in 1973.

- The National Oceanic and Atmospheric Administration (NOAA): created by Executive Order in 1970.

- The Clean Air Act: signed by Nixon in 1970.

- The National Environmental Protection Act (NEPA): signed by Nixon in 1970.

- The Environmental Protection Agency (EPA): created by Executive Order in 1970.

- The White House Council on Environmental Quality: created as part of NEPA in 1970.

And, by the way, this was back in the days when "Clean Air Act" meant "clean air"—unlike George W. Bush's "Clear Skies Initiative," which was really an invitation to pollute.

Nixon's record was truly prodigious, especially for someone who wasn't committed to protecting the environment in the first place. Whether his motives were pure or purely political, Nixon handed ownership of the environmental issue to conservatives—who promptly proceeded to throw it in the trash.

An Environmental U-Turn

Here's the mystery: For conservatives, somewhere between Richard Nixon and Ronald Reagan, ecology became a four-letter word. Republicans and conservatives not only opposed conservation legislation, they declared war on the environment and on environmentalists, dismissing them as "tree huggers," "eco-fascists," "earth muffins," or worse. "Environmentalists are a socialist group of individuals that are the tool of the Democratic Party," trumpeted the Alaskan representative

Don Young. "I'm proud to say that they are my enemy. They are not Americans, never have been Americans, never will be Americans."

Why the 180-degree change in direction? It was most likely due to a combination of factors, starting out with the basic fact that as more and more prominent liberals—such as Justice William O. Douglas, the Wisconsin senator Gaylord Nelson, and the consumer advocate Ralph Nader—spoke out in favor of environmental protection, more and more conservatives figured that as a matter of course, they had to be against it.

Many conservatives also mistakenly bought into the myth that saving the environment was inimical to fundamental conservative principles. Any restrictions on development, for example, were seen as an erosion of private property rights. Efforts to protect the environment were painted as antijobs. The environment and the economy were considered on a collision course, with Americans forced to take sides. And all environmental legislation was tarred with the brush of bigger bureaucracy and more Big Brother—in direct contradiction to the conservative ideal of smaller, less-intrusive government.

In the West, meanwhile, the big issue was the control and use of public lands. Alarmed that the Forest Service and Bureau of Land Management were reviewing millions of acres for possible designation as new wilderness areas, the governors of thirteen states began to argue for state control over what happened on federal lands. Most of that territory was covered with sagebrush anyway, they argued, good only for grazing, logging, or mineral extraction. Their campaign became known as the "Sagebrush Rebellion." They won the support of the presidential candidate Ronald Reagan in 1980. And, shortly after his election as president, Reagan declared himself a "Sagebrush Rebel."

Antienvironmental arguments were based on a false premise, of course. We know now that there is no inherent conflict between a healthy environment and a healthy economy. In fact, you can't have one without the other. But after being bombarded with antienvironmental propaganda by big business, a lot of people started to believe the environment versus economy myth—and still do.

Finally, and most significantly, there was the iron grip of special interests on the Republican Party. They wrote the campaign checks to get Republicans elected, and, once their friends were in office, they wrote the special-interest legislation. In every area, conservative

Republicans let big business dictate public policy. Oil companies blocked all efforts to limit offshore drilling. Timber companies opposed all attempts to preserve first-growth redwood forests. Builders and developers killed legislation to save our most productive farmlands. And chemical companies fought restrictions on dangerous pesticides like DDT.

On the environment, conservatives decided to adopt the golden rule: he who has the most gold, rules. And, of course, the ones with the most gold were no friends of the environment.

In just eight years, from Nixon to Reagan, official Republican Party policy changed from protecting the environment to destroying it.

Reagan Declares War on the Environment

In 1979, my wife, Carol, and I built a new passive solar home on our property in Inverness, California. Thanks to a simple matter of smart design—southern exposure, double-paned glass, concrete floors—the house keeps cool in the summer and warm in the winter. When needed, for really cold winter days, we have a backup wood stove. Our heating and cooling bill is zero.

We opted for solar because, as environmentalists, we wanted to build an energy-efficient home. We were also attracted by, and took advantage of, solar energy tax credits created by President Jimmy Carter to encourage the use of alternative sources of energy. But utilities didn't want homeowners like us to be free from big gas and electric bills. And so, to reward them for helping to bankroll his 1980 campaign, one of the first things Ronald Reagan did as president was to cancel the solar tax credits. That was just the beginning of his antienvironmental crusade.

Nobody ever accused Ronald Reagan of being an environmentalist. But as governor of California, he had at least been open-minded about environmental protection. As noted previously, he signed Peter Behr's Wild and Scenic Rivers bill. He also signed legislation authored by Behr to protect the California mountain lion. He named a leading conservationist, Ike Livermore, as his resources secretary. In his free time, he headed to his ranch to ride horses and cut brush.

But a vastly different Ronald Reagan moved into the Oval Office. What happened? Livermore later conjectured to the Reagan biographer Lou Cannon that Reagan's reversal on the environment was due to the fact that he never had to deal with environmental issues again, between the time he left Sacramento and the time he moved to Washington. Nor did he take any environmental advisers from California to Washington with him.

Something else happened, too. In his definitive biography of the fortieth president, Cannon traces Reagan's environmental U-turn on the environment to the business groups he wooed and won on his way to the White House. The more he listened to their tirades against environmentalists and government regulations, the more heated his own rhetoric became.

Campaigning in Steubenville, Ohio, on October 7, 1980, Reagan met with a group of businessmen in the steel industry. As recounted by Cannon, after they denounced "environmental regulatory overkill," Reagan chimed in. Bureaucrats in Washington, he charged, had gone beyond protecting the environment:

> What they believe in is no growth. What they believe in is a return to society in which there wouldn't be the need for the industrial concerns or more power plants and so forth. . . . I have flown twice over Mt. St. Helens out on our West Coast. I'm not a scientist and I don't know the figures, but I just have a suspicion that that one little mountain out there in these past several months has probably released more sulphur dioxide into the atmosphere than has been released in the last ten years of automobile driving or things of that kind that people are concerned about.

The next day, the Reagan campaign released a report on regulatory reform that concluded there was no need for additional controls on emissions because "air pollution has been substantially controlled." Which proved embarrassing, four days later, when Reagan returned to California. His chartered jet was unable to land at Hollywood-Burbank airport, as scheduled, because the airport had been shut down due to smog.

As president, Reagan needed someone to tackle "environmental extremists" and take the axe to environmental regulations. He found the perfect pair in James Watt and Anne Gorsuch Burford.

Reagan named James Watt, the head of the Mountain States Legal Foundation and a leading figure in the Sagebrush Rebellion, as secretary of the interior. For years, Watt had been fighting those he described as "bureaucrats and no-growth advocates who create a challenge to individual liberty and economic freedoms." They were the same forces, he vowed, that he would fight in Washington. And then, proving he was almost as good at the antienvironmental rhetoric as his new boss, Watt warned, "If we fail, we won't just see a drift toward socialism. We will see the rampant acceleration toward socialism that the liberals will bring to America."

In fact, earlier, Watt had divided people into two categories: "liberals and Americans." I guess we liberals should be happy he still counted us as "people."

Before long, Watt became the most visible, and most controversial, member of Reagan's cabinet. He carried out Reagan's antienvironmental agenda with a vengeance.

Watt's first move was to offer two hundred million acres of coastline for offshore drilling every year for five years. Do the math. This added up to one billion new acres of offshore drilling: ten times the amount of ocean property that was opened up for oil exploration and drilling in the entire history of the United States. Even some oil companies weren't sure they could drill that much, that fast.

In rapid order, Watt proposed a moratorium on new national parks, approved the use of motorcycles and trail bikes on fragile desert lands, opened up five Western national recreation areas to drilling for oil and gas, and nearly doubled the acreage available for coal mining on federal lands in Montana. He even tried unsuccessfully to undo federal protection for those five California rivers—the Eel, the Trinity, the Klamath, Smith, and the lower American—that Reagan had given state protection to in 1972.

For Watt, so far, so good. The more trouble he stirred up, the more Reagan came to his defense. "Jim Watt has been doing what I think is a common sense job in the face of some environmental extremism we've suffered from," the president responded to his critics. But then Watt went too far, even for the Reagan White House. He zeroed in on the California coastline.

One billion acres of offshore drilling still didn't satisfy Watt's appetite for exploitation of our natural resources. On top of that program, he announced that he was opening for development another eighty million acres off the coast of California, stretching north from Big Sur to the Oregon border. For Californians, he might as well have proposed building a dam across Yosemite Valley or clear-cutting Redwood National Park.

The response was immediate, loud, angry, and bipartisan. The Democratic governor Jerry Brown sued to block the sale, known as Lease Sale 53. The Republican senator Sam Hayakawa came out against it. The chairman of the California Republican Party and Reagan's 1966 campaign manager both warned the White House that Watt could cost Republicans several seats in Congress. When a federal judge blocked part of the sale, Watt was forced to back down by political powers in the Reagan White House. He announced that Lease Sale 53 was postponed until after the 1982 mid-term elections. It was never revived.

In September 1983, Watt shot himself in the foot with a careless comment about having "two Jews and a cripple" on his staff. He resigned a couple of weeks later. By that time, his friend Anne Burford was already out the door.

Thanks to Reagan, Anne Gorsuch Burford had become the first female administrator of the Environmental Protection Agency. She arrived at the EPA, however, with a different agenda than previous administrators had. As she saw it, her mission was not to protect the environment but to dismantle the EPA—and she did a pretty good job of it.

Burford served two years as the EPA administrator. During that time, she slashed $200 million from the agency's budget and cut its staff by 23 percent, effectively shutting the EPA's research and enforcement divisions. She gutted the Clean Air Act and boasted that she had reduced the EPA's book of clean water regulations from six inches to one-half inch. While at it, she also accelerated federal approvals for the spraying of dangerous pesticides and proposed dedicating a thirty-by-forty-mile area off the Delaware-Maryland coast as a site where incinerator ships could burn toxic waste.

Again, despite loud protests from environmentalists in both parties, Reagan stuck by Burford—until she was cited for contempt of Congress. She refused to turn over documents related to a possible conflict of interest in her management of the Super Fund. Burford cited "executive privilege" on instructions of the White House. But when she was slammed by the court for contempt, the Justice Department refused to defend her. Made to walk the plank, Burford resigned in March 1983.

Reagan had five more years in the White House. Yet even with the departure of Watt and Burford, the environmental damage was already done. Reagan's focus from there on out was on foreign policy. He paid little attention to domestic policy. And on the environment, he made no attempts to reverse the negative direction set at the Department of the Interior and the EPA by his first two appointees.

Thanks in large part to James Watt and Anne Gorsuch Burford, the man who had been considered so friendly to the environment as governor of California racked up the worst environmental record of any president—until George W. Bush.

An Oil Slick in the White House

How ironic. And how unfair to Ronald Reagan.

On the environment, we often think of Reagan as the most antienvironmental president of our lifetime when, in fact, George W. Bush is many times worse. "What they're doing makes the Reagan administration look innocent," said Buck Parker, the executive director of the legal arm of the Sierra Club, or Earthjustice.

Most environmental organizations agree that the Bush administration has been by far the most antienvironmental in our nation's history. Environmentalists feared the worst from a former oil man who, as governor, left Texas with the dirtiest air and the weakest environmental regulations in the nation. And, in that case, George W. Bush did not disappoint.

No president has gone after the nation's environmental laws with his level of determination. Robert F. Kennedy Jr., the president of the Waterkeeper Alliance, said flat out, "George Bush will go down in history as America's worst environmental president." A leading Republican environmentalist agreed. Complained Russell Train, the EPA administrator under President Nixon, "I think this administration is not a conservative administration. I think it's a radical administration. It represents a rollback of environmental policy going back to a period many, many years ago. It's backward."

So why hasn't Bush stirred up more environmental outrage?

For one thing, the war in Iraq and the war on terror have taken the spotlight away from environmental issues, to Bush's advantage. But Bush has also been more adept than Reagan at staying under the radar. He appointed equally bad, but less colorful, people to key environmental posts. He kept his own antienvironmental rhetoric to a minimum. And he didn't promise to gut environmental standards while campaigning for president. He simply did it, once elected.

In fact, Bush made only one promise related to the environment while campaigning for president in 2000: to add carbon dioxide to the list of emissions contributing to greenhouse gases that the federal government would regulate. Bush vowed to "establish mandatory reduction targets for emissions of four major pollutants: sulfur dioxide, nitrogen dioxide, mercury and carbon dioxide"—a statement that was actually stronger at the time than anything Al Gore had yet said on greenhouse gases.

Poor Christie Whitman. Bush was barely in office when, as his first administrator of EPA, she rushed off to Italy for a March 2001 international conference of environmental ministers in order to outline Bush's plan for reducing carbon dioxide emissions. She returned as proud as a peahen. But one week later, Bush called Whitman into the Oval Office and gave her the bad news. The coal industry wasn't happy with his decision. Neither were a handful of Republican senators. Therefore, he was dropping the plan. On March 13, 2001, Bush forced Whitman to announce that regulation of carbon dioxide would *not* be an administration priority. Promise made, promise broken. And a bad omen for what lay ahead.

Whitman was a proven environmentalist and a rare exception in the Bush administration. For the most part, when filling important environmental jobs, Bush sought out people from the coal, oil, gas, mining, or timber industries—and put them in charge of regulating the same industries from which they used to draw a paycheck. Can anybody say "fox in charge of the hen house"?

In my book *Bush Must Go,* I published the list of industry representatives who were given sensitive environmental jobs by George W. Bush. It reads like a Who's Who of special-interest lobbyists. Since nothing better illustrates Bush's determination to wage war on the environment, from the very beginning, I repeat it here:

Name	Qualifications	Job
Dick Cheney	CEO of Halliburton	Vice President
Andrew Card	Lobbyist, auto industry	White House Chief of Staff
Condi Rice	Board member, Chevron	National Security Advisor; Secretary of State
Gale Norton	Protégé of James Watt; cofounder of Council of Republicans for Environmental Advocacy, underwritten by chemical and mining industries	Secretary of the Interior
J. Steven Griles	Lobbyist for coal, natural gas, and oil industries	Deputy Interior Secretary
Mike Leavitt	Governor of Utah, worst environmental record of fifty governors	Administrator of EPA (after Whitman)
Don Evans	CEO, oil and gas company	Commerce Secretary
Ann Veneman	Board member, Calgene, specializing in genetically engineered foods	Agriculture Secretary
James Connaughton	Lobbyist for ARCO, Alcoa, and General Electric	Chair, White House Council on Environmental Quality
Mark Rey	Lobbyist, timber industry	Agriculture Undersecretary for Natural Resources
Linda Fisher	Lobbyist, Monsanto Chemical Company	Deputy Administrator, EPA

And those were just the top jobs. Bush also filled scores of lower-level offices with antienvironmental zealots who spent their entire pre-Bush careers fighting the very laws and regulations they were now sworn to protect.

With his team of polluters in place, Bush then proceeded to dismantle every environmental program that other presidents had taken years to build.

Clinton Executive Orders. Bill Clinton was notorious for waiting until the last minute to get things done. But as president, he had an ace up his sleeve: the Executive Order. In the last months of his presidency, like most presidents before him, Clinton took advantage of the opportunity to achieve by Executive Order certain goals he never got around to pursuing through legislation. Many of Clinton's actions dealt with the environment. Bush overturned every last one of them, including:

- Clinton reduced the allowable amount of arsenic in drinking water from 50 to 10 parts per billion. Bush demanded that it be kept at 50. He later reversed his own decision, keeping the Clinton standard.

- Clinton proposed new regulations limiting raw sewage discharges from pig farms and cattle lots. These regulations were suspended by George Bush in January 2001.

- Clinton adopted a new rule prohibiting the federal government from awarding contracts to companies that violate federal laws, including environmental regulations. This rule was suspended by George Bush in March 2001.

- Clinton adopted new rules phasing out environmentally damaging snowmobiles in Yellowstone and Grand Teton national parks. These rules were suspended by George Bush in June 2001.

Wilderness. Since the days of Teddy Roosevelt, our most beautiful and fragile lands have been set aside, protected from all development, for public benefit. Almost every administration since TR has added to our bank of wilderness areas, managed by the Bureau of Land Management. This president has gone backward. In April 2003, then interior secretary Gale Norton cut the new wilderness areas designated by her predecessor, Bruce Babbitt, almost in half: from 6.2 million acres to 3.2 million acres. She also rescinded Babbitt's order to review all federal lands for possible wilderness designation before opening them up to future mining, drilling, road building, or off-road vehicle use. And she ordered that 50 million acres of wilderness-quality BLM lands in Alaska could not be reviewed for possible wilderness classification unless first approved by Alaska's conservative congressional delegation—a classic case of the tail wagging the dog.

The result has been a virtual land-grab in the West by oil and gas companies. Since Norton's order, for example, the BLM has leased for oil and gas drilling 67,000 acres of proposed wilderness lands in Colorado; 190,000 acres of prime wilderness potential in Utah; and the entire 622,000-acre Jack Morrow Hills area of southwest Wyoming.

Endangered Species. One of the most far-reaching environmental laws ever passed by Congress, the Endangered Species Act was designed to protect both plant and animal species that are threatened with extinction due to uncontrolled economic growth and development. Today, some 1,326 species are on the list. Ever since President Nixon signed the bill into law in December 1973, the program, under the U.S. Fish and Wildlife Service (FWS), has thrived—until George W. Bush.

Bush has endangered the endangered species program in two ways: by ignoring it and by gutting it. Where other presidents rushed to extend federal protection to threatened plants and animals, Bush sat on his hands. According to records kept by the National Wildlife Federation, 42 species were accepted for protection under the short tenure of President Gerald Ford; 112 under Jimmy Carter; 270 under Ronald Reagan; 235 under Bush 41; and 524 under Bill Clinton. In the first seven years of the Bush 43 administration, only 58 species were added to the endangered list—and 54 were the result of litigation. The administration itself recommended only 4 species for protection.

At the same time, year after year, Bush has slashed the FWS budget, creating a backlog in the department's ability to consider newly threatened species and shutting down many of the protective programs. Which is too bad because, as the bald eagle could testify, they've been very effective. In June 2007, the bald eagle was actually removed from the Endangered Species List because federal efforts to bring its numbers back have been so successful.

The bald eagle was fortunate. It got on and off the list while there was still a program in place to save it. Now that George Bush has taken an axe to the Fish and Wildlife Service, other species may not be so lucky.

National Forests. Management of America's 191 million acres of national forest has always been a tough balancing act: how to protect the forest and the watershed, while providing for logging at the same time. For decades, timber companies were able to write their own rules. Under Bill Clinton, the pendulum started to swing more toward protection. Under George W. Bush, it's swung back the other way. Big time.

Before Bill Clinton left office in January 2001, the Forest Service adopted a new Roadless Area Conservation Rule (RARE), banning the construction of new roads—and therefore, in effect, banning logging—on 58.5 million acres of national forest lands in thirty-eight states. By the end of January, under a new president and a new director of the NFS, the new rule had been temporarily suspended. It was repealed by the Bush administration in 2005. At the same time, the Forest Service adopted new regulations that reversed proposed rules making recreation and the protection of watersheds and wildlife a priority and put the emphasis back on logging and mineral development.

Under those new rules, the Forest Service leased 52,000 acres of the Los Padres National Forest, adjacent to the city of Santa Barbara, for oil and gas drilling; opened up a 12-square-mile tract in Southern Oregon's Siskiyou National Forest to logging; and tripled the amount of old-growth redwoods that were made available to timber companies in eleven national forests in California. At the same time, both the Forest Service and the Bureau of Land Management sold off hundreds of thousands of acres of publicly owned lands to timber companies. The Bush administration replaced long-term protection of our forests with short-term profiteering.

Healthy Forests. Leasing or selling off our national forests was sure to please George Bush's friends in the timber industry, but it stirred up a storm of protests from Democrats in Congress. So Bush began to look for a way to sugarcoat massive logging on public lands. His answer: the famous "Healthy Forests Initiative."

Remember, Bush and his friends in the timber industry faced a very real problem. As just noted, before leaving office, President Clinton had designated 58.5 million acres of national forests in thirty-eight states as "roadless areas." The problem for big timber: no roads = no logging = no timber to sell. By August 2002, Bush had come up with an innovative solution: portray more logging as a way to save the forests.

And that's the "logic" behind the "Healthy Forests Initiative." As outlined, the initiative would "save" forests and "protect homes" by allowing timber companies to build new roads on public lands, in order to weed out national forests and remove young trees crowding the forest floor that might fuel more forest fires.

You have to admit, there is a certain logic behind it: if timber companies were successful in removing all the trees, they would indeed prevent forest fires—since there would be no trees left to burn. But these were remote lands, far from human habitation. In reality, the forests initiative was nothing but a license for timber companies to wipe out the best of America's remaining virgin forests, all in the name of "fuel reduction."

Environmentalists weren't fooled. The initiative was opposed by the Sierra Club, the Natural Resources Defense Council, the Wilderness Society, and other organizations. They saw it for what it was: one more attempt by George Bush to sell our resources off to the highest bidder. But Republicans in Congress swallowed Bush's plan hook, line, and sinker. They passed the Healthy Forests Restoration Act, which Bush then signed into law on December 2, 2003.

National Monuments. The Antiquities Act of 1906 allows presidents to preserve as National Monuments historic or scenic places that deserve special protection but are not considered worthy of national park designation. Some of the better known are New York's Statue of Liberty, Wyoming's Devil's Tower, California's Muir Woods, and Arizona's Navajo National Monument.

True to form, George Bush first used the Antiquities Act, not to add National Monuments, but to endanger them. Out of sixteen monuments in the West created by Bill Clinton, Bush opened up eleven to oil and gas extraction and mining for coal, gold, and silver—activities that the Antiquities Act is expressly designed to prevent. Bush defended his actions in typical Bush-speak: "There are some monuments where the land is so widespread, they just encompass as much as possible."

To give credit where credit is due, however, this is one case where George W. Bush finally got religion. In June 2006, under the Antiquities Act, he created the Northwestern Hawaii Islands Marine National Monument, encompassing 140,000 square miles—the world's largest marine protected area. Clearly, Bush did so only because no oil company was interested in the area, but still, for once we can say, "High five, George Bush!"

Drilling in Alaska. In his 2006 State of the Union speech, President Bush said, "America is addicted to oil." He's right. But his environmental and energy policies have done nothing except perpetuate our addiction to oil, starting with his determination to plant oil rigs on every last square foot of Alaskan wilderness.

It's like the story of the father who thought he could stop his son from smoking by forcing him to smoke a whole pack of cigarettes, one after the other, until he got sick of them. He tried to cure his son's addiction to smoking with smoking. Bush tried to cure our addiction to drilling with drilling.

From day one of their administration, Bush and Cheney, two frustrated oilmen, have lusted after the Arctic National Wildlife Refuge, or ANWR. This pristine slice of Alaska was set aside for federal protection by President Eisenhower in 1958. But Bush, Cheney, and their oil buddies aren't satisfied with drilling in the 95 percent of Alaska that is open to development. They insist on drilling in ANWR, too. And they've made ANWR the centerpiece of their national energy policy—even though it would produce very little oil. According to the United States Geological Survey, the economically recoverable oil from the Arctic Refuge—thirty-two billion barrels—would keep the lights on for only six months. And it would take ten years to bring that oil to market. Even at the peak of production in 2027, oil from the ANWR would supply only 2 percent of U.S. consumption.

But ANWR's not the only wild area of Alaska that Bush and Cheney have set their sights on. Their oil-and-gas-leasing plans cover virtually the entire length and width of Alaska's North Slope and Artic Ocean, both onshore and offshore—where they have already leased more than eighteen million acres to oil companies. In addition, they have offered for oil and gas leasing major parts of central Alaska's Yukon Flats National Wildlife Refuge, the third-largest reserve in the National Wildlife Refuge system and one of the greatest waterfowl breeding areas in the world. For Bush, Alaska is nothing but Texas with caribou instead of armadillos. Drill everywhere!

Energy. Drilling in Alaska was but one part of the industry-friendly, environmentally devastating energy policy put forth by the Bush administration, and it reads as if it were written in the boardroom of Enron—and probably was.

The Bush-Cheney plan called for the construction of hundreds of new power plants, a huge increase in coal production, bringing back nuclear power, and drilling for oil in the Rocky Mountains, as well as in the Alaskan wilderness. There was no priority on the development of alternative sources of energy or energy conservation because, as Cheney famously observed, "Conservation may be a sign of personal virtue, but it is not a sufficient basis for a sound, comprehensive energy strategy."

When the plan was shaped as legislation and sent to Congress for enactment, it contained so many sweetheart deals for oil and gas companies that Senator John McCain dubbed it "The No Lobbyist Left Behind Act." As signed by President Bush in August 2005, "The Energy Policy Act" provides $6 billion in tax credits for the nuclear power industry; another $6 billion, plus federal loan guarantees, to build sixteen new coal-fired power plants; and $1.7 billion in tax breaks to the oil and gas industry for new exploration. It also exempts oil and gas projects on public lands from key provisions of the Clean Water Act, the Safe Drinking Water Act, and the National Environmental Protection Act; opens up areas of the coast previously under moratorium to new offshore drilling; and, of course, sanctions drilling in Alaska's ANWR and North Slope.

Simply put, the Bush energy package is an environmental disaster. It contains nothing for the development of new, clean energy technologies. Despite Bush's rhetoric about moving beyond fossil fuels, his plan leaves us more dependent on oil, not less.

On a related energy issue, Bush refused to require U.S. automakers to produce more fuel-efficient cars. In fact, he opposed congressional efforts to increase fuel-efficiency standards from today's 27.5 miles per gallon to 33 miles per gallon over the next decade. In a stretch even for him, Bush argued that more fuel-efficient cars would mean more fatalities on the nation's highways— as if everyone responsible for traffic deaths is driving a Prius!

Under pressure to do something, Bush released his own fuel-efficiency proposal in March 2006, which environmentalists immediately dismissed as pure public relations. Bush's plan exempts pickup trucks, which account for 80 percent of all heavy private vehicles, and increases the efficiency of SUVs by only 1.8 miles per gallon over the next four years. As the Sierra Club points out, that isn't even a drop in the bucket. Without sacrificing performance or safety, we have the technology today to produce cars that get 40 miles per gallon—and doing so would save as much oil as we would import from the Persian Gulf and ANWR combined.

Clean Air. As noted previously, the Clean Air Act is part of the environmental legacy of President Richard Nixon. It is also one of the federal government's greatest success stories and is responsible for significant decreases in smokestack emissions and major improvements in air quality. But George Bush and Dick Cheney, again marching to the drums of their oil, gas, coal, and utility campaign contributors, immediately set out to roll back the clock. Fortunately, they've been blocked from doing so at almost every turn.

It's hard to believe he could do it with a straight face, but in 2001 Bush announced his deliberately misnamed "Clear Skies Initiative"—a plan that would actually make the air dirtier, not cleaner. Bush proposed replacing mandatory air pollution controls with voluntary controls, arguing that industry captains were more than willing to reduce pollution on their own, if only we asked them nicely. When that absurd proposal went nowhere, Bush decided to lean on his EPA and, like a good team player, the EPA complied.

In December 2002, Administrator Christie Whitman proposed changes in the EPA's enforcement of the Clean Air Act. Most notably, the EPA would exempt refineries and power plants from provisions of the New Source Review (NSR) regulations, which required some seventeen thousand large industrial facilities across the country to install new air pollution control equipment whenever plants were upgraded to produce even more emissions.

Environmental groups responded with outrage. Editorial pages decried the most dramatic rollback of clean air laws in thirty years. And fifteen Northeastern states sued to block relaxation of the NSR rules, which then New York attorney general Eliot Spitzer called "a betrayal of the right of Americans to breathe clean, healthy air." Adding insult to injury, the National Council of Churches issued a statement branding Bush's dirty air campaign "immoral." Congress eventually rejected the weaker NSR rules, as did the D.C. Circuit Federal Court of Appeals. The Bush administration was trying to rewrite the Clean Air Act, ruled the panel of judges, in a way that was valid "only in a Humpty-Dumpty world."

Along the way, Bush's attempts to gut the Clean Air Act claimed another victim. When EPA administrator Christie Whitman left the Bush administration, she said she was doing so in order to spend more time with her family. This was nothing but classic spin! When was the last time you or anyone you know quit a job to spend more time with his or her family? Never. Yet government people do it all the time—or so they say.

Whitman later admitted that the real reason she resigned was because she so strongly disagreed with the Bush-Cheney plan to let older industries off the hook. When she personally appealed to President Bush to drop the plan exempting power plants from installing new pollution control equipment, he refused. Whitman was forced to sign the final plan or else. "I just couldn't sign it," said Whitman. She resigned in June 2003.

An Inconvenient Truth. You know what they say about boys who grew up in the oil business: "You can take the boy out of the oil company, but you can't stop oil industry lobbyists from controlling everything the boy does afterward." Or something like that.

Oil and gas companies were the largest contributors to Bush's campaign for president in 2000. Four years later, they poured another $2 million into his reelection campaign, making him the number-one recipient of energy industry dollars. For their campaign largesse, George W. Bush let them dictate his administration's energy policy and agreed to oppose any changes in policy they did not support, even if it meant putting the planet at risk.

In the face of overwhelming evidence of the reality and danger of climate change, the extent to which Bush and Cheney not only ignored the problem, but also blocked any efforts to take corrective action, is astounding. History may well regard it as the single greatest failure of a failed Bush administration, and they certainly have many failures to choose from.

It started in March 2003, when Bush announced that the United States was officially rejecting the Kyoto Treaty on reducing greenhouse emissions, which had already been signed by 169 nations.

Still, Bush couldn't ignore demands for action on global warming, especially since two members of his Cabinet, EPA administrator Whitman and Treasury Secretary Paul O'Neill, were public advocates of the need to take global warming seriously. So Bush responded by asking the National Academy of Sciences for advice. Its report, published in June 2001, concluded that global warming was real and that human activity was a major contributing factor. Bush responded by calling for yet another study, this time by his own EPA.

When it was released, in June 2002, the much-revised and badly watered-down EPA report still proved to be a stunning endorsement of what scientists had been warning about for years. It began, "There is general agreement that the observed warming is real and has been particularly strong within the past 20 years." Even though the EPA called for only voluntary, not mandatory, changes by industry, it affirmed that human creations such as oil refineries, power plants, and auto emissions were behind climate change—and that global warming was already having a significant, negative impact on the environment.

Did EPA scientists convince Bush to take another look at climate change? Not at all. When pressed by reporters, he dismissed their report with a curt "I read the report put out by the bureaucracy."

Actually, Bush did more than that: he tried to scuttle the EPA report before it was published. Its first draft contained the ominous warning: "Climate change has global consequences for human health and the environment." That wording was dropped on orders from the White House.

But that's not all. Bush had previously installed the former oil industry lobbyist Philip Cooney as chief of staff of the White House Council on Environmental Quality and had given him explicit orders to throw cold water on any pro–global warming language that accidentally emanated from any other part of the administration. Cooney eagerly complied. In a series of e-mails, he asked the pro-business Competitive Enterprise Institute, as a favor to the Bush White House, to debunk the EPA report. Cooney himself later admitted to Congress that he had personally edited three government reports to eliminate or downplay any link between greenhouse gases and global warming. By the time Cooney was finished with the EPA report, agency scientists complained that it "no longer accurately represents scientific consensus on climate change." Cooney left the White House in 2005 to go to work for ExxonMobil.

But even under the heavy-handed Bush White House, government scientists did not give up. In August 2004, in a report to Congress, the EPA acknowledged that global warming cannot be explained by natural causes alone and that it is at least partially due to energy consumption, deforestation, and other human activities. Reporters hurried to ask President Bush what had caused the administration to change its policy. "I don't think we did," muttered the confused chief executive.

White House aides later made it official: the latest EPA report—which apparently caught Bush by surprise—in no way represented a change in administration policy. Even though the United States produces more than 20 percent of the world's greenhouse gases, and even though nineteen of the twenty hottest years on record have occurred since 1980, and even though the world's glaciers are melting before our eyes, George W. Bush would not even admit that global warming exists, let alone do anything about it.

At the same time, in a classic case of the left hand not knowing what the right hand was doing, the Pentagon released a 2004 report identifying global warming as one of the most serious threats to national security because of the anarchy that could result from massive climate change and economic collapse. Quick! Somebody tell George W. Bush.

Finally, on July 6, 2005, before leaving for a G8 meeting in Scotland, President Bush admitted for the first time that pollution generated by humans contributed to global warming. Any hopes for a change of direction were dashed, however, when Bush spent his entire time at the summit opposing mandatory emission controls proposed by the British prime minister Tony Blair and others.

Again on May 31, 2007, Bush sounded the right notes on global warming. In a Chicago speech, he declared, "In recent years, science has deepened our understanding of climate change and opened new possibilities for confronting it. The United States takes this issue seriously."

How seriously? Not very. As of this writing, the Bush administration has still proposed no new restrictions on greenhouse gases from power plants or automobiles, nor has it agreed to participate in any international agreements on climate change.

Meanwhile, the evidence keeps mounting. In late August 2007, the National Oceanic and Atmospheric Administration reported that 2006 was the second-warmest year in recorded history in the United States. After comparing the natural effects of El Niño versus the manmade effects of industrial activities, NOAA scientists discovered that you couldn't blame global warming on Mother Nature. They concluded that "2006 warmth was primarily due to human influences." But George Bush is still not listening.

He's not listening to scientists. But, more significantly, he's not listening to religious leaders, either. On global warming, this self-described born-again Christian is, in fact, ignoring the warnings of more and more Christian conservative pastors about the dangers of climate change, as well as their pleas for decisive government action. From the pulpit, they are first to declare that those who fail to take global warming seriously are neither true Christians nor true conservatives.

Protecting God's Creation

In Genesis, the first book of the Bible, there are two accounts of creation. In both, God creates the earth and all living creatures. And in both, humankind is clearly the crowning achievement of God's creation. But, as laid out in Genesis 2:15, the second account of creation features a very special responsibility that is given to man and his offspring:

The Lord God took the man and put him in the Garden of Eden to work it and take care of it.

Consider the command: "Take care of it." It is precisely that attitude toward the environment, the responsibility of stewardship, that was missing for centuries from the agenda of organized religion—but no longer.

Today, in a revolutionary move that has severed many religious conservatives from political conservatives and seriously weakened the stranglehold of the Republican Party over the religious right, many churches have banded together under the banner of environmental protection. The movement includes evangelical Christians, Catholics, Muslims, and Jews. Their argument is simple but compelling: Whatever our creed, the dual mission we all share is to love God and love our neighbor. How can we love God without loving and caring for His creation? How can we love our neighbor without loving and protecting the environment on which he or she depends on to survive? How, indeed?

Religious conservationists base their passion for the environment on the words of Scripture. Jesus often uses references to nature in his parables, from the "lilies of the field" to the "seed falling on good soil." The Psalms overflow with praise for God's creation: "The heavens declare the glory of God; the skies proclaim the work of his hand" (Psalms 19:1). And many passages in the Old Testament affirm that we honor God by caring for His handiwork: "You alone are the Lord. You made the heavens, even the highest heavens, and all their starry host, the earth and all that is on it, the seas and all that is in them. You give life to everything, and the multitudes of heaven worship you" (Nehemiah 9:6).

Churches are late arrivals to the environmental movement, to be sure. For the last forty or fifty years, for the most part, they sat on the sidelines. They weren't antienvironment; they just weren't involved in the issue. Saving the environment was not on the list of priority issues for either the religious right, primarily concerned with abortion and homosexuality, or the religious left, more focused on poverty and peace.

That began to change in 1990. Led by the late astronomer Carl Sagan, a group of international scientists meeting in Moscow published an "Open Letter to the Religious Community," arguing that global environmental problems had become so serious they demanded a worldwide religious, as well as scientific, response. The reaction was immediate and electric.

In the early 1990s, in rapid succession, appeared the Earth Ministry Organization of Seattle, the National Religious Partnership for the

Environment, the Evangelical Environmental Movement, and other religious organizations whose primary focus was environmental protection. More recently, even the pope joined the crowd.

On several occasions, Pope Benedict XVI has advised Catholics of the need to protect the environment, warning in early 2007 that "disregard for the environment always harms human coexistence, and vice versa." The pope is soon expected to release an encyclical on the environment. And speaking for the pope, Cardinal Renato Raffaele Martino, the head of the Vatican's Pontifical Council of Justice and Peace, told a 2007 Vatican Conference on Climate Change, "For environment . . . read Creation. The mastery of man over Creation must not be despotic or senseless. Man must cultivate and safeguard God's creation."

Actually, in one important way, the Vatican leads the way in reducing the human impact on climate change. In the summer of 2007, it made arrangements to replant an ancient thirty-seven-acre forest in Hungary. Now renamed the "Vatican Climate Forest," the papal trees will absorb as much carbon dioxide as the Vatican will produce each year, making the Vatican the world's first carbon-neutral state.

The involvement of churches in the environmental movement is extremely significant. For one thing, millions and millions of people can be reached through the churches, people who might otherwise remain ignorant of environmental issues. But religious belief also brings another important dimension to the debate.

Arguing that we humans, the most advanced form of life on the planet, have a special responsibility to care for the habitat we share with all creatures is one thing. But adding that we have a God-given responsibility to protect His Creation clearly takes things to another level. And that divine imperative is not limited to environmental education. It also encompasses environmental action. The message is clear: As a believer, how can you refuse to be an environmentalist? As a believer, how can you refuse to recycle, conserve energy, buy a Prius, or take the bus?

For many churches, moving into environmental issues has not been easy or automatic. One issue, in fact—global warming—has split evangelical churches right down the middle.

In January 2006, a group of young evangelical pastors petitioned the National Association of Evangelicals (NAE) to recognize climate change as a critical global problem and urge member churches to join in petitioning world governments to take corrective action. Their petition fell on deaf ears. Led by Jerry Falwell, Pat Robertson, James Dobson, Chuck Colson, Franklin Graham, the so-called Old Guard of the evangelical movement, the NAE voted against taking a stand on global warming, ruling that it was not a "consensus" issue.

But the forward-looking evangelicals didn't give up so easily. Within a week, they had regrouped and issued the Evangelical Climate Initiative, signed by 106 evangelical pastors, including Rick Warren, the head of California's Saddleback Church and one of the most influential clergymen in the country. The initiative outlines what younger pastors believe to be a moral obligation to save the planet—an obligation they will not let anyone, not even their senior evangelicals, prevent them from carrying out:

> As American evangelical Christian leaders, we recognize both our opportunity and our responsibility to offer a biblically based moral witness that can help shape public policy in the most powerful nation on earth, and therefore contribute to the well-being of the entire world. *Whether* we will enter the public square and offer our witness there is no longer an open question. We are in that square, and we will not withdraw.

Setting forth an action agenda on global warming, the Evangelical Climate Initiative makes four "claims" and urges "all who will listen" to take "the appropriate actions that follow from them."

- Claim one: Human-induced climate change is real
- Claim two: The consequences of climate change will be significant, and will hit the poor the hardest.
- Claim three: Christian moral convictions demand our response to the climate change problem
- Claim four: The need to act now is urgent. Governments, businesses, churches, and individuals all have a role to play in addressing climate change—starting now.

As may already be evident, evangelicals embrace global warming so strongly because they consider it more than just an environmental issue. They see it as an integral part of their "pro-life" commitment.

"This is a pro-life issue," says Pastor Joel Hunter, a director of the
National Association of Evangelicals, "it simply addresses life outside
the womb." They see it as directly linked to national security. And
because it's a problem that will most severely affect the world's poorest
populations, they see it as one of the most important opportunities
today to carry out the traditional Christian obligation to help the
poor—an obligation that's particularly pressing when wealthy nations
are creating the problem and poorer nations are suffering from it.
Noted John Carr, the director of the U.S. Conference of Catholic
Bishops, "There is no issue that will touch the poorest among us more.
Some of us have been doing the sinning, but others will pay the
penance."

Most interesting, for our purposes, is the fact that the active involvement of churches, especially on global warming, changes the entire
dynamic of the environmental movement. In effect, it brings things
back full circle, to a time when conservatives were taking the lead on
conservation issues.

And that's especially true of religious conservatives. By embracing
global warming as a priority issue, much to the chagrin of conservatives
like James Dobson and Pat Robertson, evangelical pastors are demonstrating that abortion and gay marriage are not the only issues
Christians care about, that alleviating poverty is still a big priority, and
that people of faith can be theologically conservative without also having to be politically conservative.

By emphasizing the environment as a God-driven issue, churches
may well put conservatives back in the driver's seat on conservation,
with a religious twist. But that's not all. They may also break the
stranglehold the Republican Party has held on religious conservatives.

The environment, in other words, may prove to be the issue that
shatters once and for all the unholy alliance that has existed between
the Republican Party and the religious right, ever since Jerry Falwell
founded the Moral Majority in 1975. Who knows? If the environment
remains an important issue in the faith-based community, and if evangelicals continue to be rebuffed by George W. Bush and other
Republican leaders on climate change, they just might look elsewhere
for candidates to support. God only knows, they might even support a
Democrat. And that would be nothing short of miraculous!

Lessons Learned

A favorite seminary professor of mine often warned, "It's a queer bird that dirties its own nest."

He wasn't talking about the environment, but he might well have been. Because we are queer birds, indeed, if we continue to dirty our own nest and think there are no long-term consequences.

Clean air and water, parks, open space, rivers, farmland, mountains, desert, and marshes: they are not ours to despoil. They are ours to enjoy, briefly, before passing them on, unspoiled, to our children and grandchildren. Preserving the planet is not a luxury, it's our God-given responsibility. Protecting the environment is not a liberal conspiracy, it's a conservative mandate—which many of today's conservatives either don't understand or simply reject.

After starting off as responsible stewards of God's creation, most conservatives have turned into its implacable enemies: treating natural resources not as gifts to treasure for long-term enjoyment, but as assets to plunder for short-term profit.

We've seen how conservatives who are in power deal with the environment. Given the opportunity to defend it, they declared war on it, instead. They don't deserve another chance, and we can't afford to give them one.

The environment is too fragile and the stakes are too high to risk any further onslaught or damage. The consequences of global warming are too severe to risk any further delay in addressing this problem.

CHAPTER 2

Restoring Honor and Dignity to Government

The conservative believes that there exists
an enduring moral order.
Russell Kirk

I think one of the great problems we have in
the Republican Party is that we don't encourage
you to be nasty. We encourage you to be neat,
obedient, loyal and faithful and all those Boy
Scout words, which would be great around a
campfire but are lousy in politics.
Newt Gingrich

I will restore honor and dignity to the
White House.
George W. Bush

Duke Cunningham is a hero. He's an
honorable man of high integrity.
Tom DeLay

I happen to be one who admires Scooter Libby.
John McCain

David Vitter is a good man.
Rudy Giuliani

God votes Republican.

Or so conservatives would have us believe. In fact, if you've swallowed the rhetoric of the religious right and the Republican National Committee (assuming there's any difference between the two), the contrast between the two parties is clear: Republicans believe in God, Democrats don't; and people who live in red states have moral values, while people who live in blue states have none.

Not so fast. As I argued in my last book, *How the Republicans Stole Religion*, neither party has a monopoly on morality. And as Senator Barack Obama reminded delegates to the 2004 Democratic National Convention: "We worship an awesome God in the blue states!"

From this nation's founding to the present, in fact, both liberals and conservatives have relied on their own moral creeds to shape the major issues of the day. Liberals oppose the immorality of the war in Iraq, the death penalty, and the fact that forty-five million Americans have no health insurance. Conservatives aim their moral outrage at abortion, stem cell research, and gay marriage. And, more and more, both liberals and conservatives recognize the moral imperative of protecting the environment.

Some people mistakenly identify our trust in moral rectitude with belief in a particular religion. Most notably, the Reverend Pat Robertson and the late Reverend Jerry Falwell, among evangelicals, have argued that the United States was founded as a Christian nation—and still is a Christian nation today.

They're dead wrong. The Founders did not want an official state religion and worked mightily to prevent the establishment of one. Many of our original settlers came to America, in fact, to escape an official state religion. And most of the Founders were not members of the Christian faith at all. They were Deists. They believed in a distant Supreme Presence who, like the proverbial clock maker, set the wheels of the universe in motion, then sat back and watched the passage of time. The Founders created a society where people were free to believe, or not believe, as they pleased.

Our civic morality is based, not on faith in God, but on faith in the inherent worth of each individual. Inspired by the great Enlightenment philosophers, our Founders embraced a nontheological, but no less compelling, code of human behavior: We live a virtuous life. We know the difference between right and wrong. We treat others with respect—

not because God told us to, but because we recognize that our fellow man, endowed with the same inalienable rights as we are, deserves it. And, by extension, we conduct ourselves in human affairs in an upright and virtuous manner—and assume our leaders will do so, as well.

In other words, we don't have to demand high moral conduct from our political leaders: we simply expect nothing less. It goes with the territory.

That theme of morality as the glue holding our democratic society together permeates the writings of political conservatives. In *The Politics of Prudence*, Russell Kirk makes it the first of his ten conservative principles: "[T]he conservative believes that there exists an enduring moral order." He identifies "the essence of social conservatism" as "preservation of the ancient moral traditions of humanity." And he warns what happens when morality is pushed aside:

> A society in which men and women are governed by a belief in an enduring moral order, by a strong sense of right and wrong, by personal convictions about justice and honor, will be a good society—whatever political machinery it may utilize; while a society in which men and women are morally adrift, ignorant of norms, and intent chiefly upon gratification of appetites, will be a bad society—no matter how many people vote and no matter how liberal its formal constitution may be.

In theory, therefore, we expect both liberals and conservatives to maintain the highest moral standards—but especially conservatives. It's not surprising when liberals fail. But conservatives? Never. Conservatives are the guardians of tradition and morality. True conservatives don't cheat, don't steal, don't lie—and never, never use public office for private gain. And since serving the public interest is an inherent part of public morality, conservatives will always put public values over private ones—and will never serve special interests over the public interest. Catering to special interests, conservatives often argue, is a liberal's game.

Oh, really? In the real world, somehow, it hasn't always worked out that way. Even prior to today's political scandals, in fact, the twentieth century's three biggest symbols of government corruption— Teapot Dome, Watergate, and Iran-Contra—all occurred under conservative, Republican presidents.

Teapot Dome

By today's standards, what happened at Teapot Dome almost seems like "business as usual." Headline: A member of the president's cabinet abuses his office for personal gain. Reaction: So what's the big deal?

But Teapot Dome was a big deal at the time because it was such a shock. For the first time in our history, a Cabinet member was ultimately sent to prison. Even today, the words "Teapot Dome" are shorthand for government corruption.

The scandal's origins lay in an important public policy. After World War I, worried that it might run out of fuel in any future conflict, the navy set aside three oil reserves on public lands, to be used only by the military in case of emergency. Two of the fields, Elk Hills and Buena Vista Hills, were in Kern County, California. The third, named Teapot Dome after a teapot-shaped rock formation located there, was in Natrona County, Wyoming.

At first, all three fields were under the jurisdiction of the navy. Then, in 1921, President Warren G. Harding appointed one of his Republican cronies, the New Mexico senator Albert B. Fall, as his secretary of the interior. One year later, Fall convinced the navy to transfer control of the properties to his department. Without seeking competitive bids, he then leased the fields to two oil executives, Henry Sinclair and Edward L. Doheny, who showered Secretary Fall with $404,000 in appreciation—the equivalent of $4 million today.

When Washington started buzzing with rumors about how the interior secretary became a wealthy man overnight, the Senate Committee on Public Lands opened a two-year investigation into the matter. Eventually, Fall was found guilty of bribery, fined $100,000, and sentenced to one year in prison.

Warren G. Harding and Teapot Dome thus became symbols of official wrongdoing, inspiring an impressionable young man from Whittier, California, to tell his parents, "I will be an old-fashioned lawyer, a lawyer who can't be bought."

History had a more ironic outcome in mind. Fifty years later, Richard Nixon and Watergate displaced Harding and Teapot Dome as shorthand for corruption in Washington, and then some.

Am I Not a Crook?

"I am not going to comment from the White House on a third-rate burglary attempt."

With those words on June 19, 1972, the press secretary Ron Ziegler attempted to eliminate any possibility of a connection between the White House and a break-in, two days earlier, at the headquarters of the Democratic National Committee in the office building of the Watergate Hotel. Poor guy. Little did he realize that his boss, President Richard Nixon, had authorized the entire operation—and would spend the next two years trying to cover it up.

It is difficult to overstate the impact of Watergate on U.S. politics. No other political event in recent history has caused such upheaval in Washington, and no politician has been trusted since. Phrases like "executive privilege," "stonewalling," "dirty tricks," "plumbers," and "cover-up" are now part of the permanent political lexicon. And variations on the famous question "What did the president know, and when did he know it?" are still invoked today when allegations of wrongdoing surface in the nation's capital.

Thanks to news accounts, several books, and the movie *All the President's Men*, the facts of Watergate are well-known. Even the identity of the enigmatic "Deep Throat" is no longer a secret. We're all familiar with the truly pathetic figure of a paranoid Nixon, assured of reelection, yet nonetheless ordering the Watergate break-in and then using all the powers of his office to cover up any connection, all the while taping the conversations that would eventually prove his guilt and cause his downfall. It has all the makings of a Greek tragedy.

Yet for Richard Nixon, Watergate was not the exception but the rule. That's what makes Nixon so interesting. This president, who was so gifted in foreign policy and who showed such leadership in the fields of housing, education, and the environment, was at the same time fundamentally corrupt.

Nixon actually believed that "When a president does it, that means it's not illegal." Or, in the original Louis XIV version, "L'Etat, c'est moi."

Nixon did not hesitate to use the powers of the presidency to secure his own political base and to destroy his political enemies. He ordered the illegal wiretapping of the phones of journalists and politicians. In addition to the Watergate break-in, he sent burglars into the office of the

Pentagon Papers leaker Daniel Ellsberg's psychiatrist. He sicced the FBI on his critics. He illegally juggled campaign funds and maintained a secret campaign slush fund in Mexico. The Nixon aide Charles Colson, inspired by his boss's take-no-prisoners approach to politics, proposed that they send their henchmen to firebomb the offices of the Brookings Institution in Washington. Nixon, showing restraint for once, declined.

In the end, few people close to Nixon escaped his downfall. Attorney General John Mitchell and the top White House aides Bob Haldeman, John Ehrlichman, and Charles Colson all served time in jail. The administration officials Gordon Strachan, Robert Mardian, and Kenneth Parkinson were also indicted for conspiring to obstruct the Watergate investigation. Dwight Chapin and Ed Reinecke were found guilty of lying to Congress and/or the grand jury.

Rather than face certain impeachment, Nixon announced on August 8, 1974, that he would resign the office of president, effective noon the following day. He was pardoned by President Gerald Ford exactly one month later.

Hopefully, we will never see a figure as personally corrupt as Richard Nixon in the Oval Office again. And yet, despite the merry band of criminals caught up in Watergate, the Nixon administration did not set the record for widespread government corruption. That distinction ultimately went to another Republican and a true conservative.

Making Deals with Terrorists

We remember Ronald Reagan not only as a likable, sunny, grandfatherly fellow, but as a manageable, albeit somewhat out-of-touch president who would never do anything wrong or tolerate any wrongdoing by members of his administration. At best, that's only half correct. If Watergate gave us the concept of "plausible deniability," Reagan perfected it.

Reagan himself may have had clean hands, but he surrounded himself with a bunch of scoundrels and merely looked the other way when they got in trouble. When he left office, no fewer than 138 members of his administration had either been indicted, convicted, or subjects of investigations into official misconduct or criminal activity. In his book *Sleepwalking through History: America in the Reagan Years*, the presiden-

tial historian Haynes Johnson concludes, "In terms of numbers of officials involved, the record of his administration was the worst ever."

We're not talking minor players, either. Many top officials of the
Reagan administration were brought down by various scandals, includ-
ing Attorney General Ed Meese, the White House counselor Michael
Deaver, Interior Secretary James Watt, Labor Secretary Raymond
Donovan, the EPA director Anne Gorsuch Burford, and National
Security Adviser Richard Allen. But the worst crime of the Reagan
years, and the one his administration will be remembered for, was the
series of events that became known as the Iran-Contra Affair.

In theory, Iran-Contra was simply a twofold business transaction:
selling arms to Iran and using profits from those arms sales to supply
weapons to the Nicaraguan contras. The problem is, both phases of
that operation were against U.S. policy and against the law. The Boland
Amendment, passed by Congress and signed into law by President
Reagan, expressly prohibited military support for the contras. On many
occasions, President Reagan repeated his pledge: "We will never make
deals with terrorists." Meanwhile, with his blessing, members of his
administration were doing both: dealing with terrorists and arming the
contras.

I first learned of the Iran-contra connection a couple of months
before it became public. In September 1986, in my job as a political
commentator for KABC-TV, I traveled to Nicaragua with a small group
of journalists from Los Angeles, organized by the peace activist Alice
McGrath. At the suggestion of a couple of journalist friends, I next flew
to San Jose, Costa Rica, where I met up with the ABC Radio stringer
Tony Avirgan.

Tony covered the Nicaraguan insurgency from Costa Rica, where
a large force of contras was based. A few months earlier, in fact, while
attending a press conference deep in the jungle called by the contra
leader and former Sandinista Eden Pastora, Tony had almost lost his
arm when a briefcase bomb exploded, killing one journalist and
wounding Pastora and several others.

Over a Chinese dinner in San Jose, Tony outlined in great detail a
chain of events whereby the CIA sold antitank and antiaircraft missiles
to terrorists in Iran and next turned around and used the proceeds to
buy arms for the contras, which they then flew into contra bases in
Costa Rica and Honduras. The entire operation, he insisted, was being

run right out of the Reagan White House. I must admit, at first hearing, it all sounded too fantastic and too evil for me to believe.

About a month later, Tony and his wife, the journalist Martha Honey, repeated the same story to an equally skeptical group of reporters at a news conference I arranged for them at the Los Angeles Press Club. As I recall, everyone listened politely, but nobody wrote or broadcast the story—even though, by this time, the first accounts of the Iran-contra connection had been reported by a Lebanese magazine and denied by the Reagan White House.

That changed suddenly, one week to the day after Tony and Martha's news conference, when Attorney General Ed Meese walked into the White House briefing room and told reporters that illegal arms sales to Iran were indeed funding illegal arms shipments to Nicaragua. The resulting uproar played out in nationally televised congressional hearings and an investigation by Special Prosecutor Lawrence Walsh.

By the time the dust settled, the list of those indicted or convicted of crimes related to Iran-Contra included the defense secretary Casper Weinberger, the national security advisers Robert McFarlane and John Poindexter, the National Security Agency staffer Colonel Ollie North, the State Department's Elliott Abrams, and the CIA officials Alan Fiers, Clair George, and Duane Clarridge. Weinberger, McFarlane, Abrams, Fiers, George, and Clarridge were given a Christmas Eve 1992 pardon by President George H. W. Bush. North's conviction was over-turned on appeal, thanks to blanket immunity given him by Congress in return for his memorable testimony.

Among top Reagan aides, only Secretary of State George Shultz opposed the Iran-contra operation from the beginning. Selling arms to our sworn enemy in order to help overthrow a democratically elected government in Central America, he argued, would amount to nothing less than "an impeachable offense." But nobody listened. And, in the end, unlike Richard Nixon, Ronald Reagan escaped impeachment only because everybody believed him when he said he had no idea what was going on in his own White House.

From a historical perspective, the Iran-contra scandal shattered the myth that conservatism and ethical behavior were synonymous. With Ronald Reagan, conservatives had finally won the White House—only to provide the most corrupt administration to date.

It was an ominous sign, indeed. Iran-Contra set the stage for the rampant corruption that was later experienced under Newt Gingrich and George W. Bush.

Newt's Contract with America

The basic theme that conservatives held higher moral standards than most politicians resurfaced in the early days of the Clinton adminis-tration, long before anybody ever heard of Monica Lewinsky. It was a moral crusade, in fact, that fueled the Republican Revolution in 1994, sweeping Republicans into power and ending forty straight years of Democratic control of Congress.

Ironically, given later disclosures, the leader of that moral crusade was the Republican congressman Newt Gingrich. His target was the Democratic Speaker Jim Wright.

Like many politicians, Wright wrote (or had written for him) a van-ity memoir, *Reflections of a Public Man*. As Speaker of the House, he was then able to persuade several labor unions to place bulk orders for the book—in return for which he would agree to speak at one of their gatherings.

In Washington, this is not an unusual practice. Full disclosure: in 2004, I made the same deal with several unions, giving free speeches in return for bulk purchases of my book *Bush Must Go*. But, of course, I was not Speaker of the House. Thanks to the then young congressman Newt Gingrich, Wright's deal cost him the Speakership.

In February 1988, Gingrich filed a complaint with the House Ethics Committee, accusing Wright of using his book appearances in order to, in effect, harness speaking fees in excess of what House rules allowed. The subsequent uproar forced Wright out of office—he resigned in May 1989—and helped to propel Gingrich into the same job, five years later.

And wouldn't you know it? Once in office, the man who got there by challenging the ethics of others became a serial ethical violator himself.

Actually, there were earlier signs that Gingrich's holier-than-thou rhetoric might backfire on him. In 1992, he had banded with a group of Republican colleagues, the "Gang of Seven," to demand an outside investigation into the House banking scandal. At the time, lax rules of the House Bank allowed members to overdraw their accounts without paying any penalty, and hundreds did so. It was, charged Newt, an abuse of power for which members should be reprimanded and severely punished. His ardor cooled, however, when it was reported that Gingrich himself had bounced twenty-two House checks.

But that was small potatoes compared to his ethical troubles as Speaker. On a variety of charges, eighty-four different ethics complaints were filed against Speaker Gingrich with the House Ethics Committee. Most were dropped after he resigned as Speaker. In the most serious case, however, Gingrich did not escape.

On January 21, 1997, the Republican-controlled House voted overwhelmingly, 395–28, to reprimand Gingrich and force him to pay a $300,000 financial penalty for violating federal tax laws and deliberately providing false information to the House Ethics Committee. The man who put himself on a moral pedestal thus became the first Speaker in 208 years to be reprimanded and penalized by the entire House of Representatives for ethical violations.

Ironically, in light of what would later happen to him, the House member who defended Gingrich most vigorously was the Texas congressman Tom DeLay, who denounced the Ethics Committee's recommendation that congressional leaders should be held to a higher standard of conduct. Debating Gingrich's fate on the House floor, DeLay thundered, "The highest possible standard does not mean an impossible standard no American could possibly reach."

As if that public reprimand were not enough, Gingrich then turned around and made his own book deal—one that made Jim Wright look like a Cub Scout. As an advance for his own memoirs, Gingrich received a hefty $4.5 million from HarperCollins, a publishing house owned by Rupert Murdoch, who was then under investigation by the Federal Communications Commission (FCC) for the possibly illegal purchase of the FOX Network. A week later, Gingrich entertained Murdoch, accompanied by FOX's top Washington lobbyist, at a strategy session in the Speaker's office. Gingrich insisted there was no connection between the big paycheck, the big meeting, and the big investigation, but few believed him. After howls of public outrage, Gingrich dropped the $4.5 million advance and wrote the book for a buck.

As the former Senate Majority Leader Robert Dole noted, Gingrich's book problems were a classic case of "live by the sword, die by the sword." Gingrich resigned as Speaker in 1998, the most ethically challenged man ever to serve in the House's top post. And that does not count his alleged sexual misconduct, which included having an affair with a Congressional staffer, while House Republicans were trying to impeach Bill Clinton for the same offense. Fortunately, for many Republicans, hypocrisy is not a capital offense.

Newt Gingrich certainly made his mark. As the most corrupt Speaker ever, he paved the way for the most corrupt Congress ever and one of the most corrupt administrations ever.

The Culture of Corruption

At the conclusion of every campaign speech as a candidate for president, the Texas governor George W. Bush raised his right hand, as if taking the oath of office, and pledged to restore "honor and integrity" to the White House. That turned out to be just another one of his broken promises, along with his pledge to be "a uniter, not a divider" (unless you count his uniting the country against him and his policies).

Indeed, during the Bush 43 administration, from one end of Pennsylvania Avenue to the other, so many Republicans were investigated, indicted, and convicted of wrongdoing that the then Democratic leader, and soon-to-become House Speaker, Nancy Pelosi dubbed it "the culture of corruption."

Republicans, of course, did not have a monopoly on corruption, although they came close. The Democratic congressman William "Dollar Bill" Jefferson was caught with $90,000 in lobbying money in his home freezer. And West Virginia's Alan Mollohan was forced to resign from the House Ethics Committee amid charges that he had funneled federal funds to home-state foundations, perhaps enriching himself in the process. But they were two lone Democrats among a crowd of corrupt Republicans.

Conservatives may talk a good game about moral values. In practice, they proved just as corruptible as anybody else, if not more so. Indeed, if George W. Bush has accomplished nothing else in office, he has proven that the phrase "conservative morality" is all too often a contradiction in terms.

Serving the Special Interests

Like almost everything else in Washington, the tone of unethical behavior was set by the White House. And while there is no evidence that George W. Bush and Dick Cheney—or, for that matter, any of their top aides—have used their White House power to enrich themselves, they did, from the very beginning, send the clear signal that under the Bush 43 administration, their cronies in big business could get anything they wanted.

It started with special treatment for an old Bush pal from Texas.

"Kenny Boy"

A few years ago, at Florida's fabulous Boca Raton Resort, I was speaking to a group of some thirty leaders of the Horatio Alger Society, when I suddenly lost my breath—and, momentarily, my train of thought. For, walking into the back of the room and taking a seat in the rear row was none other than the former Enron CEO Ken Lay.

Later, enjoying drinks and dinner with the group aboard a member's mega-yacht, I carefully avoided Lay, whom I had pilloried many times in print and on television. But Lay sought me out and insisted on beginning a conversation with me about energy conservation. I learned firsthand what an engaging personality he was and how he had charmed his way into friendships with three presidents.

The late Ken Lay is the poster boy for George W. Bush's practice of enabling and condoning corporate greed. Lay started out as one of George H. W. Bush's finance chairmen but soon shifted his loyalties to the younger Bush. He supported every one of George W.'s campaigns: for Congress, governor, and president. In 2000, he was a Bush "Pioneer," raising more than $100,000. He provided the candidate Bush with a corporate jet. He was Bush's guest for lunch at the White House the day after his inauguration. And for good reason. Under Lay's direction, Enron and Enron employees were the top contributors to George W. Bush's campaign, making a total of $602,625 in direct contributions.

Lay was rewarded for his loyalty with unprecedented access to the new Bush administration. He was the only corporate CEO to be given a one-on-one meeting with Vice President Dick Cheney in putting together the administration's energy policy. And that meeting paid off. Congressman Henry Waxman later identified seventeen policies in Cheney's final report that directly benefited Enron.

Bush appointed two Lay associates, Nora Mean Brownell and Pat Wood III, to the Federal Energy Regulatory Commission, or FERC. He also dispatched Lay to interview Curtis Herbert, his newly appointed chair of FERC. When Lay reported back that he was less than impressed, Bush fired Herbert and replaced him with Patrick Wood, Lay's handpicked candidate. But that was only the beginning. In the White House, Bush surrounded himself with no fewer than seventeen former Enron executives or consultants. It was difficult to know where Enron ended and the Bush administration began.

Small wonder, then, that Lay got help at the highest level whenever he needed it. When Governor Gray Davis requested the administration's assistance in easing temporary caps on wholesale electricity prices to help deal with California's rolling blackouts in 2000, Lay asked Cheney to say no. Cheney complied. When Enron wanted to build a new liquefied natural gas plant at Dabhol, India, both Cheney and Secretary of State Colin Powell lobbied the Indian government for him. The National Security Council even formed a "Dabhol Working Group" inside the White House.

Few corporate CEOs have enjoyed that kind of influence in any administration since the days of the banking tycoon J. P. Morgan. But Enron wasn't the only sacred cow in the Bush administration. Vice President Cheney had his own corporate pet to pamper.

HALLIBURTON—"with Two L's"

Believe it or not, there are people more cynical than I am. Unlike many of my fellow liberals, for example, I have never subscribed to the theory that the only reason nations go to war is for the financial benefit of big corporations. But there's no denying that for many firms, wars are prime opportunities for profiteering—and prime opportunities for government leaders, if they are so inclined, to give special preference to their corporate friends. When it came to war with Iraq, George Bush and Dick Cheney couldn't wait.

One price we paid for destroying Iraq, of course, was the cost of rebuilding it. It was a stiff price, indeed, and most of that payment went right into the pockets of Bush and Cheney's corporate cronies.

According to the Center for Responsive Politics, which keeps track of such things, six firms led the corporate hit parade for campaign contributions from 1999 to 2002: the Bechtel Corporation; the Fluor Corporation; Halliburton; its subsidiary Kellogg, Brown, and Root (KBR); the Parsons Corporation; and Washington Group International (WGI). Together, they spent $3.6 million in campaign contributions, of which 66 percent went to the Bush presidential campaign and other top Republican candidates.

And—surprise, surprise—guess which six firms were given the exclusive right to bid on $900 million worth of contracts to rebuild Iraq's water supply system, roads, sewers, oil pipelines, power plants, and electricity grid? You guessed it: Bechtel, Fluor, Halliburton, KBR, Parsons, and WGI. If that's not political payback, it sure looks like it. As the *New York Times* editorialized, "This looks like naked favoritism and undermines the Bush administration's portrayal of the war as a campaign for disarmament and democracy, not lucre."

The two biggest winners were Bechtel and Halliburton. Bechtel got started with a no-bid Pentagon contract to rebuild major portions of Iraq's electrical grid, power generation facilities, water and sewer systems, and airports. The firm was initially rewarded $34 million, with the understanding that the contract could soar to $680 million over the next eighteen months.

But that was still small potatoes compared to Halliburton's windfall.

On March 25, 2005—just one week after the invasion of Iraq began—Halliburton was given an open-ended contract by the U.S. Army Corps of Engineers to rebuild Iraq's oil fields. For Dick Cheney's former firm, it was the sweetest of sweetheart deals. No other firm was asked or given the opportunity to bid. And completing the job was estimated to cost up to $7 billion. Even for the Pentagon, that was a record amount of money to be handed out under a noncompetitive bid. According to the late-night comedian David Letterman, Halliburton scored so well because Cheney told the Pentagon, "When writing checks, don't forget that Halliburton has two l's!"

It wasn't long, however, before Halliburton got too greedy. Given, in effect, a license to steal in Iraq, they did so. Military officials became suspicious when they realized that KBR was charging them $2.27 per gallon for gasoline imported from Kuwait—which local merchants were selling for only $1 per gallon. It was later discovered that Halliburton had overcharged the Pentagon—meaning U.S. taxpayers—some $61 million. Halliburton paid a stiff fine, but the company is still doing business in Iraq and, most likely, still overcharging the government.

Nor was Halliburton the sole corporate gold-digger in Iraq. In late August 2007, it was reported that a U.S.-owned company operating from Kuwait had bribed army officials to win contracts in Iraq. Lee Dynamics International (LDI) paid hundreds of thousands of dollars to army contracting officers to win more than $11 million in contracts. Word of LDI's bribery scheme forced the Pentagon to investigate the details of eighteen contracts awarded to U.S. firms in Iraq, worth more than $3 billion.

In short, for the corporate pals of Bush and Cheney, the war in Iraq was the new California Gold Rush: the path to instant wealth with little, if any, government interference. For Bush and Cheney, it was the perfect quid pro quo. After all, what good's a war if you can't use it to pay back your friends?

Student Loans—at a Price

Call it American ingenuity or American greed. It required no little imagination to take a government program designed to help poor students pay for a college education and turn it into a pot of gold for special interests. Yet with the help of a compliant Congress and White House, that's exactly what happened.

Starting with G.I. loans for returning veterans of World War II, student loans are a proud American tradition. In theory, this program is one way that we, as a nation, can recognize the importance of a college education and can give every young American the chance to earn one. In practice, it's become one more way that big corporations can rip off U.S. taxpayers.

Student loans are a big business: $85 billion in 2007. And it's more complicated than it needs to be.

The federal government actually offers two student loan programs. As its title suggests, under the "Direct Loan Program," the government loans the money directly to the student and charges the lowest possible interest rate. It's cheap, it's successful, and its administrative costs are rock bottom.

Many conservatives, however, believe the government should not be in the business of making loans (or at least not loans to poor students.) So, some fifteen years ago, they established a second loan program, the misnamed "Federal Family Education Loan (FFEL) Program," which turns student loans over to private banks and lending institutions. It is a bonanza for private interests, with zero business risk.

Under the terms of the FFEL, the government guarantees banks and other private lenders that if students default on their loans, the federal government will pay them. In addition, the government offers banks additional subsidies to guarantee a profitable return on the loans. Not surprisingly, administrative costs of this program are ten times higher than those of the Direct Loan Program.

In their blind allegiance to "privatization," conservatives have created a giant sinkhole for taxpayer dollars. According to a study prepared by the Center for American Progress (CAP), for every $100 in student loans, the FFEL costs $7 more than a direct loan. That difference adds up to billions of dollars per year paid to banks and private lenders that could instead go to finance more student loans or be given as grants to colleges and universities. If only direct loans had been made from 1992 to 2005, CAP reports, taxpayers would have saved a total of $37 billion. That would mean, for example, an extra $14.4 million a year to UCLA, $27 million a year to Penn State, and $42 million yearly to the University of Texas at Austin.

Despite the obvious advantages of direct loans, to both student and taxpayer, 77 percent of all loans made today are the more expensive FFELs. Why? Indeed, why does the more expensive program still exist at all? Because banks and private lenders have such clout in Washington.

To protect their very lucrative student loan business, banks are very generous to incumbent legislators. In the 2006 election cycle, the top student lender shelled out $900,000 in campaign contributions, most of it to Republicans.

While the FFEL program operated under both Democratic and Republican administrations, it has been allowed to expand and flourish under President George W. Bush. The Bush administration, in fact, spurned several opportunities to clean up the system. In early 2001, the new Department of Education (DOE) secretary Rod Paige was presented with a plan prepared by the outgoing Clinton administration to end the practice of lenders showering universities and university officials with large gifts, or "inducements," to drum up business.

Unfortunately, like many other Clinton plans, the loan proposal was rejected. There was no way Bush was going to start his presidency by clamping down on friendly banks and lenders. Yet had his department acted then, it would have avoided the major public scandal over student loans that erupted six years later.

In 2003, someone blew the whistle on problems with student loans. Jon Oberg, a top DOE researcher just eighteen months from retirement, sent a memo to his department heads warning that lenders were walking away from the program with hundreds of millions of dollars in unearned profit—and he urged cutting off the subsidies. Oberg said he was ordered to spend the rest of his time at the department working on unrelated projects.

Finally, in 2007, after an investigation by the New York attorney general Andrew Cuomo and congressional hearings chaired by Congressman George Miller exposed the student loan industry as a corporate boondoggle, the new DOE secretary Margaret Spellings admitted there was a problem and pledged to work on new rules for the program—which would be announced in the summer of 2008, shortly before George W. Bush leaves the White House.

Meanwhile, even though Spellings promised "to improve the way the loan programs perform," the Bush administration's FY 2007 budget contains $8 billion in direct subsidies to student lenders. That same $8 billion could have been used instead to make 1.5 million new Pell grants, under the direct loan program.

One reason FFELs continued to thrive is because, under George W. Bush, the Department of Education operated a revolving door with banks and lenders. More than a dozen senior DOE officials in the loan program either worked for lenders before they joined the department or left the department to take jobs in the industry. How could there be any critical oversight of the student loan program when the Bush DOE was a wholly owned subsidiary of the loan industry?

Things were so cozy between the DOE and lenders that the man responsible for the program even had "skin in the game." Matteo Fontana was George Bush's man at the DOE in charge of overseeing lenders in the FFEL Program—until Cuomo's investigation into conflicts of interest on the part of certain college administrators revealed that Fontana, too, was personally profiting from loans he approved. Like financial administrators at Columbia University, USC, and UT at Austin, Fontana owned a significant block of shares—at least 10,500 of them, worth more than $100,000—in Student Loan Xpress, one of the largest student lenders. The resulting negative publicity forced Fontana's resignation.

Compared to the billions of taxpayer dollars siphoned off by Halliburton in Iraq, the student loan rip-offs are little more than petty theft. But they are still outrageous because they represent the adulteration of a noble public goal. The student loan scandal shows how low conservatives are willing to stoop in pursuit of the Almighty Buck.

By handing student loans over to private lenders, the government has turned a silk purse into a sow's ear. Once again, the zeal for privatization has ended up wasting taxpayer dollars, while subsidizing corporations to perform a task the government itself could do more efficiently and more cost-effectively.

With each of these examples, and more, it's clear that special interests have owned the Bush White House. But as long as Republicans were in control of Congress, special interests owned the House and the Senate, too. For corporate lobbyists, there was no end of Republican leaders ready to take their money and do their bidding. Unlike George Bush and Dick Cheney, however, Republican congressional leaders didn't stop with allowing big business interests to dictate public policy. Many of them also took advantage of their office to line their own pockets.

The Congressional Hall of Shame

Senator Bill Frist

As majority leader of the U.S. Senate from January 2003 to January 2007, Bill Frist led the debate on many health care–related issues: revising Medicare, expanding Medicare to include prescription-drug coverage, and providing protection to some forty-five million Americans without health insurance. He was the Republican Party's go-to man on health matters, with a unique ability, as demonstrated in the Terri Schiavo case, to diagnose and predict total recovery for long-time, brain-dead patients merely by watching a videotape.

There was only one problem: a huge conflict of interest. Because Frist was a major shareholder of his family's mammoth health-care business—HCA, Inc.—every one of those changes, with the possible exception of Schiavo's recovery, would have put substantial cash in Frist's own pocket.

Frist denied any conflict, insisting that his holdings were in a blind trust of which he had no knowledge and over which he had no control. He saw no need to sell his stock, he said, because he didn't even know how much stock, if any, he owned. "I think really for our viewers it should be understood that I put this into a blind trust," Frist told CNBC News. "So as far as I know, I own no HCA stock."

But Frist's story began to fall apart in June 2005, when his personal trust suddenly dumped all of his shares in HCA, Inc.—just weeks before the price of the stock plummeted. Intrepid reporters then discovered that Frist had personally given the order to sell his stock, after insisting for a decade that he had no knowledge of his holdings. Documents also revealed that the senator had received regular reports from the managers of his trust on how many shares he owned, what they were buying and selling, and other financial transactions. It wasn't a blind trust, after all. As one wag commented, it was more like a "seeing-eye dog trust."

Before he could say "buy, sell, or hold," Frist found himself the subject of two separate insider-trading investigations, by the Justice Department and the Securities and Exchange Commission. Even though no charges were ever filed, Frist declined to run for reelection when his term expired at the end of 2006. Stung by the appearance of wrongdoing, he also dropped his plans to run for president in 2008.

Speaker Dennis Hastert

How did a high school teacher and wrestling coach without a penny end up a wealthy member of Congress?

Easy. Once he got to Congress, Denny Hastert simply learned, in the immortal words of the Tammany Hall chieftain George Washington

Plunkitt, the difference between "honest graft and dishonest graft." Plunkitt explains, "My party's in power in the city, and it's goin' to make a lot of public improvements. Well, I'm tipped off, say, that they're going to lay out a new park at a certain place.

"I see my opportunity and I take it. I go to that place and I buy up all the land I can in the neighborhood. Then the board of this or that makes its plan public, and there is a rush to get my land, which nobody cared particular for before.

"Ain't it perfectly honest to charge a good price and make a profit on my investment and foresight? Of course, it is. Well, that's honest graft."

Denny Hastert couldn't have laid it out any clearer. His story is just a slight variation on Plunkitt's century-old public park scam.

In 2002, Congressman Hastert bought a 195-acre farm near Plano, Illinois. Two years later, he and a couple of friends established Little Rock Trust 225, into which Hastert transferred part of his property. Then Hastert used his influence as Speaker to secure two friendly "earmarks" in the budget: one to build the controversial "Prairie Parkway"; the second to build a highway interchange five and a half miles from that part of his farm now owned by the trust.

With highway access now secured to a formerly land-locked parcel, the land trust sold its property for $5 million—and Hastert walked away with a $2 million profit. Honest graft? Or dishonest graft? You decide.

Rick Renzi of Arizona

If imitation is indeed the highest form of flattery, then the Arizona congressman Rick Renzi is one of Denny Hastert's biggest fans. Impressed by Hastert's lucrative land deal, Renzi went out and engineered one of his own.

Renzi was first elected to Congress in 2002. Four years later, he had already been named one of the "20 Most Corrupt Members of Congress" by the nonpartisan watchdog group Citizens for Responsibility and Ethics in Washington, or CREW. He earned that distinction for consistently introducing and voting for legislation that benefited his father's defense company, ManTech International Corporation. But soon it was his own company that was in trouble.

Once elected to Congress, Renzi sold his real estate business to his partner, James Sandlin. A couple of years later, Renzi introduced legislation arranging for a swap of land owned by Sandlin with a parcel of land owned by the federal government. Sandlin subsequently sold his land for a huge profit, after which he gave Renzi a check for $200,000—which Renzi somehow "forgot" to list on his financial disclosure forms.

When details of the $200K payoff hit the news, Paul Charlton, the U.S. attorney for Arizona, opened an investigation. Federal agents raided Renzi's family business. And Renzi resigned his post on the House Intelligence Committee.

Another case of dishonest graft? We may never know. Shortly after launching his investigation into Renzi, Charlton was added to the list of U.S. attorneys targeted for firing by the White House and Attorney General Alberto Gonzales. He was fired, and the Renzi investigation suddenly disappeared.

Surely, that's the end of the list of completely out-of-control Republicans. No, actually, we're just getting warmed up. The worst is yet to come.

Randy "Duke" Cunningham

As one of 435 members of Congress, there are many ways to stand out. To make the history books, even. By being the first Muslim. The first openly gay. The youngest. Or even the oldest.

Duke Cunningham made congressional history in a way nobody else would hope to emulate: becoming known as "the most corrupt member of Congress ever." And that is really saying something!

A famous Vietnam "flying ace" first elected to Congress in 1990, the San Diego Republican Duke Cunningham served eight terms—during which he led the fight for a constitutional amendment against flag burning—before announcing in July 2005 he would not seek a ninth term. As it turns out, Cunningham was already under investigation for accepting bribes from defense contractors. In November, he pleaded guilty and resigned his seat. In March 2006, he was convicted, fined $1.8 million, and sentenced to eight years and four months in federal prison—where Cunningham sits today.

Give Cunningham credit for one thing. Over the years, many

members of Congress have seen opportunities for self-enrichment. Nobody saw or seized them as well as the Duke did.

As a member of the defense subcommittee of the House Appropriations Committee, Cunningham struck up a special friendship with the defense contractor Mitchell Wade, the president of MZM, Inc. Cunningham was good to Wade, snaring him $150 million in government contracts. In return, Wade was good to Cunningham: buying his house in San Diego for the inflated price of $1.6 million, which enabled Duke to buy a $2.5 million Rancho Santa Fe mansion; supplying Duke and his wife with $1.8 million in antiques, Persian rugs, jewelry, and other furnishings; buying him a Rolls Royce and a condo in suburban Washington; and providing him with a yacht, the *Duke Stir*, to live on in Washington harbor.

George Condon, the Washington bureau chief of the *San Diego Union*, who with his colleagues won a Pulitzer Prize for breaking the Cunningham story, told me personally that even after writing a book on the congressman, he was shocked at new evidence of Cunningham's insatiable greed. No sooner was his daughter accepted for college, for example, than Cunningham called Wade and asked him to buy her a new laptop. Wade also pitched in $2,000 for Ms. Cunningham's graduation party from college.

To make it easier for Wade and other defense contractors to play the game, Cunningham even sketched out, on congressional stationery, his very own "Bribery Menu." For each $1 million in government contracts rewarded, a $50,000 "fee" was expected. But for contractors, the bigger the contract, the better the deal. With amounts of more than $20 million, only $25,000 was due the congressman for every $1 million received. Apparently, it pays to bribe in bulk.

Forget Wilbur Mills or Jim Wright or William "Dollar Bill" Jefferson. There has never been a more corrupt member of Congress than Randy "Duke" Cunningham. And, hopefully, there never will be.

The Incredible Hulk, Ted Stevens

You may recognize Ted Stevens. He's the one wearing the Incredible Hulk necktie on the Senate floor. Some people wear a crucifix or carry a rabbit's foot. Stevens never goes into battle without first joining forces with the Incredible Hulk.

The eighty-three-year-old Stevens, who's served in the Senate longer than any other Republican, is certainly one of the most colorful members of Congress. As it turns out, he's also one of the most corrupt.

In 2003, the *Los Angeles Times* reported that Stevens had abused his position as chairman of the Senate Appropriations Committee to become a very wealthy man. According to the *Times*, Stevens invested personal funds in companies owned by Alaskan businessmen friends and then wrote preferences for those companies into the law. Perhaps because he was so powerful, perhaps because it was considered business as usual, no action was taken against Stevens.

But Stevens didn't escape so easily the next time. While investigating illegal ties between Veco Corporation, an Alaskan energy services company, and members of the Alaska legislature, U.S. attorneys discovered that the trail of corruption led into federal territory. The former Veco CEO Bill Allen had already pleaded guilty to bribing several legislators, including Stevens's son, for tax breaks to Veco. At the same time, officials learned, Allen was also showering financial favors on Alaska's senior senator.

Like many of us, Ted Stevens decided to remodel his own house. He more than doubled the size of his home, a faux ski chalet located in Girdwood, forty miles south of Anchorage. What made this remodel unusual is that it was personally overseen by Bill Allen himself and other Veco executives. And the contractor told authorities that he was instructed to send all bills not to the home's owner, but to Bill Allen at Veco.

Obviously, Stevens was most grateful. From 2000 to 2006, Veco received more than $30 million in federal contracts, thanks to its good friend in Washington. Payback? That's what the FBI and the IRS were investigating as of January 2008.

In an unrelated matter, Stevens was also under investigation by the Department of Commerce and the Department of the Interior for questionable grants to Alaska's nonprofit Sealife Center. Questions were raised when $700,000 out of $4 million given to the center was redirected to companies owned by Trevor McCabe, the former legislative director in Washington for Senator Stevens.

Nevertheless, Senator Stevens insists that he is not worried by either investigation. One presumes he is counting on the Incredible Hulk to protect him from harm.

Casino Jack and Friends

In any other Congress, the combined corruption charges against the Republicans Bill Frist, Denny Hastert, Duke Cunningham, and Ted Stevens would be enough to spark voter outrage and throw the party in power out of office. But no matter how many times Frist, Hastert, Cunningham, and Stevens were caught with their hands in the cookie jar, they were a mere sideshow to the worst congressional corruption event of all time: the buying and selling of influence by the super Republican lobbyist Jack Abramoff.

As of January 2008, the Abramoff scandal had taken down two members of Congress, ensnared several others in ongoing investigations, destroyed several political careers, and sent one top White House aide, as well as Abramoff himself, to prison—and it's still far from over.

Abramoff earned his first conservative political stripes at Brandeis University in 1980, organizing Massachusetts college campuses for Ronald Reagan. His partner was a Harvard student named Grover Norquist. After Reagan's victory, the two moved to Washington, where they teamed up with Ralph Reed to take over the College Republicans.

When Reagan left town, so did Abramoff—for a while. He traveled. He produced two Hollywood movies. But Washington politics was his first love. When Republicans took back Congress in 1994, Abramoff returned to Washington and set up his own lobbying shop. And unlike other lobbying firms, which have both Republican and Democratic partners in order to reach out to legislators on both sides of the aisle, Abramoff called his shop a "Republican lobbying" firm—created exclusively of, by, and for Republicans.

Abramoff's goal was to build the biggest and most lucrative lobbyist shop in Washington, and he soon succeeded, signing up big clients like the government of Pakistan and the Commonwealth of the Northern Mariana Islands. One of his biggest coups was making a deal to represent the Mississippi Band of Choctaw Indians, who needed help in expanding their casino operation. The Choctaws soon brought several other Indian tribes to their new lobbyist. Abramoff and associates were later accused of manufacturing grave "threats" to Indian casinos in order to scare tribes into paying higher fees to Abramoff so that he could "save" them.

To be successful, Abramoff knew he couldn't depend only on visits to House and Senate offices. So he bought two restaurants near the

Capitol, where he could wine and dine legislators. He leased four arena and stadium skyboxes, where he could entertain lawmakers at sports events. He created several charities for funneling money to legislators' favorite causes. And, while he was at it, he also purchased his own fleet of casino boats, earning Abramoff the nickname "Casino Jack."

But Abramoff was good for more than free meals, drinks, and football tickets. He hired staffers from Capitol Hill and made them rich lobbyists. He also hired wives and family members of congresspeople. He found jobs for his own staff in the Bush administration. His influence in the nation's capital was so widespread that his extended enterprises became known as the "Enron of lobbying." And he pushed his staff to bring in more and more lobbying dollars. In one typical e-mail, Abramoff gushed to a staffer, "Da man! You iz da man! Do you hear me?! You da man!! How much $$ coming tomorrow? Did we get some more $$ in?"

Along the way, Casino Jack made lots of friends in high places. But then, as with Enron, the roof started to cave in. His casino boats began to lose money, his Indian casinos faced stiff competition, and the Justice Department began an investigation into rumors that he was buying votes with campaign contributions and special favors.

Abramoff's whole operation unraveled as fast as he built it. On March 6, 2006, he pleaded guilty to mail fraud, tax evasion, and conspiracy to bribe public officials and was sentenced to five years and ten months in federal prison. He continues to cooperate with federal investigators, and already Abramoff has taken several prominent people down with him. Indeed, the list of those tarnished by him is staggering.

Tom DeLay

The outspoken House majority leader and staunch defender of Newt Gingrich resigned his post in September 2005 after being indicted for laundering federal campaign contributions to state legislative candidates in Texas. At the same time, DeLay found himself in hot water for his close ties to Jack Abramoff.

Two of DeLay's top aides, Tony Rudy and Michael Scanlon—both of whom later also pleaded guilty to bribing lawmakers—were hired by Abramoff. DeLay's wife, Christine, was put on the payroll of the Abramoff associate David Beckham. DeLay was a frequent guest at Abramoff's restaurants and skyboxes. He was treated to a luxury outing to London and Scotland, where he played golf at the legendary St. Andrews Links. He and his wife and daughter also enjoyed an Abramoff-paid trip to the Mariana Islands, where DeLay gave a speech calling the lobbyist "one of my very closest and dearest friends."

In return, DeLay blocked legislation banning sex shops and sweat shops in the Marianas. He intervened with Attorney General John Ashcroft to shut down a casino that was in competition with the Mississippi Choctaws. He killed a bill placing restrictions on Internet gambling, benefiting another Abramoff client. And to help Abramoff round up new clients, he launched the "K Street Project," whereby corporations were pressured to hire Republican lobbyists only or risk alienation from the Republican leadership of Congress.

Because of his many close connections with Abramoff, it is widely believed that Tom DeLay is one of the targets of the Justice Department's ongoing investigation. Even the *Wall Street Journal* editorialized that DeLay has a certain "odor" about him. As the *Washington Post* columnist E. J. Dionne observed, for the *Journal* to criticize DeLay is like the *Osservatore Romano*, the Vatican's official newspaper, criticizing the pope!

Bob Ney

Bob Ney, the veteran congressman from Ohio and chairman of the House Administration Committee, was Jack Abramoff's "fixer" on Capitol Hill. When his lobbyist friend was trying to buy the SunCruz casino fleet, Ney read glowing statements about Abramoff into the *Congressional Record*. When Abramoff had concerns with pending election reform legislation, Ney personally introduced four amendments to fix the problems. When Congress voted to install new wireless communication service in the Capitol, Ney made sure that a client of Abramoff's got the contract.

And Ney, like DeLay, was taken care of with frequent dinners at Signatures, parties in the MCI skybox, and a luxury golf outing to St. Andrews—this one paid for by the Capital Athletic Foundation, another one of Abramoff's so-called charities, headed by Julie Doolittle, the wife of another Republican congressman.

Unlike DeLay, however, Ney left too many obvious fingerprints. In January 2007, he was sentenced to thirty months in prison for conspiracy and making false statements to federal investigators.

Conrad Burns

If Bob Ney was Abramoff's fixer in the House, Conrad Burns was his fixer in the Senate. The senior senator from Montana was conveniently positioned as the chairman of the Senate Appropriations Subcommittee on the Interior, with jurisdiction over Indian Affairs. In a 2006 *Vanity Fair* article, Abramoff bragged, "Every appropriation we wanted from Conrad Burns's Committee we got."

And Burns, in return, got everything he wanted from Abramoff, including countless free meals at his restaurants and some $200,000 in donations from the lobbyist's tribal clients. Abramoff also gave top jobs in his lobbying firm to Burns's former chief of staff and legislative director.

Running for reelection in 2006, Senator Burns said that he regretted his association with Abramoff, and he donated the contributions received from Abramoff's clients to charity. But it was too late. His name had already been added to the list of the twenty most corrupt members of Congress. He was defeated by the Democrat Jon Tester.

John Doolittle

Julie is not the only member of the Doolittle family caught up in the Abramoff corruption scandal. Her husband, John, a Republican congressman from Northern California, is also involved. The two of them, in fact, have enough interlocking fund-raising and lobbying ties to make any FBI agent's head spin.

For starters, Doolittle's chief of staff Kevin Ring left Congress to work for Abramoff. Doolittle received more than $50,000 in campaign contributions from Abramoff clients and held a fund-raiser in his skybox. Abramoff also hired Sierra Dominion Financial Solutions, a consulting firm owned by Julie Doolittle, and made her the head of his Capital Athletic Foundation. At the same time, she was working for the Alexander Strategy Group, a lobbying firm with close ties to DeLay and Abramoff, which, through its client the Korea-U.S. Exchange Council, paid for a "fact-finding" mission to Korea by Congressman Doolittle. And Mrs. Doolittle was also the chief fund-raiser for her husband's campaign committee, for which she was paid a 15 percent commission on every dollar raised—from Jack Abramoff's clients.

Congressman Doolittle is part of the Justice Department's

Abramoff investigation. He is also reportedly under investigation for his legislative assistance to and campaign contributions from PerfectWave, a defense contractor that also gave hundreds of thousands of dollars to the former congressman Duke Cunningham. Small wonder that in 2006, John Doolittle also made CREW's most corrupt list. Or that the FBI raided the Doolittles' northern Virginia home and seized their financial records.

David H. Safavian

The lobbyist Jack Abramoff's activities were not confined to Capitol Hill. They reached from one end of Pennsylvania Avenue to the other, from Congress to the White House.

While serving in the Bush White House as head of the Office of Federal Procurement Policy in the Office of Management and Budget (OMB), David Safavian was indicted for lying to government investigators about his dealings with Abramoff, a longtime friend. When he was chief of staff for the General Services Administration (GSA), Safavian went along on that now-infamous golf outing to St. Andrews with Congressman Bob Ney—even though, at the time, Abramoff had business dealings with GSA.

Safavian lied to investigators about the trip and about his efforts to help Abramoff acquire two federally managed properties in the Washington area. He was convicted and sentenced to eighteen months in prison.

Susan Ralston

With Safavian's indictment, the Abramoff scandal moved onto the White House grounds. And with Susan Ralston's resignation, it moved into the West Wing.

Ralston had served as the executive assistant to Jack Abramoff in his lobbying firm. Because of his friendship with Karl Rove, Abramoff was able to get Ralston the same job for Rove in the Bush White House. Where, of course, she proceeded to do favors for, and extract favors from, her former boss.

In October 2006, under investigation by the White House counsel for her ties with Abramoff, Ralston abruptly resigned her job, after admitting that she had accepted expensive tickets to sports and entertainment events from Abramoff, while supplying him with insider White House information. Rove insisted that he knew nothing about it.

J. Steven Griles

With the help of his old College Republican buddy Ralph Reed, Jack Abramoff got himself named to the transition team for the Department of the Interior. In that position, he helped to convince the incoming president George W. Bush to ignore the protests of environmental organizations and name the former coal industry lobbyist Steven Griles as deputy secretary of the interior. Not that Bush needed much convincing. Once Bush heard the words *coal industry*, Griles had the job—where he proved to be a boon to Abramoff and an embarrassment to Bush.

Griles never forgot his guardian angel Abramoff. The Department of the Interior has jurisdiction over the United States' Indian tribes. So when one of Abramoff's clients wanted to prevent the construction of a casino by a competing tribe, Griles obligingly stepped in to block it—and lied about his actions in testimony before the Senate Indian Affairs Committee.

In June 2007, Griles was fined $30,000 and ordered to join other Abramoff friends in prison, serving his own ten-month sentence.

Ralph Reed

As noted earlier, during the Reagan administration, the College National Republican Committee was led by the triumvirate of Chairman Jack Abramoff, the staffer Grover Norquist, and the intern Ralph Reed.

Reed went on to become the cherub-faced, first executive director of the Christian Coalition. In 1997, he left the Coalition to form his own political consulting firm, Century Strategies, lining up such big-name clients as Microsoft and Enron (thanks to an intercession from Karl Rove).

But Reed didn't think he was making enough money. So in 1999 he e-mailed his old friend Jack Abramoff, asking for his help and advice in "humping" corporate clients—a curious turn of phrase for a born-again Christian. Abramoff came through, arranging contracts for Reed with eLottery, an Internet gambling firm, and two Indian tribes. Reed, in fact, was paid $4.2 million for leading opposition to the opening of new Indian casinos; his fees were paid by Indian tribes with competing casinos.

By this time, Reed decided that he wanted a taste of power himself. After a brief stint as the Republican state chairman of Georgia, he declared his candidacy for lieutenant governor. Ahead in all the polls and claiming the support of the Bush administration, Reed seemed a shoo-in until the Abramoff scandal broke—along with news of Reed's close business association with Abramoff. Georgia Republicans started to turn away, and the White House ignored him. In the end, only the New York mayor Rudy Giuliani campaigned for him. Reed lost by 12 points.

Ralph Reed's political career is over, but his legal troubles are not. He remains a target of the Abramoff investigation.

The Republican Sex Parade

To make matters worse, Republican congressional leaders weren't just greedy old devils. They turned out to be horny old devils, too.

In a sense, this was nothing new. We know, for example, that while Republican Party hacks were demanding Bill Clinton's impeachment, conviction, and removal from office for consensual oral sex with Monica Lewinsky, the Republican Party leaders Newt Gingrich, Dan Burton, Henry Hyde, and Bob Livingston were at the same time enjoying, or had previously enjoyed, their own extramarital dalliances.

Nor did Republicans clean up their act once George Bush moved into the White House. To the contrary. They saw Republican control of all three branches of government as a license to frolic. Shattering yet another political myth, it proved to be Republicans, not Democrats, who could not keep it zipped.

Mark Foley

Among Republican sex offenders of the George W. Bush era, the seven-term congressman from Florida was the first and the worst. That Foley was a closeted gay man was one of Washington's worst-kept secrets. What remained a secret was the fact that he preyed on underage congressional male pages.

Foley's inappropriate, and perhaps illegal, relationships surfaced in late September 2006 with the publication of explicit e-mails in which the congressman solicited sex from several young pages or asked for photographs of their private parts. Confronted by ABC News with the evidence, Foley resigned from Congress on September 29.

Compounding the outrage over Foley's actions was the fact that he served as Republican chair of the House Caucus on Missing and Exploited Children. Even more outrageous was the fact that several complaints about Foley's activities with pages had previously been made to Republican leaders, who simply ignored them. Among those who were informed that there might be a serious problem but did nothing were the House Speaker Denny Hastert, the majority leader John Boehner, the chairman of the Republican Congressional Campaign Committee Tom Reynolds, and various top staffers.

Confronted with a clear case of teen abuse, Republicans decided that they would rather coddle the abuser than protect the child.

David Vitter

Even among Republican Senators, Louisiana's David Vitter stood out as a self-described paragon of virtue. He ran for office as "Mr. Family Values." His Web site boasted of his commitment to "advancing mainstream conservative principles." As a Louisiana state senator, he demanded that Bill Clinton resign the presidency for cheating on his wife. Elected to the U.S. Senate in 2004, he became a strong proponent of teaching "abstinence only" in public schools. He led the fight for a constitutional amendment banning gay marriage because, he said, it would destroy "the most important social institution in human history."

David Vitter did everything but claim to walk on water. Until he learned one of the most important political lessons of all: if you put yourself on a pedestal, you'd better be sure you're squeaky clean.

When it came to preserving the sanctity of marriage, it turned out that Vitter wasn't practicing what he was preaching. When Deborah Jeane Palfrey, the famous "D.C. Madam" who was accused of running a call-girl ring for powerful men in the nation's capital, published the phone numbers of her regular clients, David Vitter's name popped up as the most prominent "John" on the list. According to Palfrey's records,

Vitter had started frequenting her prostitutes even before his election to the Senate. He continued once he moved to Washington, even making calls to arrange liaisons in between votes on the Senate floor.

But that was just the beginning of Vitter's problems. Next stepped forward a New Orleans woman known as the "Canal Street Madam," who revealed that years earlier, Vitter had been a frequent customer of her French Quarter brothel, enjoying the services of the prostitute Wendy Cortez. These charges were raised against him in his 2004 Senate race but were denied by Vitter.

Of course, face-to-face with his own moral transgressions, Vitter did not demand of himself the same test he once applied to Bill Clinton. He first held a tearful news conference in Louisiana, wife by his side, admitting his "mistakes." He then flew to Washington to inform members of the Senate Republican Caucus that he would not resign his seat but would stay on and fight for the values he believed in (but did not practice).

Hypocrisy often works—at least, among hypocrites. Vitter received a loud, sustained standing ovation from his fellow Republicans.

Larry Craig

One other hypocrite didn't fare so well.

Other than being a member of the Senate's famous "barbershop quartet," Idaho's Senator Larry Craig was best known as an authority on "Western" issues. A leading Senate conservative, he was also an outspoken opponent of gay rights and gay marriage. Which is okay, for a conservative—unless you run around soliciting sex from policemen in public restrooms.

Since his days in college, Craig had dealt with rumors that the gay-basher might actually himself be gay. While serving in the House, he was briefly named in an earlier, pre–Mark Foley, congressional page sex scandal. As a senator, he was accused by one gay Web site of engaging in sexual acts in the men's room at Washington's Union Station. Craig successfully denied all such accusations.

His luck ran out in a men's room at the Minneapolis–St. Paul airport on June 11, 2006, when the senator was arrested for attempting to initiate sexual activity with an undercover police officer. When, two months later, Craig returned to Minnesota to plead guilty to disorderly conduct and pay a $575 fine, the news of his arrest hit the national media.

At first, Craig offered the lamest possible excuses. In hindsight, he insisted, his actions had been misconstrued because he had a "wide stance." He should have consulted a lawyer but didn't. He should not have pleaded guilty but decided to do so only because he'd been harassed by the *Idaho Statesman*. As to his sexual orientation, Craig told the world, with his wife by his side, "Let me be clear. I am not gay. I have never been gay."

His Republican Senate colleagues didn't buy it. Straight wife-cheaters like David Vitter are one thing; gay men's room cruisers like Larry Craig are another. Senators John McCain and Norm Coleman immediately called for Craig's resignation. And the Senate Ethics Committee opened an investigation.

At first, Craig offered to resign. Then, to the consternation of fellow Republicans, he changed his mind, vowing to complete his current term in office, instead—but not run for reelection in 2008.

Sadly, when it comes to moral values, the Larry Craig incident sums up the experience of the last twelve years of conservative rule: you get the worst, or most hypocritical, behavior on the part of those from whom you expect the best.

Lesson Learned

Once again, in one more important arena, conservatives fail the test. They sell themselves as saints, yet they expose themselves as sinners.

This is not to say that conservatives are any more corruptible than liberals, but rather to say that conservatives are easily *as* corruptible as liberals and perhaps even more so. Because after a while, having proclaimed their moral superiority so loudly, conservatives actually start to believe it—and therefore blind themselves to their own shortcomings.

Human nature is weak, and temptation is always with us. As long as there are human beings elected to public office, there will always be those who take advantage of their position for money, power, or sex.

Where conservative Republicans go wrong is pretending to be holier-than-thou. Just ask them, they'll tell you. They are the party of family values. They operate according to a higher moral standard. They have a monopoly on virtue. They will restore honor and integrity to public office.

Nonsense. For a time, the American people believed them. And what did we get? No honor, no integrity, and no virtue. Instead, we were exposed to some of the most corrupt public officials and the most corrupt administrations in history.

Over and over again, conservatives had their chance to demonstrate their moral fiber. They failed, every time.

CHAPTER 3

Making Americans Safer

At the core, we are dealing with two parties that have
fundamentally different views on national security.
Republicans have a post-9/11 worldview and many Democrats
have a pre-9/11 worldview. That doesn't make them
unpatriotic—not at all. But it does make them wrong—
deeply and profoundly and consistently wrong.
Karl Rove

Time and time again, the Democrats want to have it both
ways. They talk tough on terror, but when the votes are
counted, their softer side comes out.
George W. Bush

And what I'm concerned about . . . is that as we get
farther and farther from 9/11, we've got—we seem to have
people less and less committed to doing everything
that's necessary to defend the country.
Dick Cheney

If [a Democrat] gets elected, it sounds to me like we're
going on the defense. We've got a timetable for withdrawal
from Iraq. We're going to wave the white flag there. We're
going to try to cut back on the Patriot Act. We're going to cut
back on electronic surveillance. We're going to cut back on
interrogation. We're going to cut back, cut back, cut back, and
we'll be back in our pre–September 11 mentality of being
on defense. The Democrats do not understand the full
scope and nature of the terrorist war against us.
Rudy Giuliani

S ound familiar? We've heard it time and time again since September 11, 2001. If there's a favorite trump card in the conservative's deck of dirty tricks, it's the old, rhetorical canard that Democrats are weak on national security.

It's almost a given. Every time Republicans find themselves in political peril, they fall back on the same tired old talking points. Elect a bleeding-heart liberal, they say, and you might as well hand over the country to Osama bin Laden.

Back in 2004, when it looked like the Democratic presidential candidate John Kerry might still carry the day in Ohio and across the nation, Dick Cheney warned America that voting for Kerry, a decorated Vietnam veteran, was tantamount to voting for the evildoers. "If we make the wrong choice," Cheney said, "then the danger is that we'll get hit again—that we'll be hit in a way that will be devastating from the standpoint of the United States." Elect Kerry, prophesied Cheney, and "we'll fall back into the pre-9/11 mindset. . . . I think that would be a terrible mistake for us."

Conservative scare tactics proved so successful in 2004 that, not surprisingly, Republicans went back to the well in 2006. "Conservatives saw the savagery of 9/11 in the attacks and prepared for war," Karl Rove told a New York audience early that year. "Liberals saw the savagery of the 9/11 attacks and wanted to prepare indictments and offer therapy and understanding for our attackers." Or, as the president himself put it, in a Hail Mary attempt two weeks before Election Day: "We are constantly changing to defeat this enemy. But if the Democrats were to take control, their policy is pretty clear to me. It's cut and run."

This time, of course, the politics of fear didn't work so well for the GOP. Americans were either tired of hearing it or didn't believe it anymore. Despite the shrill warnings of Bush and company, Republicans lost control of both houses of Congress, while every single Democratic incumbent in the House and the Senate was returned to office.

But it'll take more than just one midterm rout for conservatives to abandon their favorite electoral ploy. After all, it's the only issue they've got. Come 2007, they were beating the same dead horse. In announcing his candidacy for president, Rudy Giuliani summed up the party's rationale for 2008: "America will be safer under a Republican president."

Conservatives have been repeating the mantra that "Democrats are weak on national security" so often and for so long that it's become a generally accepted theory in U.S. politics. Still, saying something doesn't make it so. The fact of the matter is, the United States has been made *less* safe, not more safe, in the years since 9/11 under this Republican president.

Thanks to Bush's decision to abandon the pursuit of al-Qaeda in the mountains of Afghanistan and launch, instead, a dubious and badly managed war in Iraq, we have given the perpetrators of 9/11 a big "time out" and a license to reorganize. Already, in 2003, Bush had almost forgotten about America's enemy number one: "I don't know where bin Laden is. I have no idea and don't care. It is not important, and it is not our priority. I am not truly concerned about him." No surprise, then, that more than six years after the horror of 9/11—and more than six years after Bush promised to capture him "dead or alive"—Osama bin Laden remains at large.

In fact, Bush's war in Iraq has been a dream come true for bin Laden. The occupation not only removed from power one of his political enemies, the secular tyrant Saddam Hussein, it further destabilized the Middle East, fanned resentment of the United States throughout the Muslim world, and swelled the ranks of those who would willingly take up arms or sacrifice their lives in the battle against us.

But Iraq is only the tip of the iceberg. In chapter 6, I will document the inefficient mess Republicans have made of the Federal Emergency Management Agency (FEMA) and in chapter 7 I'll describe the bloated bureaucracy of the Department of Homeland Security. Most Americans would agree that neither agency has made us more secure. From nuclear nonproliferation to first-responder funding, from port security to airline cargo, this conservative administration has time and time again shirked its responsibility to protect Americans from harm, all the while accusing Democrats of being soft on terror.

Summer Soldiers and Sunshine Patriots

America and General George Washington faced a crisis in 1776: there was a revolution to fight, and the patriots needed every last willing soldier they could find. That's when Thomas Paine rose to the occasion, stirring men to action with his noble prose:

These are the times that try men's souls: The summer soldier and the sunshine patriot will, in this crisis shrink from the service of his country, but he that stands it NOW, deserves the love and thanks of man and woman.

Paine's words have resonated throughout history and are repeated whenever it becomes necessary for ordinary citizens to defend their nation in an hour of need. But Paine's words resonate for another reason, as well. In referring to "summer soldiers" and "sunshine patriots," Paine might as well have been talking about today's Republicans. For those most quick to accuse Democrats of cowardice usually turn out to be men who never served in the military themselves.

Case in point: Georgia's Saxby Chambliss. In 2002, Chambliss, then a member of Congress, challenged for reelection the Democratic senator Max Cleland, who had lost two legs and an arm in the Vietnam War. Proving once again that conservatives will resort to anything to win, Chambliss accused Cleland of siding with al-Qaeda—simply because he opposed Bush's plan to prohibit employees of the new Department of Homeland Security from joining a union. Chambliss even aired doctored TV ads showing Cleland alongside Osama bin Laden and Saddam Hussein. Despicable? Yes! But, it worked. Cleland lost, Chambliss won.

Speaking of "sunshine warriors," by the way, Chambliss sat out the Vietnam War because of a "bad knee." How convenient.

Of course, Chambliss isn't the only self-styled Republican "warrior" without the war record to back it up. Dick Cheney, who once accused antiwar voters of giving comfort to "al-Qaeda types," was once antiwar enough himself to seek *five* deferments from service in Vietnam. Indeed, as Tim Noah of *Slate* pointed out, Cheney's daughter Elizabeth was born exactly nine months and two days after the government started to call up childless husbands for duty. In a 1989 interview, Cheney explained that when it came to military service, he had "other priorities."

The list goes on. Karl Rove, the architect of the administration's "soft on terror" attacks, used college deferments to avoid going to Vietnam. So did countless other Republican leaders, including Rudy Giuliani, Fred Thompson, Newt Gingrich, Mitch McConnell, Trent Lott, John Ashcroft, John Boehner, Roy Blunt, Denny Hastert, Dick Armey, and Tom DeLay.

You must, however, give DeLay credit for devising the most creative spin for never serving in Vietnam. As the *Houston Press* reported it, DeLay told a 1988 press conference that so many minority youths had volunteered for well-paying military positions to escape poverty and the ghetto that there was simply no room for patriotic folks like himself.

In the end, of course, whether one actually served in the military or not is beside the point. With an all-volunteer military and no draft since Vietnam, we long ago passed the point where prior military service is a prerequisite for public office. Never having served in the military doesn't make you any less a patriot than one who has. Nor does opposing the war in Iraq. But if, like George Bush, Dick Cheney, and others, I had pulled strings to get out of going to Vietnam, I wouldn't be strutting around puffing up my chest in chickenhawk fashion, accusing Democrats of being weak-willed on matters of national security.

So why does the "weak on national security" charge stick? Well, in some ways, it *is* the Democrats' own fault. Democrats don't help themselves, for example, when they overreact. In every election cycle, Democratic candidates fall over themselves trying to prove they are as tough, if not tougher, than their opponents on national security—instead of challenging the opponents' definition of what national security really means. The current election cycle is no exception.

Afraid of being cast as soft on terror, Democrats have voted for almost everything Bush has asked for, from the Patriot Act, to the original authorization of force in Iraq, to the extension of the National Security Agency (NSA) surveillance program, to additional funding for the war in Iraq—all of which merely served to further emasculate Congress and inflate the authority of the president. In that sense, Democrats have only themselves to blame. As the former Clinton speechwriter Heather Hurlburt put it in the *Washington Monthly* in 2002, "We worry about how to position ourselves so as not to look weak, rather than thinking through realistic, sensible Democratic principles on how and when to employ military force, and arguing particular cases, such as Iraq, from those principles."

All that being said, the real reason the "weak on national security" label has stuck to Democrats is by dint of sheer repetition. It didn't start with George Bush and Dick Cheney. For more than half a century, Republicans have been saying it over and over and over again, until it's become part of the accepted wisdom in Washington. Conservatives are from Mars, liberals are from Venus. If you want better schools, call a Democrat. If you want a safer world, call a Republican.

Sounds good, except it's not true.

Remember, it was two Democrats, Woodrow Wilson and Franklin Roosevelt, who brought this nation into—and led us through—World Wars I and II. It was a Democrat, Harry S. Truman, who originally formulated the strategy of containment, implemented it as government policy, and began the battle against the totalitarian menace of Soviet communism. And in 1999, when the House majority leader Tom DeLay protested that "bombing a sovereign nation for ill-defined reasons with vague objectives undermines the American stature in the world," he wasn't talking about George W. Bush in Iraq. He was talking about President Clinton's successful military actions in Kosovo. Democrats know how to be from Mars when it's the right thing to do.

The War in Iraq: Making Us Less Safe, Not More

The real problem with Republican charges of being soft on security, however, is not how they might hurt Democrats. It's how they have hurt the country, because their tough talk has not been matched by tough action. Despite spending billions of dollars and waging war in two countries at the same time, the Bush administration has made us less safe than before September 11, not more.

Let me repeat that: George Bush has made us less safe, not more. *George Bush has made us less safe, not more.* I'll repeat it as many times as I need to. Try it yourself. It feels good. It's true. Now tell everyone you know, in case some of them haven't yet figured it out. It's your patriotic duty.

Bush has made us less safe, primarily through a disastrous foreign policy that seems designed to stir up more hostility against the United States around the world. And the centerpiece of that policy, of course, is the war in Iraq.

Countless books have been written on this subject. There's no need to repeat all the arguments here, except to point out the obvious: coming on top of the war in Afghanistan, the war in Iraq is one more example of the United States invading a Muslim country *as a solution to the problem of growing anti-Americanism in the Muslim world.*

Our invasion of Iraq and our continued occupation of Iraq attracted thousands of young Muslims to come to Iraq merely for the sport of killing Americans; spurred the creation of a whole new terrorist organization, al-Qaeda in Iraq; and drove thousands of recruits into terrorist cells around the world for the purpose of carrying out attacks against the United States and our allies. Simply put, the war in Iraq has become the recruiting poster for terrorist organizations worldwide.

Not only that. As we noted earlier, by choosing to invade Iraq instead of finishing the war in Afghanistan and tracking down the leadership of al-Qaeda, George W. Bush has given Osama bin Laden, Ayman al-Zawahiri, and their deputies more than four years so far to regroup, rearm, raise new funds, recruit new members, and plan new attacks against the United States.

There is no way the war in Iraq can be seen as making the United States safer (which is, after all, supposed to be the purpose of all just wars). That point was made most spectacularly—and embarrassingly, for the administration—by General David Petraeus, the commander of U.S. forces on the ground in Iraq, in his testimony before Congress on Tuesday, September 11, 2007. Here's the transcript of his now infamous exchange with the Virginia senator John Warner.

> Warner: "Are you able to say at this time, if we continue what you have laid before the Congress here as a strategy, do you feel that that is making America safer?"
>
> Petraeus: "Sir, I believe that this is, indeed, the best course of action to achieve our objectives in Iraq."
>
> Warner: "Does that make America safer?"
>
> Petraeus: "Sir, I don't know, actually."

The obvious follow-up question, which Warner didn't ask, is: if the war in Iraq is not making us any safer, what the hell are we doing there?

In terms of damaging foreign policy, of course, the war in Iraq doesn't stand alone in inciting hatred of everything American. But when you add the war to our continued, unconditional support of corrupt, oppressive regimes like Egypt and Saudi Arabia; blanket support for the government of Israel, no matter what actions it takes in the Palestinian Territory or Gaza; the building of what appear to be permanent American bases in Kuwait and Iraq; the denial of due process to hundreds of prisoners at Guantanamo Bay; and the existence of a secret, worldwide network of prisons for torturing Muslim prisoners . . . Well, as the Republican congressman Ron Paul dared to suggest in one presidential debate, you get some idea of why some people might be pissed off at us.

It's not that all of those policies are necessarily wrong. But, taken together, it does make one see how already suspicious minds might conclude that the United States has declared war on Islam.

Commission Accomplished?

It's not just a militaristic foreign policy that leaves us more vulnerable. Security problems caused by the war in Iraq and other foreign policy failures are compounded by security lapses in protecting the homeland.

The definitive evidence of those failures came in the final report of the 9/11 Commission. Creation of this bipartisan, ten-member panel was at first bitterly opposed by the Bush White House. Yet under the leadership of the Republican former New Jersey governor Thomas Kean and the former Democratic congressman Lee Hamilton, it soon became widely recognized for its thoroughness, objectivity, and accuracy.

The Commission's official report, released in July 2004, contained forty-one recommendations for actions that the administration and Congress should take to protect the homeland. But the Commission's members didn't stop there. Proving they meant business, they returned to Washington eighteen months later, in December 2005, and graded the government's response in a "National Security Report Card."

How well did the Republican president and the Republican-controlled Congress score in homeland security? Lousy! The Commission handed out 5 Fs, 12 Ds, 9 Cs, and 2 Incompletes. Moreover, Republicans received only one A-, for working to clamp down on terrorist financing. Commission members found no excuse for inaction, other than indifference. After all, complained the Commission member John F. Lehman, the former secretary of the navy under President Reagan, "None of this is rocket science."

Among the homeland security failures highlighted by the commission:

Airport Passenger Screening (F). "Few improvements have been made to the existing passenger screening system since right after 9/11," the Commission's final report found. For people who fly often, those meaningless "improvements" are all too familiar: long lines at security, taking off your shoes, handing over your toothpaste, and throwing out your Diet Coke—all in the name of defeating terrorists.

We would all accept these changes more willingly, if checked luggage were screened as carefully as carry-ons. It's not. The 9/11 Commission gave the Transportation Security Administration (TSA) a D on "Checked Bag and Cargo Screening," noting that "Improvements here have not been made a priority by the Congress or the administration. . . . The main impediment is inadequate funding." Especially since the no-liquids rule went into effect in September 2006, screening systems have been so overwhelmed by the increased amount of baggage being checked that airlines are reluctant to spend even more money on screening checked baggage.

Funding Formula (F). The Commission found: "Homeland security funds continue to be distributed without regard for risk, vulnerability, or the consequences of an attack, diluting the national security benefits of this important program." No kidding. In July 2006—a month after the Department of Homeland Security announced that antiterrorism money to New York City and Washington would be cut by 40 percent—the *New York Times* scrutinized the National Asset Database (NAD), a list of potential terrorist targets developed by the Department of Homeland Security to determine which cities and states should get federal antiterrorism funding. Which state ranks the highest? Think Dan Quayle and race cars.

Yes, according to the NAD, Indiana is the most vulnerable of all the states, with 8,591 potential terrorist targets—almost 50 percent more than New York (5,687) and twice as many as California (3,212). On the list of places terrorists might strike in the Hoosier

State is the Amish Country Popcorn Factory of Berne, Indiana. Also found on the NAD as natural favorites of al-Qaeda extremists are the Old MacDonald Petting Zoo of Woodville, Alabama; the Apple and Pork Festival in Clinton, Illinois; and the Sweetwater Flea Market outside Knoxville, Tennessee.

I guess the theory is that bin Laden is evil—and what could be more evil than attacking a petting zoo? Nevertheless, as the *Times* concluded, "It reads like a tally of terrorist targets that a child might have written."

Maximum effort by U.S. government to secure WMD (D). Again, from the 9/11 Commission report: "Countering the greatest threat to America's security is still not the top national security priority of the President and the Congress." In other words, George W. Bush spares no expense in dollars or American lives to track down weapons of mass destruction (WMD) that don't exist. But he ignores those that do.

In my 2004 book *Bush Must Go*, I wrote at length about Bush's evisceration of the Nunn-Lugar Comprehensive Threat Reduction Program. It remains one of the worst national security failures of this administration. Enacted by Congress in 1991, soon after the collapse of the Soviet Union, the Nunn-Lugar Act launched an aggressive program to find, deactivate, and destroy WMD stockpiles all over the newly born, chaotic Russian republics—and thus prevent a post–Cold War catastrophe occurring as a result of left-over Cold War technology. By 2001, Nunn-Lugar had destroyed 6,212 Russian nukes, 520 additional intercontinental ballistic missiles, 624 nuclear air-launched cruise missiles, and 27 missile-firing submarines, and had completely eliminated nuclear weapons from Ukraine, Belarus, and Kazakhstan.

But once George Bush was elected, Nunn-Lugar hit a brick wall. Bush cut its budget by $140 million, then shut the program down in 2002—only to reopen it under political pressure in 2003. Campaigning for reelection in 2004, he pledged $451 million for Nunn-Lugar, even though its cosponsor, the Republican Richard Lugar, estimated that the program needed $2 billion to be successful. One year later, Bush had already cut its budget back to $409 million; for 2008, he had projected only $348 million.

Despite all of Bush's rhetoric about WMD, the world's most

successful plan to eliminate the threat posed by leftover Soviet nuclear weapons and other WMD faced the death of a thousand cuts until Democrats took control of Congress in January 2007. The very first bill introduced and passed by the new Democratic House under Speaker Nancy Pelosi was a measure to implement the recommendations of the 9/11 Commission, including a revamping of Nunn-Lugar—for which the Senate later tossed in an additional $100 million.

Coalition Standards for Terrorist Detention (F). The Commission reports: "U.S. treatment of detainees has elicited broad criticism, and makes it harder to build the necessary alliances to cooperate effectively with partners in a global war on terror." The Bush administration's contempt for civil liberties and basic human rights has made all Americans, and particularly those in harm's way, less safe in the war on terror. By their violation of the Geneva Conventions, secret network of prisons, and practice of torture, Bush & Co. have only given our enemies increased ammunition to fuel their ranks.

Scholarship, exchange, and library programs (D). This failing grade, along with the D given by the 9/11 Commission on "support [of] secular education in Muslim countries," reflects the administration's all-too-narrow view of the war on terror.

A wise old saying goes, "When your only tool is a hammer, every problem looks like a nail." George W. Bush scorns diplomacy as weakness, views educational programs as bleeding-heart liberal attempts to "offer therapy and understanding for our attackers," and believes the war on terror can be won solely through U.S. military might. He has made zero effort to support educational or modernization efforts in the Muslim world.

No Safe Port

While most attention since September 11 has been paid to air travel, the security of U.S. ports has been sadly neglected. Three months after 9/11, the Customs Agency announced its "Container Safety Initiative," a plan to begin screening all containers coming into U.S. ports from the largest foreign ports. Yet not until 2005 did the Bush administration provide any funding.

The result: as of February 2006, only 6 percent of eleven million containers entering U.S. ports every year were being screened, leaving 94 percent that could be filled with just about *anything*. They could be filled with linoleum siding, T-shirts, toys, or computer parts. They could also contain illicit drugs, illegal immigrants, or a WMD. Who knows? A couple of years ago, ABC's Brian Ross actually smuggled components for making a nuclear bomb, hidden inside a container, into a U.S. port—twice!

Still, neither Bush nor the Republican Congress would get behind a comprehensive port security bill. "It has been almost five years since the attacks of 9/11," the Port of Seattle CEO Mic Dinsmore testified before the Senate, "and I must say that I still do not sleep well knowing all the vulnerabilities in our port security system. While some progress has been made, it is not enough. The rate at which containers are screened is abysmal, and the controls we have for allowing persons to get onto our marine terminals are almost embarrassing."

But then, in February 2006, President Bush did something to change all that. Did he go before a nationwide television audience, decry the dangers of our lax port security, and announce tough efforts to fix the problem? Not exactly. Instead, he and the Department of Homeland Security endorsed the $6.8 billion sale of six U.S. ports— New York, New Jersey, Philadelphia, Baltimore, New Orleans, and Miami—to Dubai Ports World, a firm owned by the United Arab Emirates (UAE).

Say what you want about George Bush, but any man who comes up with a plan to sell our most important ports to an Arab firm in the name of homeland security gets serious points for creativity.

Unknown to most Americans, management of these ports was already in foreign hands—namely, the British firm Peninsular & Oriental Steam Navigation Co. But now, with approval of this deal, control of our major East Coast ports would be handed over to the UAE—a nation from which two of the 9/11 attackers hailed and through which much of the 9/11 funding was laundered and a nation that recognized the Taliban and is a supporter of the terrorist organization Hamas.

Bush was hammered by leaders of both parties for selling U.S.

assets to Dubai. But the political furor was defused when DP World pulled out, agreeing to divest the ports to a U.S. firm the following month. In the wake of "Dubaigate," Congress passed a port security bill mandating $7.4 billion in increased inspection spending and screening for nuclear weapons. The bill did not, however, mandate the screening of all foreign containers heading for the United States—which means that our ports are still where we are most vulnerable.

It's clear, however, that President Bush still did not get the message. In April 2006, he approved a deal for the UAE-owned Dubai International Capital to purchase from Doncasters Group Ltd. nine military plants that manufacture turbine blades for U.S. tanks and airplanes.

Mass-Transit Malaise, Nuclear Nightmare

Unfortunately, it's not just the ports. This administration has also failed to protect critical infrastructure and transportation systems around the country, from trains to mass transit to nuclear plants.

We've seen attacks on rail and subway systems in Tokyo in 1995, Moscow and Madrid in 2004, London in 2005, and Mumbai in 2006. Obviously, we could be next. And yet, although the United States' mass-transit systems carry sixteen times more passengers every day than its planes do, the Bush administration has persistently neglected them in its homeland security strategy. A 2005 Brookings Institution report found that the government had invested only 1 cent per passenger on mass transit security, as compared to $9.16 per passenger for airlines.

Some cynics might suggest that's because a few hundred dead subway riders would mean a few hundred less Democrats. But I don't think that's fair. A lot people who ride the subway don't vote at all.

Transportation experts estimate that it would cost $6 billion to secure the United States' mass transit systems. As of 2006, Bush had offered less than $600 million of that and has slated only $150 million for security improvements in his FY 2007 budget. "When it comes to security," William Millar, the president of the American Public Transportation Association, told USA Today, "public transportation riders are treated as second-class citizens by the federal government."

Perhaps the worst security nightmare would be a terrorist attack on a nuclear power facility, twenty-one of which are located within five miles of a major airport. Yet in the wake of September 11, the Bush administration has basically ignored the question of nuclear reactor security. In 2002, the Massachusetts congressman Ed Markey released a review of the nuclear power industry, called "A Hard Look at the Soft Spots in Our Civilian Nuclear Reactor Security." His investigation determined that the Nuclear Regulatory Commission (NRC) had no clue how many foreign nationals work at nuclear reactors or how much is spent on security at individual reactors.

Finally, in 2005, Congress directed the NRC to upgrade its security regulations for nuclear reactors within eighteen months. Yet a 2006 study by Congress's General Accounting Office found that—in keeping with the Bush administration's usual approach to problem solving—the NRC had cut back its regulations in response to industry pressure. The United States' nuclear reactors remain sitting ducks and easy terrorist targets.

Run for the Border

Despite the fact that we are a nation of immigrants, nothing gets a conservative's blood boiling faster than the idea of an illegal immigrant. Given all the tough talk on immigration from people like Lou Dobbs and Tom Tancredo, you'd think that if there's one thing conservatives should be able to get right, it's border security.

But that's not the case. Even with immigration, Republicans have made a mess of things—failing to keep us safe by not securing the border. Most Republicans, for example, insisted that the answer lay in building the biggest possible fence. They actually passed legislation to do so, but then never built the fence!

Give Bush credit for something. At least he knows it's not that simple. As the former governor of a border state, Bush has tried to push his party in the right direction on immigration. Working with Democrats in Congress, he fashioned a comprehensive immigration bill that upgraded border security, while at the same time starting a temporary worker program, imposing stiff penalties on employers who hire undocumented workers, and creating a path to citizenship for millions of illegal immigrants already in the country.

But this was one case where right-wing conservatives refused to go along with their president. Given a choice between securing the border or demonizing immigrants, Republicans in Congress opted for the latter. Accusing Bush of trying to force "amnesty" on the country, they killed his bipartisan immigration plan and replaced it with—nothing.

Our southern and northern borders thus remain basically unprotected, as a 2007 report from the Government Accounting Office confirmed. Should they choose to do so, the next group of terrorists seeking to attack U.S. targets won't have to go to the trouble of hijacking planes to cross the border. They can simply walk across.

Caveat Emptor

Because they did so once, we assume the next group of terrorists that strikes the United States will try to do it again by hijacking an airliner. Or, perhaps, by smuggling WMD inside a container ship. Unfortunately, as we should have learned by now, terrorists aren't that predictable. They might instead target our food supply or the flow of consumer goods, where we are particularly vulnerable, as recent events have proved.

The millions of Chinese-made, lead-painted toys recalled by Mattel in 2007, the Chinese-made toothpaste that contained diethylene glycol and killed fifty-one people in Panama, and yes, even the tainted Chinese-made pet food that killed an unknown number of animals in March 2007—these are all security issues, too. It's not all about flying planes into buildings. Consumer and product safety is also an important homeland security issue—and one that conservatives have long ignored, mainly because of their aversion to anything that smacks of government regulation. For them, cheap products are just good business, and companies should be able to produce and sell whatever they want. Consumers beware!

Nowhere is this laissez-faire attitude toward consumer protection more evident than at the Consumer Product Safety Commission (CPSC) under George W. Bush.

The CPSC was established in 1972, with the mission of protecting the public "against unreasonable risks of injuries associated with consumer products." For many years, it was a strong watchdog agency, but manufacturers resented the increased level of oversight and pressured conservative Republicans to hamstring the agency.

Ronald Reagan responded by cutting the consumer protection workforce in half. George W. Bush has tried to finish it off altogether. Charged with assuring the safety of $1.4 trillion in consumer products at a time when the United States is increasingly flooded by cheap imports, the CPSC is now down to 420 workers, including only one lone scientist assigned to test imported toys.

As Bush did with other agencies, he undermined the effectiveness of the Consumer Product Safety Commission by appointing anticonsumer activists to its leadership. As chairman, he named Hal Stratton, who, as a former New Mexico attorney general, had refused to join consumer protection lawsuits because, he said, other state attorneys general were just trying "to impose their own anti-business, progovernment regulation views" on manufacturers.

When Stratton resigned in 2006, Bush tried to replace him with Michael Baroody, a former senior lobbyist for the National Association of Manufacturers, but neither he nor Baroody could survive the public outrage that followed. Baroody withdrew his name from consideration, and Commissioner Nancy Nord, a former official of the U.S. Chamber of Commerce, was named acting chair of CPSC. In October 2007, in the wake of the children's toys scandal, Nord nevertheless opposed legislation to increase the authority of the agency, double its budget, and expand its staff—which makes strong enforcement all the more difficult, and which makes us all the more vulnerable to terrorist threats from an entirely different direction.

Who Will Protect This House?

While the GOP talks a tough game on security, it took a Democratic Congress to act.

As noted earlier, the very first bill introduced and passed by the House of Representatives under Speaker Nancy Pelosi, H.R. 1, implemented many of the 9/11 recommendations that Republicans had ignored, muddied, or avoided.

In addition to revamping Nunn-Lugar and other WMD nonproliferation programs, H.R. 1—finally—mandated the inspection of *all* port containers within five years and *all* airline cargo within three years. In addition, it declared that DHS would now allocate Homeland Security grants according to risk and not to political pressure. It provided extensive funding for increased educational and diplomatic ventures abroad, such as the Muslim Youth Opportunity Fund, to expand our arsenal of tools in the war on terror. And it established grants, as the 9/11 Commission recommended, to promote rail and mass transit security and provide first responders with more shared, up-to-date systems of communication. Congress sent the bill to President Bush with a 371–40 vote in the House of Representatives and an 85–8 vote in the Senate. It is now the law of the land.

Carrying out the recommendations of the 9/11 Commission is a big step, but Democrats can't rest on their laurels just yet. The threats are too real, the risk is too great, and—to date—the response has been too weak. As demonstrated by the continuing carnage in Iraq, the overextended state of our armed forces, the gaping holes in the protection of our homeland, growing anti-Americanism around the world, and the continued freedom of Osama bin Laden, the challenges to our safety and security are very serious.

Both at home and abroad, George W. Bush has failed to protect this nation. The United States needs new leadership that will make us safe again. On national security, we need a new president who will not just talk the talk but walk the walk.

Lesson Learned

Conservatives are right about this: in the end, there's no more important function of government than to protect and defend the homeland. For unless we are secure in our cities and our homes, we can achieve none of our goals and aspirations. That was true before September 11, 2001, but it's all so much more apparent today.

Ever since 9/11, Republicans have tried to make homeland security their number-one issue. President Bush doesn't make a speech on any subject without invoking September 11. Republicans held their 2004 national convention in New York City, evoking the memories of Ground Zero and September 11. And the not-so-subtle message of all Republican candidates for Congress and president boils down to: We may not be so good on health care, Social Security, stem cells, education, or the environment—but you can trust us on homeland security. You can trust us to keep you safe.

Except they haven't.

In August 2007, the Center for American Progress and *Foreign Policy* magazine released the results of their third annual "Terrorism Index," a survey of more than a hundred top national experts from across the political spectrum. Among their key findings:

- 91 percent of the experts think the world is becoming more dangerous for Americans.

- 84 percent of the experts do not believe the United States is winning the war on terror.

- Nine in ten experts believe the war in Iraq has had a negative impact on U.S. national security.

- 83 percent of the experts, including 64 percent of conservatives, say the troop surge in Iraq is having either a negative impact or no impact at all on U.S. national security.

In other words, even here, on this most important of all issues, conservatives have failed to deliver. They talk tough on security, but tough talk is no substitute for real protection. Until January 2007, conservatives were in charge of the White House and Congress. Yet despite all their harsh antiterrorist rhetoric, they have failed adequately to protect our cities, ports, railways, refineries, and power plants. Our borders are still not secure. The recommendations of the 9/11 Commission are still not met. Meanwhile, conservatives have pursued a pointless war in Iraq that has stirred up even more hostility toward the United States— making us less safe, not more.

You could not come up with a more compelling argument for why conservatism doesn't deserve a passing grade as a governing philosophy. Conservatives can't even get right the one governmental responsibility they admit is most critical of all.

There is nothing more important than protecting the homeland. Yet at this, too, conservatives have failed. Our national security is on the line. The stakes are too high. The risks are too great. We can't afford to give conservatives another chance.

CHAPTER 4

A Safeguard against Tyranny

The executive shall never exercise the legislative and judicial
powers, or either of them, to the end that it may be a
government of laws and not of men.
John Adams

The accumulation of all powers, legislative, executive, and
judiciary, in the same hands, whether of one, a few, or many,
and whether hereditary, self-appointed, or elective, may
justly be pronounced the very definition of tyranny.
James Madison

When the president does it, that means that it's not illegal.
Richard M. Nixon

To those who scare peace-loving people with phantoms
of lost liberty, my message is this: Your tactics only
aid terrorists, for they erode our national unity
and diminish our resolve.
John Ashcroft

The president needs to have his constitutional powers
unimpaired, if you will, in terms of the conduct
of national security policy.
Dick Cheney

If this were a dictatorship, it'd be a heck of a lot easier—
as long as I'm the dictator.
George W. Bush

E ver since our Founders first declared independence from the "long train of abuses and usurpations" that marked the reign of King George III, Americans have grappled with the issue of executive power. And, on executive power, like many other constitutional issues, where you stand depends on where you sit.

In a nutshell, here's the broad outline:

The Founding Fathers envisioned and created a legislative body that was one of three equal branches of government, yet the most powerful of the three.

Working with Congress to carry out the laws of the land, they also created a strong but circumscribed chief executive.

True to the Constitution, conservatives have traditionally always argued for a president with limited powers.

Over the years, several presidents of both parties have asserted the need to act above or even outside the law, in times of national emergency.

George W. Bush and Dick Cheney have sought to establish a unitary executive with unlimited powers, thus turning the Constitution—and conservatism—upside down.

A President, Not a King

Ever since they walked into the West Wing, George W. Bush, Dick Cheney, and their conservative compadres have argued for what they call a "unitary executive," by which they mean a president who doesn't have to worry about the niceties of running back to Congress for permission—who doesn't even have to worry about obeying the law—especially in time of war.

As explained by the Bush mouthpiece Bill Kristol, the publisher of the *Weekly Standard*:

A key reason the Articles of Confederation were dumped in favor of the Constitution in 1787 was because the new Constitution—our Constitution—created a unitary chief executive. The chief executive could, in times of war or emergency, act with the decisiveness, dispatch and, yes, secrecy, needed to protect the country and its citizens.

Unfortunately, either Kristol ignores his history or decides purposely to distort it. Because that's the exact opposite of what the Founders were thinking about when they first used the term *unitary executive*. They were trying to limit executive authority, not expand it. After all, as enshrined in the list of grievances that make up our Declaration of Independence, they had only recently prosecuted a revolution to free themselves from the arbitrary dictates of an unchecked executive power.

In debates among delegates to the Constitutional Convention, the phrase *unitary executive* meant one president, as opposed to a small governing body. Delegates were split on the issue. Virginia's Edmund Randolph feared that having but one president would burden the new nation with the "fetus of monarchy." Based on his belief that it would be harder for a group of men to seize power than for one individual to do so, he proposed instead a panel of three leaders, one from each area of the country. Pennsylvania's James Wilson and New York's Alexander Hamilton countered that a single executive would be the best "safeguard against tyranny."

Jefferson, of course, was not present in Philadelphia, but he had already expressed his distrust of a powerful executive:

Experience hath shewn, that even under the best forms of government those entrusted with power have, in time, and by slow operations, perverted it into tyranny.

On this question, Wilson and Hamilton won the day (although Hamilton lost his wish that the president be elected for life!). At the same time, having just severed ties with a monarchy, the Founding Fathers carefully and deliberately designed our system of government so that the authority of the executive office would be strictly limited. Not only were powers separated among the three branches of government, but the legislative branch, not the executive branch, was considered paramount. James Madison summed it up as succinctly as possible in Federalist 51: "In republican government, the legislative authority necessarily predominates."

In his book *A Necessary Evil*, the American historian Garry Wills pointed out that any doubts about the dominant role of Congress are resolved merely by reading the Constitution:

> Lawmaking is a society's highest function: it sets the rules by which all things are to be done or judged. It precedes in time and dignity the execution or adjudication of the laws. Without prior legislation, there is nothing to be executed or adjudicated. The other two functions necessarily serve the first. That fact is implied or asserted in every part of the Constitution.

Congress, after all, can impeach members of the judiciary and executive branches; neither of them can touch members of Congress. The president can veto a bill, but Congress can override him. The Supreme Court can declare a law unconstitutional, but Congress can start the amendment process or rewrite the law to make it constitutional.

The supremacy of Congress applies even during time of war. Yes, there is only one commander in chief. But only Congress, not the president, can declare war. And only Congress has the constitutionally mandated responsibility "to raise and support armies . . . to provide and maintain a navy" and "to make rules for the government and regulation of the land and naval forces."

In other words, regarding the way our government is meant to work, Congress always gets the last word—even if it decides not to use it. Congress may choose not to impeach an outlaw president, for example, but it still retains that power. And even though Congress long ago abdicated its unique authority under the Constitution to declare war, it could still seize it back if it ever decides to do so.

Our Founding Fathers wanted a chief executive with carefully defined and limited powers. And, at one time, so did conservatives.

Conservatives and the Office
of President

The idea of a constitutionally constrained presidency was one of the central tenets of conservatism from the founding of the republic until the late twentieth century; it was part and parcel of their reverence for tradition, their belief in human fallibility, and their desire for smaller, more responsive government.

One of the main reasons that conservatives in Congress resisted the United States' entry into World Wars I and II was because they feared the vastly increased presidential powers that would inevitably accrue to Wilson or Roosevelt following a declaration of war, with no ability of Congress to rein them in. Leading the initial opposition to World War II was "Mr. Republican," the Ohio senator Robert Taft.

Taft was later praised by the conservative icon Russell Kirk for insisting that war must be a last resort. His stand at the time was important, Kirk wrote, because war tends to "make the American President a virtual dictator, diminish the constitutional powers of Congress, contract civil liberties, injure the habitual self-reliance and self-government of the American people, distort the economy, sink the federal government in debt, and break in upon private and public morality."

I imagine it brings Kirk no comfort in the afterlife to know how stunningly correct he was. To buttress Taft and steer future debates over presidential initiatives, Kirk set forth what he considered the conservative creed on executive power:

> The conservative endeavors to so limit and balance political power that anarchy or tyranny may not arise. In every age, nevertheless, men and women are tempted to overthrow the limitations upon power, for the sake of some fancied temporary power as a force for good—so long as the power falls into his hands. . . .
>
> Knowing human nature for a mixture of good and evil, the conservative does not put his trust in mere benevolence. Constitutional restrictions, political checks and balances, adequate enforcement of the laws, the old intricate web of restraints upon will and appetite—these the conservative approves as instruments of freedom and order.

The evolution of conservative thinking toward executive authority is outlined in an essay called "Conservatives and the Presidency," which appeared on the Cato Institute's blog in July 2005. As Cato scholars pointed out, no less a conservative icon than William F. Buckley Jr., writing in the pages of the *National Review*, once conservatism's sacred scripture, consistently identified the executive branch as the locus of the New Deal's liberal activism and hailed Congress as the "conservative" branch of government. His colleague James Burnham warned that the rise of activist presidents could bring about "plebiscitary despotism for the United States in place of constitutional government, and thus the end of political liberty."

Ironically, even Barry Goldwater, best remembered for his hardline stance toward the Soviet Union, was a strong proponent of a tightly bound chief executive. It sounds like a contradiction, but if Goldwater was considered an extremist for wanting to "lob one into the men's room of the Kremlin," he was also somewhat of an extremist in wanting to tame the powers of any president. In accepting his party's nomination, he told delegates to the 1964 Republican Convention:

> Those who seek absolute power, even though they seek it to do what they regard as good, are simply demanding the right to enforce their own version of heaven on earth. And let me remind you, they are the very ones who always create the most hellish tyrannies. Absolute power does corrupt, and those who seek it must be suspect and must be opposed.

Contrary to what some people later argued, Goldwater was not merely talking about foreign dictators. As evidenced by his 1964 campaign manifesto, "My Case for the Republican Party," he was also warning about the accretion of presidential power in the United States. Some conservatives go along with a stronger chief executive, Goldwater observed, maybe because they like the results achieved with more power. But this conclusion, he warned, was dangerous:

> This is nothing less than the totalitarian philosophy that the end justifies the means. . . . If ever there was a philosophy of government totally at war with that of the Founding Fathers, it is this one.

Shortly after Goldwater's lopsided defeat in 1964, however, the ground began to shift. Fellow conservatives not only scurried away from Goldwater as a politically viable leader, they began to abandon elements of his conservative governing philosophy as well—particularly his belief in a constitutionally limited president.

The winds of change had actually begun to blow much earlier, from the daring foreign adventures of Teddy Roosevelt at the turn of the century to the robust attempts of Harry Truman to contain atheistic communism in the early Cold War. A strong, independently acting chief executive was now seen as something that might be tolerated— but still only rarely and usually only in the field of foreign policy.

By the mid 1970s, however, conservatives had managed a flip-flop on presidential power worthy of Mitt Romney. In November 1974, the *National Review* reversed itself, running a cover story—"The Presidency: Shifting Conservative Perspectives?"—in which the conservative writer Jeffrey Hart argued that only a strong executive could fight against a growing federal bureaucracy and an increasingly powerful national press corps. And this was one year after Richard Nixon was forced to resign over Watergate.

For conservatives, the presidency, not Congress, was now considered the "conservative" branch of government. And the more Richard Nixon asserted executive privilege, the more conservatives liked him. Indeed, M. Stanton Evans, a conservative contributor to *Human Events* magazine, quipped, "I didn't like Nixon *until* Watergate."

So, in a strange twist that was about to get stranger, conservatives were now champions of robust executive power despite having watched one of their own be forced to resign the presidency for abusing that power.

Perhaps because Democrats had controlled the House and the Senate for so long, conservatives now began to complain about the "imperial Congress," no longer about the "imperial presidency."

By the time Ronald Reagan came to power in 1980, conservatives had stopped bemoaning the dangers of a powerful executive. To the contrary: faced with evidence of extraconstitutional behavior in the Iran-Contra Affair—where Reagan secretly defied a congressional ban on funding the contras in Nicaragua, and the Reagan aide Ollie North hailed the president as the "sole organ" of U.S. foreign policy—conservatives barely batted an eye. And in August 1981, when Reagan summarily fired striking air traffic controllers, conservatives went ga-ga over the assertion of executive power. The columnist Robert Novak wrote that Reagan's performance was "likely to reverse the dangerous erosion of presidential power at a time the Western World has maximum need for a strong presidency."

Conservatives were so enamored with Reagan that they even tried to repeal the Twenty-second Amendment, allowing him to seek a third term. Under President Clinton, conservatives were equally unsuccessful in attempting to repeal the War Powers Act, proving their willingness to cede more power to any president—even to a Democrat.

This push for a powerful president with powers far exceeding those outlined in the Constitution is a far cry from what was envisioned by the Founders. And it set the stage for the claim of unbridled presidential power asserted by George W. Bush.

As we will see, however, Bush was not the first president to rush down this path.

Power to the President

While both the Founders and pre-Nixon conservatives were understandably loathe to depend on presidential self-discipline, choosing to place their faith instead in constitutional proscriptions, the last defense against executive abuse in our history has always been personal restraint. Some presidents had it, most did not.

Indeed, it must be an awesome experience, walking into the Oval Office for the first time and knowing you're the most powerful person on the planet. And it must be awfully tempting to think, Since I'm the president of the United States, why should I have to bother checking in with that pesky Congress or Supreme Court? Especially in time of war?

Sadly, that temptation has proved impossible to resist for more presidents than not, including those who were most vociferous in their demands for a chief executive with strict limits on power.

Our very first president's term in office was scarred by an ongoing feud between Secretary of State Thomas Jefferson and Secretary of the Treasury Alexander Hamilton over the powers of the central government in general, and the powers of the presidency in particular. Hamilton championed a robust federal government; Jefferson fought for the weakest government and chief executive possible.

Once he assumed the presidency himself, however, Jefferson took a different view. On his inauguration day, March 4, 1801, Jefferson voided twenty-five out of forty-two judicial appointments that had been made by his predecessor, John Adams, and confirmed by the U.S. Senate. His initiative triggered a lawsuit that resulted in the famous *Marbury v. Madison* decision, establishing the doctrine of judicial review.

But Jefferson was just getting warmed up. To ensure that U.S. ships would retain navigation rights on the Mississippi River and, more to the point, to double the size of the fledging United States and give his "empire for liberty" room to grow, Jefferson also negotiated the Louisiana Purchase—even though, as a strict constructionist, he did not believe the president had the constitutional authority to make such a deal, and even though he feared that doing so would erode states' rights by increasing the power of the federal executive.

On executive authority, even Thomas Jefferson preached one thing but practiced another. (Of course, he did so on slavery, too). But he was not the only one. Andrew Jackson—who was branded "King Andrew I" by his Whig adversaries—defied an order of the Supreme Court regarding the independence of the Cherokee Indian Nation of Georgia. "John Marshall has made his decision," Jackson reportedly said, "now let him enforce it."

Abraham Lincoln didn't defy Congress and the courts; he simply ignored them. Lincoln's break with Congress and the Constitution came early in his term. In late April 1861, just two weeks after the first shots were fired in the Civil War, Lincoln suspended habeas corpus in the crucial border state of Maryland.

Nor did he wait for, or even seek, the approval of Congress for other initiatives taken as commander in chief of the Union forces: proclaiming a blockade of Southern ports, extending the period for volunteer enlistment, increasing the size of the army and the navy, and entrusting public funds to private individuals for the purchase of arms and supplies. He subsequently, kind of, apologized for his actions in a famous July 4, 1861, address to Congress:

> It was with the deepest regret that the Executive found the duty of employing the war-power, in defence of the government, forced upon him. He could but perform this duty, or surrender the existence of the government.

Whether strictly legal or not, Lincoln defended acting out of public necessity to hold the government together and expressed the wish that Congress would subsequently ratify his decisions. Speaking in the third person of himself as president, he told Congress, "In full view of his great responsibility, he has, so far, done what he has deemed his duty. You will now, according to your own judgment, perform yours."

So when George W. Bush defends his warrantless National Security Agency (NSA) wiretaps and asks Congress to authorize them, after the fact, one could actually argue—and right-wing commentators often do—that all he's doing is channeling President Lincoln!

Until Bush, no Republican president had waved the big stick of presidential power more proudly than Teddy Roosevelt. Still the youngest man ever to become president, he turned political theories regarding the powers of the chief executive on their head. Tradition taught that presidents were limited to those duties clearly spelled out in the Constitution. Roosevelt argued just the opposite: that the president was free to do whatever was not clearly banned by the Constitution.

And he governed accordingly, asserting the right of the United States to intervene in the internal affairs of Latin American countries and encouraging Panamanian revolutionaries to win their freedom from Colombia, in order to facilitate construction of the Panama Canal. Roosevelt even tried, by executive order, to impose a new system of phonetic spelling on the United States.

Did Roosevelt believe he was breaking new ground? No way. In his mind, he was merely following what he called the "Lincoln-Jackson" philosophy of presidential power. Roosevelt explained,

> I declined to adopt the view that what was imperatively necessary for the nation could not be done by the President unless he could find some specific authorization to do it. My belief was that it was not only his right but his duty to do anything that the needs of the nation demanded unless such action was forbidden by the Constitution or by the laws.

You can almost see the smile on TR's face as he denies overstepping his bounds:

> Under this interpretation of executive power, I did and caused
> to be done many things not previously done by the President
> and the heads of the departments. I did not usurp power, but I
> did greatly broaden the use of executive power.

I hereby nominate this for "understatement of the century"!

And yet, as robust as they were in flexing their presidential muscle, Lincoln and Teddy Roosevelt still take a backseat to Woodrow Wilson and Franklin Roosevelt. When German submarines started to attack U.S. shipping, the Wilson government asked for near-dictatorial powers from Congress to raise and equip an army to fight on foreign soil. It conscripted nearly three million men into the army via the newly passed Selective Service Act and created the War Industries Board, led by the financier Bernard Baruch, to set the production quotas, the priorities, and the prices of all war materials. FDR was also given much leeway by Congress in declaring emergency measures to lift the country out of the Depression and, later, to wage war simultaneously in Europe and the Pacific.

Roosevelt was willing to work closely with, and even show public deference to, Congress—as long as it gave him what he wanted. Otherwise, he warned, "In the event the Congress should fail to act, and act adequately, I shall accept the responsibility, and I will act." Motivated by the same sense of reality as Lincoln, Roosevelt reminded Congress, "The President has the power . . . to take measures necessary to avert a disaster which would interfere with winning of the war."

With Roosevelt, the stage was set for the modern imperial presidency. And his immediate successor, Harry S. Truman, rose to the occasion. An unlikely president, Truman was an even more unlikely dictator, but he often governed like one.

Harry Truman was the first president to take the United States to war without a declaration of war by Congress. But, interestingly enough, the former senator from Missouri did not send U.S. troops to defend South Korea in defiance of Congress. He actually did so with Congress's blessing.

Truman regularly consulted congressional leaders, asked to address a joint session of Congress, and had his own staff prepare a draft congressional declaration of war. But he was told not to bother. With the exception of a few lone voices like Robert Taft, Democratic and

Republican leaders assured him that both the Constitution and the UN Charter gave him, as president, the authority to act unilaterally. Advised the Democrat Tom Connally, the chair of the Senate Foreign Relations Committee, "If a burglar breaks into your house, you can shoot at him without going down to the police station and getting permission."

Of course, it's not likely to take a few years and cost a few thousand U.S. casualties and a few billion dollars to shoot a burglar, but otherwise this makes total sense.

In the name of homeland security, Congress thereby surrendered its primary role and influence in the conduct of foreign affairs, especially in time of war—a role it has never regained.

Truman was less successful in attempting to use his wartime powers to seize U.S. steel mills, a bold move that was shot down by the Supreme Court. But, even though unsuccessful, he set an example of unilateral executive action that has been emulated, at least to some extent, by every president since.

After Truman, the president who was most quick to assert unlimited authority was Richard Nixon—with one big difference. Truman used the powers of the presidency to serve the public good; Nixon abused the powers of the presidency to save his political hide.

Like presidents before him, Nixon took advantage of the cover of war to stretch his executive authority, most infamously by secretly extending the war in Vietnam into neighboring Cambodia. In his case, however, Congress did not simply go along. Members of both parties joined to adopt the War Powers Act of 1973, limiting the war-making authority of the president—and placing it into law over President Nixon's veto.

As if a secret war were not bad enough, Nixon really went wrong by siccing the CIA and the FBI on his political enemies and then using federal agencies to block the resulting investigation. This, of course, resulted in his ultimate downfall, as the other two branches of government rose up against his flagrant abuses of executive power. And yet, to the very end—and even long after his resignation, in his interview with the British talk-show host David Frost—Nixon argued that somehow, presidents didn't have the same obligations toward the law as all the rest of us.

It is quite obvious that there are certain inherently governmental actions which if undertaken by the sovereign . . . are lawful but which if undertaken by private persons are not. . . . But it is naive to attempt to characterize activities a President might authorize as "legal" or "illegal" without reference to the circumstances under which he concludes that the activity is necessary.

Nixon didn't just govern like an emperor. He tried to fill the White House with all the trappings of an imperial presidency. In 1969, while visiting India, Nixon was so impressed by the regal uniforms worn by Indian troops escorting his horse-drawn carriage that as soon as he returned home, he ordered the same regulation dress for uniformed Secret Service agents guarding the White House. Visitors to the Nixon White House were henceforth greeted by officers dressed as if they'd just stepped out of a sixteenth-century French palace: chocolate-brown uniforms with white tunics, draped with gold braid, and topped with sharply sloped hats.

Secret Service agents complained that the fancy dress made them look "pompous" and like part of an "imperial guard," but to no avail. The uniforms were worn at the White House until the day Nixon resigned—at which point they were packed away, hopefully never to be seen again.

Regal uniforms on the Secret Service. That may be the only manifestation of the imperial presidency George W. Bush has not adopted. In every other respect, Bush has out-Nixoned Nixon.

The Seeds of Change

Whatever George W. Bush believed about the limited powers of the presidency, all that changed on September 11, 2001.

At least, that's how the story goes. Bush started out believing in a "humble" foreign policy and a "constitutionally limited" chief executive. (Of course, when he was selected, he had a lot to be humble about.)

Then came 9/11—and both George Bush and Dick Cheney suddenly realized that traditional conservative teachings about limits on executive power no longer applied. Legal opinions crafted by Attorney General John Ashcroft, Deputy Assistant Attorney General John Yoo, and the White House counsel Alberto Gonzales fed the new ideology: in order to protect the homeland against new acts of terror, the president had to be prepared to act immediately, without consulting Congress—and even outside the law if necessary. That was the lesson of September 11.

That's how the story goes. And it's wrong.

Bush and Cheney didn't "come to Jesus" about the need to expand executive authority after 9/11. Nine months earlier, they walked into the Oval Office determined to do so. September 11 was not their reason for operating outside the law; it was their excuse.

Cheney, in fact, had been working for more than three decades, ever since he served as Gerald Ford's chief of staff, to bring back the unfettered presidential powers once enjoyed by Ford's predecessor, Richard Nixon. As a member of Congress in the ensuing years, Cheney led a band of House Republicans who strongly defended Ronald Reagan's end runs around the law on behalf of the Nicaraguan contras—much as he would later defend George W. Bush's extralegal actions in fighting the so-called war on terror.

In 2002, now vice president, Cheney told ABC News that the presidency was "weaker today as an institution because of the unwise compromises that have been made over the last thirty to thirty-five years." And on December 20, 2005, when questioned about Bush's warrantless NSA spying program, Cheney directed reporters back to a minority report of Congress's Iran-Contra Committee—a report written at his direction by the staffer Michael Malbin. That "obscure text," said Cheney, was "very good in laying out a robust view of the president's prerogatives with respect to the conduct of especially foreign policy and national security matters."

"Yes, I do have the view that over the years, there had been an erosion of presidential power and authority," Cheney acknowledged. Most conservatives would see that as a *positive* development, but not Cheney.

The world today demands a different approach, said Cheney. And he was determined to force the change: "[T]he president of the United States needs to have his constitutional powers unimpaired, if you will, in terms of the conduct of national security policy."

As the action of a "strong, robust executive" in the war on terror, Cheney upheld Bush's warrantless NSA wiretapping as "totally appropriate and consistent with the constitutional authority of the president."

And so Cheney laid down the tracks on which the Bush train

would run. When you can defy both the law and the courts and tap everyone's phone in the name of the war on terror, there is nothing you can't do.

The Bush-Cheney Empire

From the beginning, Bush and Cheney asserted broad executive powers under their new definition of the term *unitary executive*.

As already noted, when debated by the Founders in Philadelphia 1787, a "unitary executive" meant one president, rather than a committee of three. When used in the Bush White House, however, it meant one president with near-absolute power—again, especially in time of war. Today, times have changed, argued Deputy Assistant Attorney General John Yoo. "We are used to a peacetime system in which Congress enacts the laws, the president enforces them, and the courts interpret them. In wartime, the gravity shifts to the executive branch."

How far can the president go in exercising his power? The Notre Dame Law School professor Doug Cassel posed a hypothetical in a December 2005 debate with Yoo:

> Cassel: "If the president deems that he's got to torture somebody, including by crushing the testicles of the person's child, there is no law that can stop him?"

> Yoo: "I think it depends on why the president thinks he needs to do that."

Early in the administration, Yoo was joined in providing legal justification for asserting broad executive powers by Cheney's legal counsel David Addington, who would later replace indicted-for-perjury Scooter Libby as the vice president's chief of staff. Addington preached his own version of the unitary executive called "The New Paradigm," a constitutional theory of virtually limitless executive authority. By that theory, Jane Mayer wrote in her July 3, 2006, profile of Addington in the *New Yorker*, "the President, as Commander-in-Chief, has the authority to disregard virtually all previously known legal boundaries, if national security demands it."

And why not? They'd long ago already breached the bounds of prudence and reason.

Dick Cheney's Energy Task Force

Actually, the Bush administration's first opportunity to exercise either the unitary executive authority or the New Paradigm came long before September 11 and had nothing to do with crushing children's testicles. It was all about secret meetings on energy.

In his second week in the White House, President Bush created a task force known as the National Energy Policy Development Group, chaired by Vice President Dick Cheney, and ordered it to come up with a new national energy policy. In so doing, task force members held more than forty meetings with energy industry lobbyists, and Cheney himself sat down for one-on-one meetings with several energy CEOs. Task force members also held one—one!—meeting with representatives of environmental organizations, but only after their draft report had already been published.

To this date, however, except for that one meeting with environmentalists, no one knows for sure which industry representatives met with Cheney or the task force, what they recommended, or which of their recommendations ended up in the administration's final report.

Why not? Because Cheney successfully invoked executive privilege. Just a few years earlier, as the CEO of Halliburton, Cheney had written a personal letter to Vice President Al Gore, complaining about the Clinton administration's proposal to toughen air pollution standards. Any change in environmental regulations must be "addressed in full and open debate," Cheney stated in a letter that was obtained under the Freedom of Information Act by the Center for Public Integrity.

But now Cheney argued just the opposite. As a member of the executive branch and one of the president's key advisers, he was required to reveal neither whom he met with nor what they discussed. And the courts backed him up, even though they had ruled just the opposite in regard to the records of First Lady Hillary Clinton's task force on health policy.

No doubt, Cheney and company will vigorously defend the next Democratic president's right to hold secret meetings . . . when unicorns frolic in a land of sunshine and candy canes.

Visitors Chez Dick and Lynne

By 2006, Cheney's penchant for secrecy had expanded from whom he met with in the White House to whom he partied with in his home.

For years, and by law, Secret Service records have been treated as public records, based on the principle that the public has a right to know who is entering the president's house, the White House, and the vice president's house, the Naval Observatory. In September 2006, however, Cheney upset the applecart.

In a letter from his counsel, Shannen W. Coffin, Cheney informed the Secret Service that he, not the Service, was the official keeper of the records, and therefore he could, and would, refuse to divulge the names of religious conservatives he had met with in his home, as well as the identity of those who attended any other social or business events at the Naval Observatory. Instead, Cheney insisted that his visitor log be considered part of official presidential records, which won't be released to the public until long after the Bush administration is gone, when nobody any longer cares.

Cheney ultimately lost the battle in December 2007 when the conservative federal judge Royce C. Lamberth ruled that White House and Naval Observatory visitor logs are public records, subject to disclosure, and therefore may not be kept secret.

In his attempts to maintain secrecy, Cheney argued that he enjoyed special privacy protections because he is a member of the executive branch. Except when he isn't.

Cheney Takes On the National Archives

Dick Cheney had already proved that he would stop at nothing in order to govern in secret: he was willing to defy Congress, the courts, the media, and public opinion. In taking on the National Archives, he proved that he was even willing to defy an Executive Order signed by his own commander in chief.

In 2003, George W. Bush updated and signed an Executive Order, originally signed by Bill Clinton in 1995, requiring "any entity within the executive branch that comes into the possession of classified information" to report annually to the Information Security Oversight Office of the National Archives on which documents it is keeping classified and which it is declassifying. The order may seem to require nothing more than a mindless and time-consuming shuffling of paper, but it was intended by both Clinton and Bush to keep track of and protect the integrity of classified documents—while making sure that no classified information was inadvertently released.

In 2001 and 2002, Cheney's office complied with the order. Then, suddenly, in 2003, he refused to cooperate any longer. Employees of the National Archives sought to inspect his offices in order to check on compliance, but Cheney's staff blocked the doors. When National Archives officials complained, Cheney asked Congress to abolish the office. Congress declined.

Assuming that Bush, not Cheney, is the real president (no small assumption, I know!), what was Cheney's justification for refusing to obey an Executive Order issued by his own boss? The man who once argued that he did not have to reveal the names of those he met with in his home or office because he *was* a member of the executive branch now argued that he did not have to reveal what his office was doing with classified documents—because he was *not* a member of the executive branch. After all, said Cheney, he had an office in the Capitol Building, which he used on those rare occasions when he presided over the Senate.

You must admit, you have to admire his chutzpah! The vice president's main office is actually located in the *Executive* Office Building, directly alongside the White House. How could Cheney seriously claim he was not part of the executive branch? The White House press secretary Tony Snow couldn't explain it and wouldn't even try. Late-night comedians had a field day suggesting that Cheney constituted his own, independent, one-man "Fourth Branch of Government."

The issue was finally resolved when Democrats threatened to cut from the president's budget all funds for operations of the vice president's office. After all, since he wasn't part of the executive branch, he wouldn't need any executive branch funding. At which point, Cheney threw in the towel and agreed to work with the National Archives.

Strangely enough, Cheney wasn't the first top Bush administration official to try to bury his papers. He may have been inspired by previous attempts at secrecy by President Bush himself.

Get Your Hands off My Papers

It used to be that at every level of government—local, state, and fed-eral—conservatives could always be counted on to push for greater openness and transparency in government. More often than not, con-servative legislators were authors of so-called sunshine laws to open up government meetings and documents to public scrutiny.

After all, the president is our employee. He works for us, the citi-zens. And so we own everything the president writes or has written for him, as president.

That changed with Richard Nixon and continued with George W. Bush, neither of whom felt that they answered to anyone, especially not to "the people."

Just two months after taking office, Bush signed an Executive Order blocking the release of sixty-eight thousand pages of confiden-tial communications between President Reagan and his advisers, including documents relating to the roles of top administration offi-cials in the Iran-Contra Affair.

Under terms of the 1978 Presidential Records Act, those papers were supposed to be routinely released twelve years after the end of the Reagan administration—and the Reagan Library had expressed no concern.

Nonetheless, Bush acted unilaterally to block their release, perhaps to protect the reputations of former Reagan officials then holding jobs in the new Bush administration—or, more likely, the reputation of his own father, Reagan's vice president, who had thus far managed to escape culpability in the Iran-Contra Affair.

In terms of squelching presidential papers, that was just a hint of what was to follow.

In November 2001, Bush signed a second Executive Order that, in effect, reversed the 1978 Presidential Records Act. Under Bush's new edict, instead of papers being released automatically after twelve years, presidential documents may be released only when both the cur-rent president and the former president agree. Furthermore, if the current president disagrees with their release, he may veto the decision of the former president.

It's even more one-sided than that. If a former president has died, the current president may designate someone else—anybody! wife, child, mistress, or gardener—to speak for the former president regarding the release of his presidential papers. As the George Washington University professor of law Jonathan Turley noted, this provision allows the president to extend the right to invoke executive privilege "to anyone of his choosing: a half-wit nephew or a drinking buddy."

Before any approval may be granted, however, Bush's new order first specifies that historians or researchers seeking access to presidential papers must establish a "demonstrated, specific need to know," as opposed to a formerly held "right to know."

In other words, by Executive Order, George W. Bush has changed the rules covering the release of presidential papers from a question of the people's right to know to the president's right to suppress.

The order, in effect, permits some of the nation's most important government documents to be kept secret forever. It allows a president to perpetuate his misrepresentations to the American people. And, having been signed shortly after September 11, it enables George W. Bush to hide from the public all records of the questionable, if not illegal, actions he has taken in the name of the war on terror.

A Blank Check for George W. Bush

Up to this point, the efforts by George Bush and Dick Cheney to flex their executive muscles were almost laughable.

Indeed, had their attempts been limited to insisting on holding secret meetings, hosting secret dinner parties, or keeping presidential papers secret, they would have been remembered as determined, but relatively harmless, players in expanding presidential authority: irritants to future historians, but little more.

Then came September 11, which Bush and Cheney immediately seized as the excuse they'd been looking for to exercise near-dictatorial powers. Through a blitzkrieg of executive decisions, they jettisoned the Geneva Conventions on the treatment of prisoners of war, set up a secret network of torture prisons around the world, suspended the rule of law on people suspected of having terrorist ties, ordered wiretaps on virtually all domestic and international telephone calls, decided for themselves which new laws they would obey and which ones they would not—and, of course, misled the nation into an unauthorized and illegal war.

It all started on September 18, 2001, when a shocked and angry Congress understandably authorized the president to respond by military force to those who had attacked U.S. soil a week earlier.

The language of the Authorization for the Use of Military Force (called AUMF, after the sound you make when you first get the liberty knocked out of you) is very straightforward:

> [T]he President is authorized to use all necessary and appropriate force against those nations, organizations, or persons he determines planned, authorized, committed, or aided the terrorist attacks that occurred on September 11, 2001, or harbored such organizations or persons, in order to prevent any future acts of international terrorism against the United States by such nations, organizations or persons.

But from the beginning, its meaning was cloudy and its application was stretched by devious White House lawyers far beyond anything Congress ever intended.

Redefining the Word *Patriot*

For this power-hungry White House, though, not even the AUMF was enough. After all, it could be construed as authorizing emergency powers only against enemies overseas. What about enemies, or those suspected of having ties to our enemies, lurking here in the United States? Attorney General John Ashcroft was ready with the answer.

Three days after 9/11, Ashcroft marched up to Congress with a request for expanded police powers that he said the Justice Department needed to fight the war on terror. He gave his proposal a fancy name: the "Uniting and Strengthening America by Providing Appropriate Tools Required to Intercept and Obstruct Terrorism Act of 2001"—or, simply, the USA Patriot Act.

It sounds like the carefully crafted result of months of investigation, research, and congressional hearings. Not so. It was actually a 342-page grab bag of measures that the Justice Department had previously tried to wrestle out of Congress but failed. As the conservative Georgia congressman Bob Barr told Ashcroft, "You are just trying to use September 11 to get extraordinary new police powers through Congress that you could never get otherwise."

Time would prove Barr correct. We subsequently learned that there had been ample warnings to both the CIA and the FBI about the presence of al-Qaeda terrorists inside the United States and their plans to strike U.S. targets, using hijacked aircraft. The problem was not that law enforcement agencies didn't have enough tools to track them down. The problem was they didn't use the tools they had.

Nevertheless, just forty-five days after September 11, Congress passed the entire 342-page Patriot Act after only minimal debate. Most members had not even read the bill. In the Senate, the vote was 98–1. Only the Wisconsin Democrat Russ Feingold dared vote against it.

The Patriot Act turned this country into as close to a police state as we've ever been. It gives the FBI broad new police powers that can be used against law-abiding citizens, as well as against terrorism suspects. It authorizes the government to search our medical records, tax records, and library records without probable cause or without first getting a court order. And it gives the FBI authority to break into our homes or offices, under the so-called "sneak and peek" provision, and conduct secret searches without telling us for weeks, months, or ever. Big Brother rules!

In a lame attempt to make the Patriot Act appear less draconian, Congress attached a sunset clause, under which the Justice Department's extraordinary new powers dissolved on December 31, 2005. What a joke. Civil liberties were once again crushed by phony national security arguments. Under intense lobbying from the White House, as December 2005 approached, Congress simply rolled over and passed Patriot Act II—keeping all the controversial provisions of the earlier law intact.

War on terror or not, the Patriot Act so blatantly violated the basic freedoms enshrined in the Bill of Rights that it was bound to be challenged in the courts. It was. And it lost.

In September 2007, two different federal courts ruled provisions of the Patriot Act unconstitutional. A New York court denied the FBI's use of "national security letters," rather than judicial warrants, to obtain phone and computer records. And a Portland, Oregon, judge struck down the FBI's use of secret searches and unauthorized wiretapping to gather criminal evidence. Several legal challenges are still pending. It is only a matter of time before the entire Patriot Act is ruled unconstitutional.

But George W. Bush didn't need the Patriot Act in order to start tapping phones without a court order.

Reach Out and Touch Someone

On October 7, 2001, after the Taliban refused to turn over al-Qaeda's leaders to U.S. authorities, American forces began an aerial bombing campaign of targets in Afghanistan. The war in Afghanistan was a legitimate act of self-defense against an enemy that attacked us on September 11. It was the first public presidential initiative taken under the Authorization for the Use of Military Force. Only much later did we learn that Bush had also secretly assumed powers under the AUMF to launch a new round of wiretaps by the National Security Agency (NSA).

On December 16, 2005, the *New York Times* reported that sometime early in 2002 (the exact date is still unknown), President Bush ordered the NSA to conduct surveillance of all telephone calls and e-mails between a person in the United States and a person overseas—without first getting a warrant from the court, as required by the 1978 Foreign Intelligence Surveillance Act, or FISA. Existence of the program was confirmed by Attorney General Alberto Gonzales on December 19, 2005.

Editors of the *Times* later admitted they had known of the program for more than a year—meaning well before the 2004 election—but sat on the story at the request of the White House. Bush aides insisted that its publication would undermine national security—the first, but hardly the last, time the Bush White House would play on fear to defend its executive overreach after 9/11. The Bush administration is still doing so today.

A public uproar followed. Civil libertarians cried foul. The former Nixon White House counsel John Dean called Bush worse than his old boss. Members of Congress of both parties blasted Bush for failing to obey the law, especially since the FISA court was so liberal in handing out warrants. Only a handful of times in almost thirty years had the court ever said no. And besides, the law provided for emergencies such as this one. In cases where the administration felt that it couldn't afford to wait until the court convened to begin collecting information, FISA allowed a seventy-two-hour warrantless grace period.

In other words, there was no reason at all that Bush could not both expand wiretapping and still obey the law. Except, of course, that obeying the law would interfere with Bush and Cheney's determination to use 9/11 as a pretext for operating above the law.

The White House defended the lawless NSA program with a litany of lame excuses. FISA was an "old law," argued President Bush; therefore, he was not bound to obey it. FISA was broken and needed fixing, complained the then White House counsel Alberto Gonzales. Actually, though, the administration didn't ask Congress to fix the legislation because Bush & Co. didn't think Congress would agree. If they had only known terrorists were planning an attack against the United States *before* 9/11, argued administration officials, they might have prevented it. Of course, the CIA and the FBI both knew the 9/11 hijackers were in the United States—the president himself was warned of a terrorist attack on August 6, 2001—they just did nothing about it.

The central defense offered by the administration was much more far-reaching and much more troubling. Following an opinion authored by Deputy Assistant Attorney General John Yoo, the White House argued that Bush did not have to obey the FISA law because the AUMF that was passed by Congress on September 18 gave him carte blanche authority to do whatever was necessary to prevent another terrorist attack, even override the Constitution and the law.

Bush's official response to the whole controversy, in fact, was neither to admit he had overstepped his bounds nor to seek additional authority from Congress but instead to launch a criminal investigation into who leaked the story to the *New York Times*. As of this writing, that investigation continues, unresolved. But based on members of the administration who have since expressed doubts about the legality of the program, there are plenty of potential suspects inside Bush's own Justice Department.

Indeed, historians will always cite as one of the most colorful moments of the Bush administration a surprise visit by the then White House counsel Alberto Gonzales and the chief of staff Andrew Card to Attorney General John Ashcroft's hospital room at George Washington University Hospital on March 10, 2004. They weren't just stopping by to drop off flowers.

Before entering the hospital for emergency gallbladder surgery, Ashcroft had turned the reins of power over to Deputy Attorney General James Comey. He and Comey agreed that the warrantless NSA wiretaps, now up for reauthorization, were illegal—and the Justice Department would no longer support them.

Having learned that Gonzales and Card were en route to GWU, Comey rushed to the hospital and arrived before them. According to Comey's account, when the two top White House officials entered Ashcroft's room, they asked him, although he was still somewhat under sedation from surgery, to reverse his position. Ashcroft lifted his head from his pillow, pointed to Comey, and told them, "He's the man in charge." At which point, without even acknowledging Comey, Gonzales and Card turned and left the room. When word of the hospital visit got back to the Justice Department, thirty top officials threatened to resign in protest over the White House's attempt to bypass official authority and proceed with an illegal program. Perhaps one of them called the *New York Times* instead.

With Ashcroft unwilling to play ball, the White House simply reauthorized the spying program without Department of Justice certification. Which brings us back to the central point of this whole debate.

The visit to Ashcroft's hospital room is more than a docudrama. It raises the key question of the Bush administration: who decides when something is illegal and when it's not? In the Bush White House, as in the Nixon White House, the answer is clear: the president decides. If he says it's legal, it's legal. Not even Congress, whose job it is to make the law—and not even the attorney general, whose job it is to enforce the law—can clip the wings of presidential power.

Lest there be any doubt about where the administration stood, its assertion of unlimited executive authority was confirmed by a Justice Department "White Paper" issued on January 19, 2006. Widely believed to have been written by Alberto Gonzales, who was soon to replace John Ashcroft as attorney general, the document described the NSA spying program as both "lawful and consistent with civil liberties." In a phrase dripping with monarchial tones, the presumed-author Gonzales wrote that the combination of Article II of the Constitution and the AUMF passed by Congress placed the president "at the zenith of his powers." Then, in the same words used earlier by Ollie North to justify Ronald Reagan's illegal funding of the contras,

Gonzales named Bush as "the sole organ of the Nation in foreign affairs."

To put it mildly, not everyone in the other two branches of government saw it the same way. In their first test in the courts, Bush's warrantless wiretaps flunked badly. In August 2006, ruling in a lawsuit brought by the American Civil Liberties Union and other civil liberty organizations, U.S. District Judge Anna Diggs Taylor ruled that the NSA program violated privacy, free speech rights, and the separation of powers—and was also illegal under FISA. "It was never the intent of the framers to give the president such unfettered control, particularly where his actions blatantly disregard the parameters clearly enumerated in the Bill of Rights," Taylor wrote in a forty-three-page opinion. "There are no hereditary Kings in America and no powers not created by the Constitution. So all 'inherent powers' must derive from that Constitution."

In Congress, reaction ranged from hearings probing the legality of NSA wiretaps to demands for Bush's impeachment. Even several Republican senators, led by Pennsylvania's Arlen Specter, insisted that Bush must comply with the FISA law or seek necessary amendments from Congress.

Once Democrats took control of both the House and the Senate in 2006, a showdown between Congress and the White House seemed certain. As indeed it was. That showdown came in the last week of July 2007. As members of Congress rushed to get out of town for their summer recess, the administration suddenly warned of an increase in "chatter" among terrorist suspects and argued that they needed more wiretap authority, not less.

This was the opportunity Democrats had been waiting for. The NSA spy program was up for renewal and Democrats were in charge. They could either give George Bush another blank check or force him to obey the law.

And what did they do? After almost two years of bitching, complaining, and threatening impeachment, they folded. With the votes of sixteen Senate Democrats, Congress not only authorized Bush's past illegal wiretapping, it gave him expanded authority to monitor phone calls and e-mails in the future—*without* first having to get a warrant from the FISA court.

Which just confirms what history had already proved: no matter how much Congress or the courts might kick and scream, whenever a president asserts extraordinary executive power, he usually gets away with it—the Constitution be damned.

Just Call Them "Enemy Combatants"

In the weeks following September 11, the Justice Department rounded up hundreds of young men of Middle Eastern origin, branded them terrorist suspects, and detained them in secret locations for months, without any charges being filed and without giving them the right to contact their families or talk to lawyers. Not one of them was found to have any connection to the terrorist attacks of 9/11. Many were discovered to have visa problems and were deported. The rest were eventually released.

Civil libertarians complained about denying these detainees, whether U.S. citizens or not, the due process of law guaranteed by the Constitution. But from a Bush administration that was scornful of any limitations of the law, this was just a taste of what was to follow.

No sooner did U.S. forces arrive in Afghanistan than they started to detain individuals suspected of having ties to al-Qaeda or the Taliban. As the war proceeded and more and more suspects were rounded up, questions arose: Where to keep these suspects? And how to treat them?

Where? Send them to a special prison set up in the U.S. Navy base at Cuba's Guantanamo Bay.

How to treat them? Following a presidential order signed on November 13, 2001, and a January 2002 directive from Defense Secretary Donald Rumsfeld, hold them indefinitely, file no charges against them, and deny them the right to see a lawyer or appear in court to challenge their detention. And, while we're at it, torture the hell out of them.

You have to give Bush, Cheney, and Rumsfeld a certain amount of credit. No weak-kneed liberal could have come up with so brazen, or illegal, a plan.

At its peak, Gitmo housed 775 prisoners from Afghanistan and Iraq. The idea that they should be accorded the protections of the

Geneva Conventions, ratified by the United States in 1949, was tossed aside by the White House counsel Alberto Gonzales. On January 25, 2002, Gonzales advised Bush that "the war on terrorism is a new kind of war, a new paradigm [that] renders obsolete Geneva's strict limitation on questioning of enemy prisoners and renders some of its provisions quaint."

For Gonzales, the way to get around the Geneva Conventions was simple. Don't call the captives "prisoners of war." Instead, designate them "enemy combatants" or "unlawful combatants." That way, all rules applying to the treatment of prisoners are off.

No sooner had the first prisoners arrived at Gitmo—bound in shackles, draped in black hoods, and housed in outdoor cages—than howls of protest were heard around the world about their inhumane treatment. Red Cross officials visited the camp and alleged acts of torture. Amnesty International denounced Gitmo as "the gulag of our times."

Yet the White House refused to budge. Dismissing the Amnesty International report as "absurd," President Bush called the Guantanamo prisoners "killers." John Ashcroft called them "uniquely dangerous." Donald Rumsfeld justified whatever treatment they received as appropriate for the "most dangerous, best-trained, vicious killers on the face of the earth." And Dick Cheney told CNN's Wolf Blitzer that Guantanamo proved what a great country we are:

> There isn't any other nation in the world that would treat people who were determined to kill Americans the way we're treating these people. They're living in the tropics. They're well fed. They've got everything they could possibly want.

The administration also defended its broad authority to deny prisoners at Guantanamo access either to a civil trial or a standard military trial according to the Uniform Code of Military Justice. Instead, by Executive Order, Bush set up a system of military commissions where terrorism suspects would be tried in secret courts, with none of the protections afforded by U.S. law: no right to challenge their detention, no right to know the specific charges against them, no right to see the evidence against them, no right to present witnesses in their defense, no right to cross-examine government witnesses, and no right to be in the courtroom for their entire trial.

Again, the White House defended its actions as keeping with the president's consitutional war-making powers and the AUMF approved by Congress.

The courts vehemently disagreed.

The first blow came on June 28, 2004, in *Hamdi v. Rumsfeld*, when the Supreme Court reversed the District Court and ruled that while the administration had the right to detain terrorism suspects indefinitely, prisoners also had the right to challenge their detention in court. Even non-U.S. citizens, ruled the court, could not be denied the right of habeas corpus.

That was followed by an even bigger blow on June 29, 2006, when the Supreme Court struck down both the military commissions created by the Bush administration and the broader assertion of presidential authority on which the administration based its actions. Bush had only two choices, said the court in its *Hamdan v. Rumsfeld* decision: either follow standard military justice, or get new authority from Congress. For good measure, the court also ruled that no matter what George Bush called the U.S. prisoners held at Guantanamo Bay, the provisions of the Geneva Conventions did indeed apply to them.

A chastened Bush promised that henceforth he would abide by the "quaint" Geneva prisoner protections. At his request, Congress also enacted the Miltary Commissions Act of 2006, establishing somewhat more acceptable rules for trying terrorist suspects. But legal questions and challenges remain. As of this writing, not one Guantanamo Bay inmate has been tried before a military commission.

Meanwhile, after being held at Gitmo for more than five years, 420 prisoners have been released and returned to their native countries. Another 150 are scheduled for release. That will leave about 200 in detention, of which charges have been filed against only 70. So much for Rumsfeld's characterization of those caught up in Guantanamo as "the worst of the worst."

Out of all the fuss over Guantanamo Bay, did the Bush administration learn anything about due process? Apparently not. On January 18, 2007, Attorney General Alberto Gonzales told the Senate Judiciary Committee there is no express right to habeas corpus contained in the U.S. Constitution.

Get Thee to a "Black Hole"

One reason the Bush administration wasn't too concerned about criticism of its treatment of prisoners at Guantanamo Bay: it deflected attention from even worse conditions they were saving for the really big fish.

As it turns out, the "worst of the worst" weren't confined at Gitmo after all. They were sent to one of a secret network of CIA-run prisons, located around the world in friendly countries that either condoned or were willing to ignore torture.

Existence of the Bush torture palaces was first reported by the *Washington Post* on November 2, 2005, after the then CIA director Porter Goss requested that CIA employees be exempt from legislation pending in Congress to ban, and slap stiff penalties on those guilty of, cruel and degrading forms of treatment of prisoners. Any enterprising reporter might well wonder, What is the CIA up to?

As the *Post* reported, the CIA was up to torture. On September 17, 2001—six days after September 11—President Bush signed a covert action order authorizing the CIA to kill, capture, or detain al-Qaeda suspects anywhere in the world. The agency immediately established secret prisons in eight countries, from Thailand to Afghanistan, which soon held the hundred highest-ranking al-Qaeda operatives captured.

There were actually two tiers of prisons. The first tier, which housed the thirty most "high-value" captives, were located in Eastern European democracies (a.k.a. the old Soviet bloc) and manned by the CIA. Among their numbers were Abu Zubaydah, a top al-Qaeda operative captured by Pakistani forces in March 2002, and Khalid Sheikh Mohammed, who claimed to have planned the entire September 11 operation. The second tier housed seventy captives considered less dangerous, who were rounded up under a process known as "rendition" and flown to Egypt, Jordan, and Morocco, to be worked over by those countries' own agents.

The CIA prisons might have been secret, but there was no secret about why they were located overseas. Holding suspects indefinitely and in secret is illegal in the United States, and so are the "enhanced interrogation techniques" such as "waterboarding" that prisoners were subjected to. Indeed, U.S. military officers had been court-martialed for waterboarding as recently as the Vietnam War.

By 2005, after a U.S. court confirmed that waterboarding was, indeed, an illegal form of torture, the CIA started to have second thoughts. Its agents had not only used waterboarding in at least two cases, but they had also videotaped the entirety of both operations. Once the existence of the tapes became known, members of Congress, Justice Department officials, and the then White House counsel Harriet Miers all advised the CIA not to destroy the tapes. But—in a move Richard Nixon would have been proud of—the CIA did so, anyway.

In spite of the controversial history of waterboarding, the establishment of the foreign-based prisons and the interrogation techniques used in them were personally approved by the president of the United States.

Ironically, torture is also illegal in those democratic countries of Eastern Europe that agreed to host the CIA's black holes—which is why several of them were shut down once their presence became public knowledge.

Existence of the CIA torture cells was first acknowledged by President Bush in September 2006, when he announced that he was emptying out the prisons and sending the remaining fourteen high-value suspects, including Khalid Sheikh Mohammed, to join other terrorist suspects at Guantanamo Bay. At the same time, Bush asserted his right to reactivate the prison network and reemploy "enhanced interrogation techniques" whenever he deemed it necessary.

What about legislation recently passed by Congress that expressly forbids the use of torture in U.S. prisons anywhere on the planet? No problem, said Bush. He just won't obey that part of the law.

When a Signature Is Not Really a Signature

If anybody knows anything about both the horror and the ineffectiveness of torture as an interrogation technique, it's John McCain. During six years in the Hanoi Hilton, McCain was brutally tortured by his Vietcong captors and ended up confessing to anything they demanded, just to get some physical relief.

It was not surprising, then, that—once word of those secret CIA torture chambers became public, on top of reports of abuse at Gitmo and Abu Ghraib—McCain led a campaign to make any form of torture by U.S. officials a crime. Torture is not only cruel and inhumane, argued McCain, it is useless in extracting believable intelligence. But, he said, there was an even more important reason for acting to ban torture. He deplored "what we lose when by official policy or by official negligence we allow, confuse or encourage our soldiers to forget . . . that which is our greatest strength: that we are different and better than our enemies."

The White House vociferously opposed the McCain amendment and threatened a veto. Vice President Cheney went to Capitol Hill and personally lobbied Republican senators against any limits on interrogation techniques. All to no avail. In the end, the vote was 90–9. Forty-six Republicans joined forty-three Democrats and one Independent in approving McCain's antitorture legislation.

And what did President Bush do? He signed it. Because when signing any legislation with which he did not completely agree, he had long ago figured out how to have his cake and eat it, too: it's called a "signing statement."

Technically, a signing statement is like a postscript: a presidential addendum to any law he signs asserting his power to ignore those portions of the law that conflict with *his interpretation* of a president's constitutional authority. In other words, it's a way for the president to sign a law while adding: "P.S. I have no intention of actually obeying this law!"

Although signing statements are legal and have been used by every president since James Monroe, Bush has made them routine. From Monroe through Bill Clinton, presidents have resorted to signing statements fewer than six hundred times. As of November 2007, Bush 43 alone has issued more than eight hundred signing statements on issues of major importance.

As documented by the *Boston Globe*, Bush's use of signing statements includes:

- On four occasions, Congress passed legislation forbidding U.S. troops from engaging in combat in Colombia. In signing each bill into law, Bush declared that he did not have to obey the restriction because he was the commander in chief.

- By act of Congress, the Energy Department cannot fire whistle-blowers who give information to Congress. In his signing statement, Bush said that he or his appointees would decide the fate of whistle-blowers.

- Congress orders the Justice Department to report on how the FBI is using the Patriot Act to search private homes and papers. Bush says that he will decide what the FBI tells Congress.

- Congress says that the military cannot add to its files any illegally gathered intelligence, in violation of the Fourth Amendment. Bush insists that only he as commander in chief can tell the military what to do with intelligence gathered.

But Bush's most flagrant use of the signing statement came at 8 p.m. on December 30, 2005, after an elaborate White House signing ceremony of McCain's antitorture legislation. After hurriedly dropping his opposition to the bill and welcoming Senator McCain to the Oval Office for a personal mea culpa, Bush signed the legislation with great fanfare. With his signature, it was now illegal for Americans to engage in the "cruel, inhuman, and degrading" treatment of detainees held here or abroad.

What those who attended the ceremony missed was a signing statement posted later that evening on the White House Web site, announcing that the president would follow the new law only "in a manner consistent with the constitutional authority of the president to supervise the unitary executive branch . . . and consistent with the constitutional limitations on the judicial power." In other words, Bush alone would determine when the provisions of this bill interfered with his war-making powers—and when they did so, he would freely ignore the law.

It is tempting to laugh off Bush's overdose of signing statements as the desperate attempts of a hapless president to be taken seriously. "Hey, look at me," Bush seems to be crying out. "I'm here, too." If only it were that simple.

The signing statements are much more significant than that and much more dangerous. They are George W. Bush's attempt to rewrite the Constitution. As adopted, the Constitution clearly assigns to Congress the power to write the laws and to the president the duty "to take care that the laws be faithfully executed." George Bush asserts the authority to decide which laws, or portions of laws, he will execute and which he will not. And, so far, he's been getting away with it.

In that context, Bush's signing statements are no aberration. They are an integral part of a five-year strategy on the part of George Bush and Dick Cheney to expand the powers of the presidency at the expense of Congress and the courts. That is their goal. That is their passion. That is their mission. And it explains so many things about the Bush presidency.

> Why does President Bush keep open the gulag at Guantanamo Bay prison?
>
> Why does he reserve the right to torture U.S. prisoners?
>
> Why does he assert the right to tap our phones, read our e-mail, and track what books we take out of the library?
>
> Why does he refuse to obey the FISA law?
>
> Why does he block access to presidential papers?
>
> Why does he insist on deciding which laws he will obey and which ones he will not?

Answer: Because he can. That's what's behind every move Bush and Cheney make. No matter what public excuse they offer or how many times they hide behind September 11, their goal is not to win the so-called war on terror. It's to push the limits of executive power and to expand the power of the presidency for its own sake. Unfortunately, the balance of power got lost in the process.

Bottom Line: Lessons Learned

It's important to remind ourselves that the conservatives' dedication to smaller government isn't just about paying less in taxes. It's mainly about an idea that started in the Constitution with the Third Amendment: limiting how much the government can tell us what to do.

And here again, we see a serious betrayal of that fundamental principle in which conservatives throw traditional conservatism out the window and go to the opposite extreme, screwing everything up in the process.

They did it on government spending. They did it on the size of government. They did it on foreign policy. They did it on states' rights. And they did it on presidential power.

Clearly, early conservatives were on to something. In the immortal words of Lord Acton: "Power corrupts, and absolute power corrupts absolutely." Give a man any power, and he lusts for more. The Founding Fathers were therefore correct to limit the authority of the chief executive in order to prevent any future leader from assuming dictatorial powers.

As the country grew bigger, however, and as the world grew smaller, circumstances changed. Even early in our history, it became apparent that there were times when immediate, decisive executive leadership was demanded—when, to defend the nation, a president might have to take actions not foreseen or specifically provided for by the framers of the Constitution.

But those extraconstitutional bursts of presidential activity were rare and were always accompanied by subsequent review and approval by Congress or the Supreme Court . . . until George W. Bush. In what can only be called an outlaw administration, he and Dick Cheney have pushed presidential power to the limits, defying Congress and the courts, trashing the Constitution, and thumbing their noses at the law. Theirs is an imperial presidency, and George W. Bush is a dictator in everything but title.

Once again, entrusted with power, conservatives have fallen short. Their basic philosophy has proved inadequate to the task. Their attempts to govern have ended in disaster.

CHAPTER 5

Avoiding Pointless Foreign Adventures

The great rule of conduct for us in regard to foreign nations is
in extending our commercial relations, to have with them as little
political connection as possible. . . . It is our true policy to steer clear
of permanent alliances with any portion of the foreign world.
President George Washington, 1796

Peace, commerce, and honest friendship with all nations—
entangling alliances with none.
President Thomas Jefferson, 1801

Wherever the standard of freedom and Independence has been or
shall be unfurled, there will her heart, her benedictions and her
prayers be. But she goes not abroad, in search of monsters to destroy.
She is the well-wisher to the freedom and independence of all.
She is the champion and vindicator only of her own.
President John Quincy Adams, 1821

I do not believe any policy which has behind it the threat of military
force is justified as part of the basic foreign policy of the United
States except to defend the liberty of our own people.
Senator Robert Taft, 1951

Our prospects in the world of the twenty-first century are bright—
supposing we Americans do not swagger about the globe,
proclaiming our omniscience and our omnipotence.
Russell Kirk, 1993

I think the United States must be humble. We must be proud
and confident of our values, but humble in how we treat nations
that are figuring out how to chart their own course.
Candidate George W. Bush, 2000

As one can see from the previous quotes, when George W. Bush campaigned for president, way back in 2000, on the promise of a noninterventionist foreign policy, he was following a path laid down by our Founding Fathers more than two hundred years ago and embraced by conservatives ever since.

Having won our freedom from an imperial power that planted its flag and imposed its will on peoples around the globe, the last thing our Founding Fathers intended was to create another monster. They believed instead that other nations, suitably impressed by the example of our "city on a hill," would adopt our democratic values on their own, rather than have American ways forced on them at gunpoint.

For the fledging United States, the Founders charted a different approach. Other nations had friends and enemies, as dictated by their own "entangling alliances," but we would be friends with all. Other nations fought to force their values and customs on neighboring countries, but we would respect the right of countries to chart their own course. Other nations sought war, but we would work to preserve the peace.

Indeed, that was one of the reasons why, from the beginning, conservatives fought to maintain a smaller, weaker federal government: not only to allow states more freedom, but to prevent troublesome foreign excursions. The division of powers among the three branches of government was established in order to make federal initiatives more difficult to undertake. And constitutional limits on the executive were designed specifically to tie the hands of a trigger-happy war president.

As James Madison noted in a letter to Thomas Jefferson:

The Constitution supposes what the history of all Governments demonstrates, that the executive is the branch of power most interested in war and most prone to it. It has accordingly with studied care vested the question of war in the Legislature.

Going to war without a declaration of war by Congress—or continuing to prosecute a war without the support of Congress—requires an imperial presidency. Which, of course, is just what we have today, as detailed in chapter 4.

As we saw, there were occasional glaring exceptions to the rule, especially during the Cold War. But, for the most part, traditional wisdom held true. Conservatives were less likely to intervene in foreign affairs; liberals, more likely. Conservatives were less likely to use force; liberals, more likely.

Although George W. Bush turned that tradition upside down, non-intervention in the affairs of other nations remained the dominant theme of an authentic conservative foreign policy for most of our history.

Conservatives and Foreign Policy

Throughout 2002 and early 2003, the Bush administration put forth many arguments to justify war with Iraq, and most of them later proved to be falsehoods. But for the leading conservative scholar Michael Ledeen, a former consultant to the Pentagon and the State Department, the case for invading Iraq was much simpler:

> Every ten years or so, the United States needs to pick up some small crappy little country and throw it against the wall, just to show we mean business.

No statement better illustrates how far today's so-called neocons have strayed from classic conservative thinking on foreign policy. Although, in truth, it's more like every few years we feel the need to strike a hornet's nest with a stick, just to show that we can survive a hundred little stings.

According to Russell Kirk, the defining conservative virtue is prudence. (And you thought it was bloodlust for terrorists!)

In foreign policy, prudence means maintaining a strong defense, yet acting only when the national interest of the United States is clearly and directly threatened—and otherwise letting nations conduct their own affairs and determine their own courses of action. With the exception of the Spanish-American War, where the United States seized Guam, Cuba, and the Philippines in a misguided and short-lived attempt to catch up with the European colonial powers system, that's the way things used to be. In fact, by their imperial tendencies in the Spanish-American War and beyond, President McKinley and his successor, Teddy Roosevelt, were accused of betraying the time-honored ultimatum laid down to other nations by President James Monroe in 1823: You stay out of our affairs, and we'll stay out of yours.

With few exceptions, that determination not to interfere in European wars remained the foundation of U.S. policy until the start of the Cold War. Even as the storm clouds of World Wars 1 and II gathered over the free world, for example, U.S. conservatives were reluctant to abandon the "stay out of foreign wars" tradition laid down by the Founding Fathers. They opposed FDR's lend-lease program and his deal to sell used U.S. destroyers to Britain. And, at the time, the isolationists enjoyed the support of a significant number of Americans.

Thirty years earlier, the story had been much the same. As late as 1916, two years after "The Great War" had begun to devastate Europe, Woodrow Wilson successfully won the presidency on the slogan "He Kept Us Out of War." Of course, Wilson eventually reneged on that promise and instead famously called for the United States "to make the world safe for democracy." But he did so—and the U.S. public supported him—only after Germany had attacked and sunk our own vessels in the Atlantic, and word had leaked of the infamous Zimmerman telegram, a German proposal for Mexico to attack the United States.

Franklin Roosevelt faced the same challenge leading up to World War II. For years, he, too, was unsuccessful in convincing Americans to assist our allies. As a result, we ignored the pleas of France and England for troops on the ground until Japan attacked our own fleet at Pearl Harbor.

Ever since, conservative critics of the United States' involvement in the great wars have been too easily dismissed as "isolationists" or "obstructionists," but they were speaking from principle, not from weakness or fear. Following Senator Robert Taft's equation that the primary goal of foreign policy was "to protect the liberty of the American people," they believed that the use of force should be limited to those cases where our nation was directly attacked. They recognized the danger of a president assuming near-dictatorial powers during wartime. And they questioned the assertion, even then, that our mission was to prance around the globe like Johnny Appleseed, planting little trees of democracy.

Every time I visit the magnificent Franklin Roosevelt Memorial along the Tidal Basin in Washington, D.C., I am moved by the last words etched on its granite walls, those goals for the world set by FDR in his 1941 State of the Union address: "Freedom of Speech. Freedom of Worship. Freedom from Want. Freedom from Fear." Yet, conservatives asked, as important as those freedoms are to Americans, is it really our charter to make them universally recognized? And could we justify war by an understandable desire to share freedom with others? Ten years later, in his book *A Foreign Policy for Americans*, the conservative leader Robert Taft explained his lack of enthusiasm for Roosevelt's challenge: "I pointed out then that the forcing of any special brand of freedom and democracy on a people, whether they want it or not, by the brute force of war, will be a denial of those very democratic principles which we are striving to advance."

And remember, that was the *conservative* objection.

Don't think that Taft was a pacifist. Once the United States became engaged in World War II, Taft, like Americans everywhere, supported the war. Yet his conservative misgivings about foreign engagements remained, and he never abandoned what he saw as his duty to question Roosevelt's conduct of the war. On December 19, 1941—just twelve days after Pearl Harbor and eleven days after the United States declared war on Japan, Taft gave a defiant speech to the Executive Club of Chicago in which he promised to continue to speak out:

> As a matter of general principle, I believe there can be no doubt that criticism in time of war is essential to the maintenance of any kind of democratic government. . . . Too many people desire to suppress criticism simply because they think that it will give some comfort to the enemy to know that there is such criticism. If that comfort makes the enemy feel better for a few moments, they are welcome to it as far as I am concerned, because the maintenance of the right of criticism in the long run will do the country maintaining it a great deal more good than it will do the enemy, and will prevent mistakes which might otherwise occur.

How timely those words appear, more than sixty years later. How important that lesson, now more than ever.

In affirming the right of, and the need for, Americans to criticize the government, even and especially during wartime, Taft was absolutely right. By the time the war ended, however, a major sea change had occurred in U.S. foreign policy. Germany and Japan weren't the only ones to lose World War II. So did Taft and other noninterventionist conservatives.

Conservatives and the Cold War

After World War II, the United States did not crawl back into its shell. In many ways, we could not.

We wanted to help even our enemies rebuild, hence the Marshall Plan. We wanted to protect our European allies from future threats, hence NATO. We wanted to prevent World War III from breaking out anywhere on the globe, hence the United Nations. And we wanted to prevent the spread of communism, hence the policy of containment.

U.S. military force was now planted in every corner of the globe, and we would never disengage. What President Eisenhower later called the "military industrial complex" was already firmly in place. And under what became known as the "lessons of Munich," any antiwar sentiments or questioning of our military priorities were easily branded as appeasement of the enemy.

The United States was now a, if not *the*, global power, up against the unexpected and menacing new totalitarian ideology of the Soviet Union. In the face of this threat to world security, we had an almost-universally accepted obligation to be anywhere and everywhere engaged, standing up against the threat of totalitarianism. What was a true-blue conservative to do?

With the beginning of the Cold War, conservatives were pressured to join liberals in fighting the scourge of "godless communism," which they did, willingly. So much so, in fact, that anticommunism became the new glue of the conservative movement. It kept all the disparate factions of the Republican Party together and explains the deep support for the hateful tactics of Senator Joseph McCarthy.

Still, for a while, some conservatives tried to stem the tide. Ever the prophet of doom, Robert Taft warned that the NATO pact obligated the United States to go to war anytime that any country made an armed attack against any one of twelve nations: "Such an alliance is more likely to produce war than peace." And conservatives expressed concern over the eventual loss of U.S. sovereignty under the United Nations, which is a persistent worry of conservatives even today.

But those voices for a less-expansive foreign policy were getting weaker and weaker. And in 1952, when the war hero Dwight D. Eisenhower defeated Robert Taft for the Republican nomination for president, they were forever marginalized. The debate between conservatives and liberals was no longer over whether or not to engage the enemy, but over who would get there first with the most firepower.

Indeed, for fifty years, the unifying factor of foreign policy in the United States was opposition to communism. Nobody doubted the threat. Nobody doubted the need to respond. Few dared dissent.

If communism was the threat, containment was the answer. The policy was first suggested in 1946 by George F. Kennan, the then deputy head of the U.S. mission in Moscow, in a "long telegram" to Secretary of State James Byrnes. While confirming the expansionist goals of the Soviets under Stalin, Kennan suggested that in response, the United States adopt a policy of preventing the spread of communism to noncommunist nations by "containing" it within the Soviet Union's borders.

One year later, Kennan's proposal became official U.S. policy. Britain had informed the United States that it could no longer afford to provide economic aid or maintain troops in Greece and Turkey. Either the United States would step into the breach, or both nations, considered "ripe plums for Soviet picking," would be the next to fall under the hammer and sickle.

President Truman rose to the occasion. In an eighteen-minute speech to a Joint Session of Congress, he announced a bold new foreign policy, committing the United States to "support free peoples who are resisting attempted subjugation by armed minorities or by outside pressures."

Once again, Senator Taft led token opposition, but fear of communism trumped the voices of conservatism. Aid to Greece and Turkey, the first application of the new expansionist foreign policy, was approved by the Senate, 67–23. The House vote was even more one-sided, 287–107.

And thus was born the Truman Doctrine. It led to U.S. support for regimes around the world, not all of them the finest company to keep. But the doctrine remained in effect until the end of the Cold War, embraced by every president who followed Truman, both Democrat and Republican.

Truman, in fact, took the policy of containment far beyond where Kennan originally intended it, from a passive to an active and aggressive approach to future threats. In 1950, he signed a National Security Council directive, NSC-68, which stated, "Our position as the center of power in the free world places a heavy responsibility upon the United States for leadership. We must organize and enlist the energies and resources of the free world in a positive program for peace which will frustrate the Kremlin design for world domination." So now, instead of merely containing communism, we would attempt to roll back communism anywhere in the world—including, ultimately, in the jungles of Vietnam.

On foreign policy, there was at this point little difference between Democrats and Republicans, liberals and conservatives. The Democrat Woodrow Wilson took us into World War I; the Democrat Franklin Delano Roosevelt took us into World War II. The Democrat Harry Truman launched the Truman Doctrine, under which he engaged the United States in the Korean War. Using the same rationale, the Democrat John F. Kennedy followed Dwight D. Eisenhower in sending advisers, and later troops, to Vietnam—triggering a war that was continued and expanded by the Democrat Lyndon Johnson and the Republican Richard Nixon.

Democrats, in fact, had led the United States into so many foreign wars that Senator Bob Dole, running as Gerald Ford's vice-presidential nominee in 1976, accused them of being the war party. When asked about Ford's 1974 pardon of Richard Nixon, Dole famously replied,

> Well, it is an appropriate topic, I guess, but it's not a very good issue any more than the war in Vietnam would be or World War II, or World War I, or the war in Korea, all Democrat wars, all in this century. I figured up the other day, if we added up the killed and wounded in Democrat wars in this century, it'd be about 1.6 million Americans—enough to fill the city of Detroit.

And what were Republicans doing in the meantime? Supporting the Democrats! What little criticism there was of the United States' increasing use of military force around the world came no longer from conservatives but from liberals. In fact, conservatives took advantage of setbacks in the Cold War—such as the first Soviet A-bomb and "the loss of China" in 1949—and, later, growing opposition to the Vietnam War among Democrats, to turn the Republican Party into the war party. In so doing, conservatives turned traditional conservatism on its head. They no longer urged restraint; they fanned the flames. They no longer resisted the war hawks; they tried to out-hawk the hawks.

In his acceptance speech at the 1964 Republican Convention, Barry Goldwater accused Democrats of being soft on communism, and he made an ominous promise: "I want to make this abundantly clear—I don't intend to let peace or freedom be torn from our grasp because of lack of strength or lack of will—and that I promise you Americans. I believe that we must look beyond the defense of freedom today to its extension tomorrow."

Later that same year, in a nationally televised speech on Goldwater's behalf, the actor Ronald Reagan underscored the same willingness—almost eagerness—to take up arms:

> Admittedly, there's a risk in any course we follow . . . , but every lesson of history tells us that the greater risk lies in appeasement, and this is the specter our well-meaning liberal friends refuse to face—that their policy of accommodation is appeasement, and it gives no choice between peace and war, only between fight or surrender. If we continue to accommodate, continue to back and retreat, eventually we have to face the final demand—the ultimatum.

Now, before moving on to the situation today, it's important to recognize two key points about U.S. foreign policy during the Cold War.

First, the Truman Doctrine worked.

Yes, containment worked. Even when the United States faced a far, far greater danger than it does today, with thousands of nuclear missiles pointed at and capable of reaching and destroying U.S. cities, the Soviet Union dared not launch one of their missiles for fear of certain, massive retaliation.

Ironically, containment also worked against Saddam Hussein. In fact, the argument for containing Hussein was made most forcefully by the then secretary of defense Dick Cheney in August 1990, as President George H. W. Bush assembled coalition forces to drive Iraqi troops from Kuwait: "It should be clear to Saddam Hussein that we have a wide range of military capabilities that will let us respond with overwhelming force and extract a very high price should he be foolish enough to use chemical weapons on United States forces." Later, called to defend Bush's decision not to pursue Iraqi forces all the way to Baghdad, Cheney commented, "The question in my mind is how many additional American casualties is Saddam worth? And the answer is not very damned many."

Eleven years later, Cheney still cited containment as the most effective way to deal with Hussein. While Americans were in a state of shock over terrorist attacks on the twin towers and the Pentagon, and before George W. Bush had decided to invade Iraq, the now vice president Cheney dismissed any need to worry about the Iraqi dictator. "Saddam Hussein's bottled up," Vice President Dick Cheney assured the nation on *Meet the Press—five days after September 11.*

Second, there were no preemptive strikes.

Again, for more than fifty years, the United States was literally under the gun, with enough nuclear warheads to destroy any U.S. city, locked and loaded, ready to head our way at a moment's notice. At the same time, Soviet troops were massed on the borders of several European countries and communist guerrillas directly threatened our allies in Southeast Asia.

Yet during that time, no U.S. president—not Harry Truman, not Ronald Reagan—asserted the right of the United States to launch a preemptive strike or a preventive war against a nation that had not first attacked the United States. That dismal policy was a post–Cold War, George W. Bush invention.

Indeed, for all his tough talk, Reagan demonstrated one other show of restraint. After 241 marines were killed in Lebanon in 1983, he retaliated but resisted the temptation to subdue and occupy the country. Instead, realizing that he had placed marines in the middle of a civil war in a country of no vital interest to the United States, he admitted his mistake and pulled the marines out.

Only in today's world could we think of Ronald Reagan as a beacon of military restraint.

The Birth of the Neocons

The Cold War did make one other significant impact on U.S. foreign policy: it gave birth to a band of hardliners, known as "neoconservatives," who later played a major role in shaping George W. Bush's worldview and became the principal architects of his war in Iraq.

So where did neoconservatives come from? They are liberal refugees from the Cold War. The leading neocons, in fact—Irving Kristol, Jeane Kirkpatrick, Bill Bennett, Michael Novak, Paul Wolfowitz, Richard Perle, and others—all started out as Democrats. Cold War Democrats. They were followers of Woodrow Wilson, Franklin Roosevelt, Harry Truman, and Senator Henry "Scoop" Jackson. Hardliners on foreign policy. Fierce anticommunists. Strong supporters of Israel.

When George McGovern was nominated for president in 1972 under the slogan "Come Home, America," the nascent neocons felt abandoned by the Democratic Party. So they gravitated to the Republican Party with the stated goal of making it like the Democratic Party they once knew and loved. Wrote Irving Kristol, known as the "godfather" of the neoconservative movement,

> [T]he historical task and political purpose of neoconservatism would seem to be . . . to convert the Republican Party and American conservatism in general, against their respective wills, into a new kind of conservative politics suitable to governing a modern democracy.

And so, within the Republican Party, a new force was born, guided by former Democrats, to lead the fight against the Evil Empire. But then the unexpected happened: the Evil Empire collapsed. The threat of galloping communism suddenly disappeared. And neoconservatives were left without an enemy to destroy . . . but only temporarily.

With the fall of the Soviet Union, the enemy that animated the new militant conservatism disappeared. Without the specter of communism, what was the justification for a huge military and an aggressive foreign policy? The American right needed a new monster to destroy.

Searching for a New Enemy

It is impossible to exaggerate the impact of the collapse of the Soviet Union on U.S. foreign policy and on the conservative movement. As Gertrude Stein might say, suddenly there was "no there there."

It's like the EPA waking up and discovering there's no longer any air pollution or water pollution to clean up. What is it supposed to do now?

Neither George H. W. Bush nor Bill Clinton, the first post–Cold War presidents, figured out how to organize our foreign priorities. On occasion, both used military force. Bush "liberated" Panama, pushed Saddam Hussein out of Kuwait, and sent marines into Somalia. Clinton retaliated against Iraq for attempting to assassinate Bush 41, bombed Milosevic forces in Bosnia and Kosovo, sent marines to Haiti, and launched Cruise missiles at suspected al-Qaeda targets in Sudan and Afghanistan.

But without a unifying theme or enemy, it seemed that U.S. foreign policy was adrift. There was no new central purpose, no new yardstick by which to measure when and where the United States should intervene in the "New World Order," no new rules for when the use of force was justified and when it was not.

Nobody felt this lack of purpose more strongly than our friends the neoconservatives, who had migrated to the Republican Party in order to destroy dragons but now found no dragons to destroy. This presented a real problem. What's the point of being a champion of freedom and justice if you don't know whom to kill for it?

Answer: If you are given no dragon, invent one. Take a legitimate but smaller danger and magnify it into a monolithic global scare. Noted Irving Kristol in 1996,

> With the end of the Cold War, what we really need is an obvious ideological and threatening enemy, one worthy of our mettle, one that can unite us in opposition.

For some time neocons had to settle for a deep-seated hatred of Bill Clinton, specifically, and Democrats, more generally—but only until 9/11 provided the answer they were looking for. In response, George W. Bush declared a perpetual state of war. And now the shoe was on the other foot. This time, liberals—all of whom signed on for the war in Afghanistan—were pressured to stay on board and join conservatives in support of Bush's never-ending "war on terror." Sometimes, history does repeat itself.

Taming the Taliban

The first response to 9/11 was a straight shot: they attacked us, and we retaliated.

The nineteen hijackers had been trained, funded, and organized by the al-Qaeda terrorist organization, led by Osama bin Laden, from training camps in Afghanistan. The U.S. government asked Mullah Mohammed Omar, the leader of the Taliban, to capture and turn over al-Qaeda's leadership. He refused. So we invaded Afghanistan, overthrew the Taliban, and installed Hamid Karzai as the country's new president.

The war in Afghanistan began with bombing strikes by U.S. and British forces on October 7, 2001. For all practical purposes, that first phase of the war ended with the fall of Kabul on November 12. And there was little, if any, opposition—at home or in the global community.

In fact, the UN Security Council was never asked to approve the invasion of Afghanistan because it was considered a legitimate act of self-defense under Article 51 of the UN Charter. Within days of September 11, Pakistan was the only country that still recognized the Taliban. U.S. and British forces were joined by troops from Australia, Canada, Denmark, France, Germany, Italy, the Netherlands, New Zealand, and Norway, among others. The war in Afghanistan was supported by 88 percent of the American people.

But then the straight line took a bad curve: from Afghanistan to Iraq. By the spring of 2002, coalition forces, still pursuing Osama bin Laden and his al-Qaeda in their mountain hideouts on the Afghan-Pakistan border, were suddenly called off the hunt—because George W. Bush had a new target in mind and a new policy in hand.

In short, we took our eye off the ball, with tragic results.

It's clear now that the decision to abandon Afghanistan and invade Iraq was a mistake of devastating consequences. While the United

States has been bogged down in Iraq, the Taliban have reemerged as a powerful force, dominating most of the country outside of the capital of Kabul—where Hamid Karzai remains in power only because of the presence and protection of U.S. troops. Opium production, formerly banned by the Taliban, is once again the country's number-one cash crop—Afghanistan provides 90 percent of the world's opium—and opium profits are now used by the Taliban to fund its military operations. Most disturbingly, according to the Bush administration's own National Intelligence Estimate, al-Qaeda has also taken advantage of U.S. involvement in Iraq to rebuild, rearm, and make new plans for terrorist attacks against the United States. In July 2007, the Bush White House announced that al-Qaeda, still led by Osama bin Laden, was as strong as it had been before September 11.

No one has ever been as good at losing a war they'd already won as the current Republican leadership.

But, of course, as we now know, invading Iraq was not just a sudden change of direction on Bush's part. It's where the neoconservatives wanted him to go in the first place.

Targeting Saddam Hussein

In his book *The Price of Loyalty*, Paul O'Neill relates the shock he experienced at his first meeting of the National Security Council in January 2001, ten days after Bush's inauguration, where "Topic A" was getting rid of the Iraqi leader. "From the very beginning there was a conviction that Saddam Hussein was a bad person and that he needed to go." Important questions like why, how, and why now were never asked, said O'Neill, describing Bush's role in meetings as "like a blind man in a roomful of deaf people."

Two days later, the National Security Council met again. Among other items, members were handed a memo titled "Plans for post-Saddam Iraq."

Again, this was January 2001—eight months before 9/11! But neocon designs on Iraq go back much earlier than that.

In 1996, the conservatives Richard Perle, Douglas Feith, and David Wurmser wrote a policy paper for Benjamin Netanyahu, Israel's new prime minister. It urged "Bibi" to reject the Oslo peace accords negotiated by Yitzhak Rabin and adopt a new, aggressive foreign policy based on "the principle of preemption." It would start by toppling Saddam Hussein.

> Israel can shape its strategic environment, in cooperation with Turkey and Jordan, by weakening, containing, and even rolling back Syria. This effort can focus on removing Saddam Hussein from power in Iraq—an important Israeli strategic objective in its own right.

My favorite part of that paper is the idea of "shaping the strategic environment." In other words, since you might someday have a war anyway, you should start out now by triggering the kind of wars that will produce the right environment to win the wars that lie in the future. Figure that out and you're a modern-day Nietzsche. Or a current-day Perle.

Two years later, having failed to convince Netanyahu to attack Iraq, Perle and fellow neoconservatives, under the banner of the Project for the New American Century (PNAC), turned to President Bill Clinton. On January 26, 1998, they wrote Clinton a letter urging him to use his State of the Union address to declare the overthrow of Saddam Hussein as the new "aim of American foreign policy" and to begin military operations, since "diplomacy is failing." Were Clinton to so act, they promised their full public support. Joining Perle as signatories were Bill Bennett, Paul Wolfowitz, Robert Kagan, William Kristol, Elliott Abrams, Richard Armitage, and Donald Rumsfeld: a gang of neocons one wag dubbed "The Monkees," after the legendary 1960s pop-rock band.

What else do they all have in common, other than being dead wrong?

Within three years, most of those Iraq hawks would be members of the new Bush administration. But even before they took office, the fellow neocon David Wurmser, then still a resident fellow at the American Enterprise Institute, resurfaced, urging the United States and Israel to undertake a whole series of preemptive strikes:

> Israel and the United States should . . . broaden the conflict to strike fatally, not merely disarm, the centers of radicalism in the region—the regimes of Damascus, Baghdad, Tripoli, Teheran,

and Gaza. That would establish the recognition that fighting either the United States or Israel is suicidal.

We shouldn't rush into this, Wurmser cautioned. But we should be ready and waiting for the first opportunity. In a chilling premonition of things to come, he added, "Crises can be opportunities." Wurmser published his paper on January 1, 2001—*eight months before September 11.*

The sweeping war aims of neoconservatives are so divorced from reality they are staggering. They also represent the total repudiation of authentic conservative foreign policy as set forth by Robert Taft, Russell Kirk, and, lately, by Pat Buchanan and Robert Novak. Not without reason did Kirk describe neocons as "often clever, never wise."

How did neoconservatives succeed in reversing two hundred years of a noninterventionist conservative foreign policy? Easy. They met a total know-nothing in foreign policy named George W. Bush. Richard Perle described his first encounter with the then Republican candidate for president:

> The first time I met Bush 43, I knew he was different. Two things became clear. One, he didn't know very much. The other was he had confidence to ask questions that revealed he didn't know very much. Most people are reluctant to say when they don't know something, a word or a term they haven't heard before. Not him.

That's our George in a nutshell.

Neoconservatives filled this blank slate with plans for preemption, starting with Iraq. And Bush rewarded them by handing out top posts in his administration: Donald Rumsfeld became the defense secretary; Paul Wolfowitz, his deputy; Douglas Feith, the under secretary of defense for policy; and Richard Perle, the chairman of the Defense Policy Board Advisory Committee. Richard Armitage was named the deputy secretary of state, while David Wurmser bounced from the State Department to the Department of Defense to the White House. Elliott Abrams moved into the number-one position at the National Security Council. Bill Kristol—the chief organizer of the neocons—remained outside the administration, fanning the flames of war from the editorial pages of Rupert Murdoch's *Weekly Standard*.

So, all but one of the pieces for war in Iraq were in place. Neocons were in positions of power and influence. Bush was primed to carry out their designs. Plans for regime change in Iraq were already circulating in the Bush White House. The only thing missing was a pretext for invasion, which Osama bin Laden would soon provide.

Within hours of September 11, Paul Wolfowitz was advising President Bush to forget about Afghanistan and invade Iraq instead.

The very next morning, the White House counterterrorism chief Richard Clarke was stunned to return to work and find al-Qaeda already off the agenda. In his book *Against All Enemies*, Clarke related,

> I expected to go back to a round of meetings examining what the next attacks could be. . . . Instead I walked into a series of discussions about Iraq. At first I was incredulous that we were talking about something other than getting Al Qaeda. Then I realized with almost a sharp physical pain that Rumsfeld and Wolfowitz were going to take advantage of this national tragedy to promote their agenda about Iraq. Since the beginning of the administration, indeed well before, they had been pressing for a war with Iraq.

What was the rationale for invading Iraq after we had been attacked by terrorists operating from inside Afghanistan? For Rumsfeld, according to Clarke, it was very simple:

> Rumsfeld complained that there were no decent targets for bombing in Afghanistan and we should consider bombing Iraq, which he said had better targets.

As crazy as the preoccupation with Iraq seemed to Clarke, who had been trying without success for more than eight months to get President Bush and National Security Adviser Condoleezza Rice to take the threat of al-Qaeda seriously, he soon discovered that Rumsfeld and Wolfowitz were not alone. That same evening, September 12, the president himself pulled Clarke aside and told him to investigate any links between Iraq and 9/11. When Clarke protested that there was no known connection between Saddam Hussein and al-Qaeda, Bush insisted, "See if Saddam did this. See if he's linked in any way." Rumsfeld and Wolfowitz had successfully poured the poison into Bush's ear.

The next step was a September 15 meeting of the Bush Cabinet at Camp David to settle on a plan for how to respond to the attacks of September 11. According to Bob Woodward in *Bush at War*, Wolfowitz again stressed the advantages of invading Iraq over Afghanistan. Woodward summed up his argument: "Afghanistan would be uncertain. . . . In contrast, Iraq was a brittle, oppressive regime that might break easily."

And on September 20, before Bush had even announced his plans for retaliation, neoconservatives outside the administration sent him an ultimatum. In an open letter to the White House, the conservative luminaries Bill Bennett, Norman Podhoretz, Jeane Kirkpatrick, Richard Perle, William Kristol, and Charles Krauthammer told Bush that in response to September 11, he must target Hezbollah for destruction, retaliate against Syria and Iran if they refused to sever ties with Hezbollah, and overthrow Saddam Hussein. Failure to attack Iraq, they warned, would amount to "an early and perhaps decisive surrender in the war on international terrorism."

There you have it. Nine days after 9/11, Bush was called a wimp if he didn't invade Iraq. Where's Robert Taft when you need him?

In the end, Bush decided against the neoconservatives' hoped-for invasion of Iraq, but only temporarily. He didn't reject it; he only shelved it. Either directly or indirectly, he told Rumsfeld, Wolfowitz and others, Let's take care of Afghanistan first. Then we'll do Iraq.

Even before U.S. and British forces dropped the first bombs on Afghanistan, in other words, the decision to invade Iraq had already been made—and put, temporarily, on ice.

Meanwhile, Bush had to come up with some rationale for toppling Saddam Hussein. And what better place to unveil it than West Point.

The Bush Doctrine

In his first State of the Union address after 9/11, on January 29, 2002, while U.S. forces were still at war in Afghanistan, President Bush made it clear that he didn't intend to stop there. He branded three nations that had nothing to with 9/11—Iraq, Iran, and North Korea—as the "Axis of Evil." And he issued a warning to all three:

> We'll be deliberate, yet time is not on our side. I will not wait on events, while dangers gather. I will not stand by, as peril draws closer and closer. The United States of America will not permit the world's most dangerous regimes to threaten us with the world's most destructive weapons.

Bush's harsh words sent chills through the United States' foreign policy establishment—and through what few traditional, noninterventionist conservatives, now dubbed "paleo-conservatives," were left. Whoa! What was going on? Was Bush actually talking about a first strike against Iraq, Iran, and North Korea?

Yes, he was. In a commencement address to West Point graduates on June 2, 2002, President Bush put forth a completely new foreign policy for the United States. Merely defending the peace is out; extending the peace is in. Containment is out; preemptive war is in. Merely protecting the United States from terrorism is out; eliminating terrorism anywhere on the planet and forever is in.

No longer content with defending U.S. interests when threatened, the United States now asserts the right to launch a first strike anytime, anywhere, and overthrow any government we believe may sometime pose a threat to the United States, to one of our allies, or to the cause of freedom. In the words of George W. Bush at West Point:

> Containment is not possible when unbalanced dictators with weapons of mass destruction can deliver those weapons on missiles or secretly provide them to terrorist allies. . . . If we wait for threats to materialize, we will have waited too long.
>
> The war on terror will not be won on the defensive. We must take the battle to the enemy, disrupt his plans, and confront the worst threats before they emerge. In this world we have entered, the only path to safety is the path of action. And this nation will act.

What happens if we invade another country to confront a serious threat, only to discover that the facts were wrong, there were no

weapons of mass destruction, and there was no serious threat after all?
Well, then we justify the invasion as spreading the advance of freedom.
From the same commencement address:

> We will defend the peace against threats from terrorists and
> tyrants. We will preserve the peace by building good relations
> among the great powers. And we will extend the peace by
> encouraging free and open societies on every continent.

And there's nothing any other nation can do about it. As the only
superpower, Bush promised the cadets at West Point, we will act to
prevent even our friends from acquiring enough military strength to
compete.

> Competition between great nations is inevitable, but armed
> conflict in our world is not. . . . America has, and intends to
> keep, military strengths beyond challenge—thereby making
> the destabilizing arms races of other eras pointless, and limit-
> ing rivalries to trade and other pursuits of peace.

Wow! Officially, "The Bush Doctrine" now replaces "The Truman
Doctrine." It is breathtaking in its scope, especially coming from a so-
called conservative. It asserts U.S. supremacy in every corner of the
globe. It's what Pat Buchanan calls "Pax Americana." It's everything
that Woodrow Wilson used to preach—and everything that conservatives used to fear.

Instead of keeping the United States out of pointless foreign adventures, Bush has declared that jumping into them with both feet is now
our top priority.

Nothing is more critical of the Wilsonian, now Bushian, vision of
planting democracy around the globe than the words of the conservative icon Russell Kirk. "We suffer from the notion that Democracy must
be instituted throughout all the world, at whatever cost," Kirk wrote in
The Politics of Prudence. He continued, "To expect that all the world
should, and must, adopt the peculiar political institutions of the United
States—which often do not work very well even at home—is to indulge
the most unrealistic of visions." Such naive thinking, Kirk pointed out,

led us into war in Vietnam. And we're repeating the same mistake today in Iraq and Afghanistan.

As if anticipating George W. Bush and his arrogant foreign policy, Kirk warned in 1993, "Our prospects in the world of the twenty-first century are bright—supposing we Americans do not swagger about the globe, proclaiming our omniscience and our omnipotence." Had he read Bush's speech nine years before it was delivered?

Yet now, ironically, a conservative Republican president had decreed as official foreign policy the very activist, interventionist, preemptive, global, exporting-democracy agenda once advocated by the Democrat Woodrow Wilson—which Republicans had spent decades opposing. In the name of fighting Islamic fundamentalism, the repudiation of the conservative agenda was now complete and the United States was now in a state of perpetual war. As Pat Buchanan lamented, under George W. Bush, the Republican Party "has embraced a neo-imperial foreign policy that would have been seen by the Founding Fathers as a breach of faith."

Most Democrats were critical of the new Bush Doctrine, but more for political, not philosophical, reasons. What surprised me was how few conservative voices were heard in opposition to the new plan for global U.S. hegemony. Among conservative columnists, only Pat Buchanan and Bob Novak questioned Bush's overreach, for which they were branded anti-Israel, if not anti-American. But let me tell you a little secret about Buchanan and Novak, as someone who knows them well. Sometimes they get it right.

Other politicians and pundits simply put short-term political expediency over long-term conservative convictions, swallowing Bush's lame excuse that "September 11 changed everything." Nowhere was the political sell-out more apparent than in the early debates among Republican candidates for president in the spring and summer of 2007. Of the ten presidential hopefuls onstage, only Congressman Ron Paul dared to suggest that Bush was leading the nation and conservatives in the wrong direction. Here's Ron Paul on MSNBC, May 3, 2007:

> I'm suggesting very strongly that we should have a foreign policy of non-intervention, the traditional American foreign policy, and a Republican foreign policy. Throughout the 20th Century, the Republican Party benefited from a non-interventionist

foreign policy. Think of how Eisenhower came in to stop the Korean War, think of how Nixon was elected to stop the mess in Vietnam. How did we win the election in the year 2000? We talked about a humble foreign policy, no nation-building, don't police the world. That's conservative, it's Republican, it's pro-American, it follows the Founding Fathers and, besides, it follows the Constitution.

When Paul suggested, in a subsequent debate, that we might consider the United States' actions around the globe to help us understand why some people hate us, some Republican leaders suggested that he be banned from all future debates.

Yet Ron Paul was right, and not just for political reasons. There are glaring, substantive problems with the combined policy of first strike and global democratization. First, if it's a valid policy for the United States, then it's valid for every other nation. By asserting that doctrine—in light of a perceived, not necessarily a real, threat—North Korea could invade South Korea, India could invade Pakistan, Israel could invade Iran. And off we go. Second, there's also the question of the slippery slope. Twenty-two out of twenty-two Arab nations have no democratic form of government. Do we therefore have the right to invade them all? Third, democracy is messy by nature. Give people the right to vote, and sometimes the wrong people, for our purposes, will get elected. We learned that yesterday in Algeria; we're learning it again today in Iraq.

The biggest problem, of course, is that we're ignoring the lessons of history, all of which argue against the success of invading and occupying powers. Experience should teach us that in dealing with other nations, intervention is not the solution. Intervention is the problem.

"Those who cannot remember the past are condemned to repeat it," said the philosopher George Santayana. In *Where the Right Went Wrong*, Pat Buchanan put it this way:

With our MacArthur Regency in Baghdad, Pax Americana will reach apogee. But then the tide recedes, for the one endeavor at which Islamic peoples excel is expelling imperial powers by terror and guerrilla war. They drove the Brits out of Palestine and Aden, the French out of Algeria, the Russians out of

Afghanistan, the Americans out of Somalia and Beirut, the Israelis out of Lebanon.

We have started up the road to empire and over the next hill we shall meet those who went before. The only lesson we learn from history is that we do not learn from history.

But George W. Bush, with no foreign policy experience and scant knowledge of previous attempts at empire building, was not one to let history stand in the way.

He repudiated his own call for a "humble" foreign policy. He rejected everything conservatives once proudly stood for. He laid down the foundation for perpetual, preemptive war.

Less than a year later, Bush first applied his new doctrine. In Iraq. And we know the tragic result.

Lessons Learned

Once again, given a chance to govern, this time on foreign policy, conservatives screwed up royally. In fact, they got it wrong twice. Once, by being too passive; the second time, by being too aggressive.

It seems that most Republicans today wouldn't know their enemies from a hole in the ground—even if Saddam was hiding in it.

As Hitler's forces rolled across Europe, crushing freedom in their path, U.S. conservatives insisted it was none of our business. Yet after the Cold War, the collapse of communism, and the rise of Islamic fundamentalism, conservatives said that the policy of containment was no longer good enough because the whole world was our business. In the first case, they were simply naive. In the second, in the world we live in today, they are reckless.

Clearly, the classic, conservative, hands-off approach to foreign policy advocated by Robert Taft no longer applies. The world is too dangerous today. There are too many threats to global or regional stability, either from rogue nations or from stateless terrorist organizations. The United States must maintain a strong military presence, and there are times when we must take the lead and intervene. Pushing Saddam Hussein out of Kuwait is a prime example.

But George W. Bush's policy of asserting our right to intervene any-where, anytime, whenever we feel like it, is not the answer, either. It is a tremendously dangerous policy that will bog U.S. forces down in one unwinnable conflict after another and will only stir up more resent-ment against us—as, indeed, it already has. By adopting the right of "first strike," we have created a monster that will embolden outlaw regimes to strike out against their neighbors—and that will someday be used against us.

For the future security of the republic, we can't trust a conservative finger on the button, ever again.

CHAPTER 6

Cutting Waste, Fraud, and Abuse

That government is best which governs the least,
because its people discipline themselves.
Thomas Jefferson

It is time to check and reverse the growth of
government, which shows signs of having grown
beyond the consent of the governed. It is my
intention to curb the size and influence
of the Federal establishment.
Ronald Reagan

My goal is to cut government in half in twenty-
five years, to get it down to the size where
we can drown it in the bathtub.
GOP lobbyist Grover Norquist

159

Hurricane Katrina was the perfect storm: a lethal combination of nature's force and man's incompetence.

The third-deadliest hurricane ever to strike the United States, Katrina caused devastation along the Gulf Coast up to a hundred miles from the storm's center. But the storm made a direct hit on, and did the worst damage to, the historic city of New Orleans. Eighty percent of the city was flooded, some neighborhoods under twenty feet of water. No emergency services were available. The entire city had to be evacuated, yet most roads leading into and out of the city were under water and thousands of residents had no transportation. Twenty-six thousand people sought refuge in the massive Louisiana Superdome. Ten thousand more holed up in the city's Convention Center, where they quickly ran out of food and water.

These horrors aside, Katrina was more than a natural disaster. It was a natural disaster followed by a government-response disaster. What destroyed New Orleans and the Mississippi coast was not just the physical damage caused by Hurricane Katrina; it was the human damage caused by utter incompetence.

More than any other recent event, Hurricane Katrina reveals the fatal flaws behind the conservative governing philosophy. When you don't believe government can solve problems in the first place, it will never be able to. When you believe the primary function of elected officials is to neuter government, even its ability to deliver essential services, government will never be there when you need it.

In short, Hurricane Katrina has become an exemplary case study of how not to govern. Conservatives, by their own admission, set out to "drown government in a bathtub." Instead, they succeeded in drowning a great American city.

FEMA—or "Fix Everything, My Ass!"

What do conservatives believe in?

Ask any conservative, consult any conservative guidebook, and you'll get the same answer: more than anything else, number one in anybody's book, conservatives believe that the smaller the government, the better. Assuming, that is, that they believe in any government at all.

Fred Thompson made that a central plank of his presidential campaign. "Recent public surveys have found that wasteful federal spend-ing is the leading cause of low public confidence in government," he wrote on his Web site. "The American people want value for their money—good service for the least amount of money. They don't want a hollow government or one with grandiose missions that can't deliver the goods. They want a smaller one that gets results."

A smaller government. It sounds good in theory, but when conser-vatives put that in practice, their drive to shrink the size of government has, time and time again, resulted in unmitigated disaster for millions of Americans who count on the government to deliver.

Indeed, as the tragedy of Katrina proved, if there's one word that, more than any other, sums up the failure of the conservative governing policy, it's *FEMA*.

And if there's one word that sums up the incompetence of George W. Bush's administration—other than Iraq, of course—it's *FEMA*.

In the wake of Hurricane Katrina, FEMA (Federal Emergency Management Agency), a robust and effective agency of federal crisis response under President Clinton, came to stand for an unprepared, unresponsive, uncaring federal government under George W. Bush. Or, as an angry retort scrawled on a wall by one frustrated resident of New Orleans put it bluntly: "Fix Everything, My Ass!"

Yet most Americans still don't understand that it was no accident that FEMA collapsed in the wake of the Category 5 hurricane that struck the Gulf Coast on August 29, 2005. FEMA did not simply fail by happenstance. Under George W. Bush, it was deliberately designed to fail, as part of his conservative determination to privatize and min-imize the role of federal government.

FEMA is one of many government agencies that our Founding Fathers never imagined. You won't find any mention of it in the Constitution. For the first two hundred years of our history, states and cities were expected to handle their own emergencies—and they did.

Gradually, however, state and local governments began to lean and count on federal help. One major turning point came after the disas-trous Mississippi floods of 1927. In the White House at the time, Calvin Coolidge embodied the conservatives' distrust for government. "If the federal government were to go out of existence," he observed (in a long sentence, for him), "the common run of people would not detect the difference."

In April 1927, when the levees broke and the Mississippi over-flowed its banks, destroying crops and cities, Coolidge at first refused to act. Under increasing pressure to do something, he finally ordered a federal investigation, headed by the then commerce secretary Herbert Hoover, and eventually signed legislation reimbursing local governments for flood damage. From that day on, the federal role in helping state and local governments to recover from natural disasters was firmly established, although back then that responsibility was still spread among dozens of different agencies.

Fast forward fifty years. In 1979, persuaded by his former colleagues in the National Governors' Association, President Jimmy Carter brought all of the assorted federal disaster relief agencies together under the roof of a new government agency, FEMA.

With no clear direction, FEMA was dysfunctional from the beginning. Neither Ronald Reagan nor George H. W. Bush did anything to improve it. By 1992, its reputation was so bad that Congress was ready to abolish it. A congressional report dismissed FEMA as "a political dumping ground, a turkey farm, if you will, where large numbers of positions exist that can be conveniently and quietly filled by political appointment."

Bill Clinton determined to change that. A former governor himself, he knew how much states, rightly or wrongly, had begun to count on federal agencies for emergency assistance. So, he brought in as the new head of FEMA James Lee Witt, the former head of the Arkansas Office of Emergency Services. Clinton also underscored the importance of FEMA by making Witt a member of his Cabinet. Together, they transformed FEMA from being the butt of a Republican joke into a model of good, efficient government.

Under Clinton, Americans came to depend on James Lee Witt's FEMA to deliver. And it did, countless times. Witt reported directly to Clinton. Witt's FEMA provided immediate, effective relief for victims of hurricanes in Florida, tornados in Arkansas, brush fires in Arizona, and earthquakes in California. Witt proved that the federal government could play an important role in helping state and local governments to cope with natural disasters. His work was repeatedly praised by governors and mayors. Witt proved that the government could do the job.

Then another governor stepped in, promising to undo everything

Bill Clinton had done, both good and bad, for the sheer reason that they were "Democrat accomplishments." In so doing, George W. Bush turned a proud example of government at its best into a sad display of government at its worst.

He began by putting his former chief of staff and the Bush-Cheney 2000 campaign manager, Joe Allbaugh, in charge of FEMA. Unlike James Lee Witt, Bush's political crony Allbaugh had zero experience in disaster management. Not only that, Allbaugh didn't believe that the government should be in the disaster business to begin with.

It all started out rosy enough on March 5, 2001, at Allbaugh's swearing-in ceremony. President Bush praised FEMA as "an example of government at its best" and expressed his confidence in FEMA's new director: "When the worst happens in America, I can assure you folks will be confident when Joe Allbaugh arrives on the scene." For his part, Allbaugh stressed the unique importance of the agency's mission: "FEMA has the opportunity and a responsibility to affect families in a positive way when they need help the most. There can be no higher calling in this service. There can be no higher calling for our country."

Okay, sounds like he's off to a good start. Yet just two months later, May 2001, Allbaugh was in front of a congressional committee ridiculing the work of the agency: "Many are concerned that federal disaster assistance may have evolved into both an *oversized entitlement program* and a disincentive to effective state and local risk management" (italics added). Don't look to us for help, he continued: "Expectations of when the federal government should be involved and the degree of involvement may have ballooned beyond what is an appropriate level."

Instead, Allbaugh encouraged cities and states to rely on faith-based organizations like the Salvation Army and the Mennonite Disaster Service. In other words, when you see a hurricane or a tornado coming, get down on your knees and pray!

By that time, of course, the handwriting for FEMA's demise was already on the wall. In April 2001, the White House budget director Mitch Daniels had already announced the administration's goal of downsizing FEMA and turning many of its functions over to private businesses.

So naturally, when Allbaugh resigned as director of FEMA in March 2003, he created a consulting company, one of whose special services was advising private clients on how to get lucrative disaster-relief contracts.

Among his first accounts: KBR, or Kellogg, Brown & Root, a division of Halliburton.

Have you noticed how every story that begins with Halliburton ends in disaster?

Before he left office Allbaugh had already succeeded in rendering FEMA ineffective. While Allbaugh was still the director, President Bush had cut FEMA's budget, stripped it of Cabinet status, and hidden it deep in the bowels of the Department of Homeland Security (DHS), a massive, inefficient new government agency created in response to September 11—because if you can't trust the people who brought us color-coded terrorist threats, whom can you trust?

Like every other DHS transplant, FEMA was also given a new mission: whatever their responsibilities before 9/11, FEMA's employees were told that their principal focus must now be on helping to fight Bush's global war on terror. Helping states to recover from natural disasters gave way to protecting the United States from terrorism. And, of course, as a relatively minor player in the war on terror, instead of reporting directly to the president, FEMA's director now had to compete with more than a hundred different department heads for attention.

You could almost hear the wheels in Bush's brain spinning: "Surely, if we're going to cut the fat around here, the best place to start is with those people who help out in national emergencies."

Not that FEMA's new director could get much attention anyway, no matter how hard he tried. Allbaugh took care of that, too. He persuaded President Bush to appoint his deputy as his successor, someone even more unqualified than Allbaugh.

That candidate, Michael Brown, had two qualifications for joining FEMA: he was a Republican Party activist, and he had been Joe Allbaugh's college roommate. "You're hired!" Otherwise, his only professional experience was serving as the commissioner for the International Arabian Horse Association, where his job was, as you might expect, running horse shows. He was fired from that tough gig in early 2000 for what the *Boston Herald* called "a spate of lawsuits over alleged supervision failures."

No problem in a Republican administration, however. Allbaugh tapped his old buddy Brown—as close to a horse thief as you could find—to be FEMA's deputy and later lobbied Bush to make Brown his successor as the director of FEMA. Yes, less than two years after getting fired from his job running horse shows, Michael Brown was in charge of domestic emergency management for the federal government—protecting us against fires, floods, hurricanes, tornados, earthquakes, and terrorism. Apparently, Homer Simpson was too busy to take the job.

Once in charge, Brown continued the hiring pattern set by his predecessor, Joe Allbaugh. Brown named Patrick Rhode as chief of staff at FEMA: Rhode had been a former advance man for the Bush-Cheney 2000 campaign. Brown's deputy chief of staff was Scott Morris, a media strategist for Maverick Media, which produced Bush's 2000 TV commercials. Neither man had any experience with disaster relief.

But failed horseman that he was, Brown still got one thing right. To his credit, he recognized the risks inherent in shifting the primary focus of FEMA from emergency preparedness to terrorism. Such a move, he argued, would make a mockery of FEMA's motto "A Nation Prepared." Furthermore, he warned, turning FEMA into simply one of many other antiterrorism agencies would "fundamentally sever FEMA from its core functions, shatter agency morale, and break long-standing, effective, and tested relationships with states and first responder stakeholders." The inevitable result of the 2003 reorganization, he predicted, would be "an ineffective and uncoordinated response" to the next natural disaster.

Hurricane Katrina

Enter Katrina in August 2005. And Brown was proved right. All the ingredients for a massive government failure were in place.

With 1,836 lives lost and $81.2 billion in property damage, Hurricane Katrina ranks as the costliest natural disaster in U.S. history. Yet given the mistakes made by the Bush administration, leading up to and following Hurricane Katrina, it's a wonder the cost wasn't still higher.

Consider the following:

- In 2004, the State of Louisiana requested federal funding to protect New Orleans. Bush's FEMA turned them down.
- In 2004, the U.S. Army Corps of Engineers requested $62 million to repair and upgrade the levees around New Orleans.

President Bush provided less than $11 million. He vetoed all funds requested in 2005. Apparently, to him, this wasn't a valid function of government.

• Katrina struck New Orleans on August 29, 2005. As early as August 27, the National Hurricane Center had predicted that Katrina would strike the Gulf Coast with catastrophic force. Yet it wasn't until thirty-six hours after Katrina slammed New Orleans that the DHS secretary Michael Chertoff declared the hurricane an incident of national significance. Chertoff said he didn't act sooner because he read a headline in the newspaper stating "New Orleans Dodged the Bullet."

• Despite early warnings, Director Brown did not order FEMA units to New Orleans until five hours after the hurricane had already struck. It took them days to arrive. Brown also admitted that he knew nothing about ten thousand people stranded in the Convention Center until he saw it on CNN. Nevertheless, President Bush went out of his way to praise Brown and his team with the now infamous remark: "Brownie, you're doing a heck of a job!"

• Immediately, President Bush took charge, flew to New Orleans, and personally directed relief efforts . . . Yeah, in your dreams! Unfortunately, that's not the way it happened. In fact, Bush remained on his ranch for another two days after the hurricane, neither saying nor doing anything about it. Flying thirty thousand feet over New Orleans on his way back to Washington on Air Force One, Bush looked down and told aides, "It's devastating. It's got to be doubly devastating on the ground." Oh, really?

Four days after Hurricane Katrina, in trying to defend his administration's pitifully inadequate response, President Bush told ABC's Diane Sawyer, "I don't think anyone anticipated the breach of the levees." Yet the video of administration briefings held on August 28 and 29 shows Max Mayfield, the director of the National Hurricane Center, specifically warning both Bush and the Homeland Security secretary Chertoff that the levees surrounding Lake Pontchartrain were in the direct path of the storm and might be topped.

After investigating the government's inadequate response to Katrina, a Special Committee of House Republicans, appointed by Speaker

Dennis Hastert, concluded, "Katrina was a national failure, an abdication of the most solemn obligation to provide for the common welfare." Yet looking at the official follow-up to Katrina, it's obvious that members of the Bush administration didn't learn much from their mistakes.

Three years after Katrina struck, the Lower Ninth Ward, the poorest and hardest-hit neighborhood of New Orleans, is still a disaster zone. Hundreds of homes have not been rebuilt. Many businesses remain closed. The few residents who have moved back live with the double threat of environmental pollution and crime. With the city's most popular tourist destinations, the French Quarter and the Garden District, back in business, the Lower Ninth seems to have been forgotten.

Not even the levees protecting New Orleans received the attention they merited. The federal government has spent $6 billion on temporary repairs to the system of levees. But the Bush White House announced that it would wait until completion of an Army Corps of Engineers study in December 2007 before deciding whether to rebuild the levees to withstand another Category 5 hurricane—the level of protection necessary, say state and local officials, before residents will feel comfortable moving back into their homes.

FEMA, meanwhile, has been busy holding a fire sale of its used or surplus trailers. To provide temporary housing for families who lost their homes in Hurricane Katrina, FEMA originally spent $2.7 billion to buy 145,000 mobile homes at a rate of $19,000 each. But only half of them were ever used. The rest never made it anywhere near New Orleans or Mississippi. Twenty thousand still sit empty in a field outside of Hope, Arkansas. Others are parked in Selma, Alabama; Madison, Indiana; Cumberland and Frostburg, Maryland; Edison, New Jersey; Carnes and Purvis, Mississippi; Jasper and Texarkana, Texas; and Fort Pickett, Virginia.

Travel to one of these locations and you can pick up a used or virgin FEMA trailer for as little as five thousand bucks—if you dare. There is, you see, one other problem. The particular brand of mobile home purchased by FEMA has been found to contain wood paneling with an unusually high concentration of formaldehyde—which is not only a toxic gas, but also a known human carcinogen. In fact, air quality tests of forty-four FEMA trailers conducted by the Louisiana Sierra Club found formaldehyde concentrations as high as 0.34 parts per million—a level nearly equal to what a professional embalmer would be exposed to in a mortuary. No wonder locals call them "toxic tin cans."

FEMA didn't just waste money on toxic trailers. A June report by the Government Accountability Office concluded that the agency had wasted between $600 million and $1.4 billion on "improper and potentially fraudulent individual assistance payments." For example, government auditors found that debit cards distributed to Katrina victims were used to pay for such items as Dom Perignon champagne, season tickets to the New Orleans Saints' games, and adult-oriented entertainment. Well, after all, it is New Orleans. "Laissez les bons temps rouler!" FEMA also double-deposited funds in the accounts of five thousand lucky debit card holders, out of a total of eleven thousand.

Since these funds at least made it into the hands of some New Orleans residents, this is as close as the Bush administration came to a Katrina "success story."

New Oraq

In truth, though they would never admit it, Katrina worked out just as George W. Bush, Joe Allbaugh, and Michael Brown had planned. With FEMA defunded, derailed, and demoralized, the department was bound to fail at its first real test—and be forced to bring in private companies to do the work FEMA previously handled itself.

No surprise, then, that within days of Katrina's knock-out punch, private construction firms showed up in Baton Rouge with their hands out for federal contracts. No surprise that the most prominent figure on the scene, lobbying for his clients, was the former FEMA director Joe Allbaugh. And no surprise that five out of six of the first noncompetitive government contracts went to five firms that had also received no-bid contracts for work in Iraq: CH2M Hill; Bechtel; the Fluor Corporation; Kellogg, Brown & Root; and the Shaw Group—the latter two are clients of Allbaugh's. The same brand of Bush crony capitalism that worked so well in Baghdad was merely transferred to New Orleans.

This wasn't the only comparison that was made to Baghdad. In fact, the government's response in New Orleans so mirrored the response in Baghdad that some people who had experienced both started to call the city "New Oraq." In both New Orleans and Baghdad, of course, the absence of a strong federal presence created a power vacuum and ensuing chaos.

Early in the cleanup process, the freelance journalist David Enders provided this chilly report to *Mother Jones*: "At times it is hard to ignore the comparisons between Baghdad (where I was less than a month ago and have spent more of the last two years) and New Orleans: The anarchy, the looting, some of it purely for survival, some of it purely opportunistic. We watched a flatbed truck drive by, a man on the back with an M-16 looking up on the roofs for snipers, as is common in Iraq. Private security contractors were stationed outside the Royal St. Charles Hotel; when asked if things were getting pretty wild around the area, one of them replied, 'Nope. It's pretty Green Zone here.'"

The other significant Iraq connection was dependency on the National Guard. Unfortunately for the residents of New Orleans, the highly trained and experienced front line of emergency responders, both personnel and equipment, was largely missing in action, because it had been sent halfway around the world, to Iraq. Forty percent of Mississippi's Guard and 35 percent of Louisiana's—about six thousand troops total, together with equipment—were on duty in Iraq.

For the record, Guard spokesmen denied that they were shorthanded. But can anybody deny that six thousand additional trained citizen-soldiers would have made a big difference—in both states? And, of course, we saw the same serious problem with a shortage of available National Guard troops and heavy equipment when a killer tornado leveled Greensburg, Kansas, in May 2007.

Soon Forgotten

Would the embarrassing failure of FEMA lead to an admission of error or some attempts to correct the problems? Forget it.

Within months after Katrina, Congress passed legislation that, among other provisions, required that any new FEMA director have a minimum of five years in disaster management experience. When President Bush signed the bill, however, he attached a presidential signing statement declaring that he did not feel bound by the five years' experience requirement. (As we saw in chapter 4, such "above the law" signing statements are often used by Bush.)

Perhaps reflecting on his own limited track record before becoming president, Bush sees inexperience as a job qualification for becoming director of FEMA. Which, from his point of view, makes sense. After all, if your intention is that government can do no good and must be minimized, why does it really matter who runs it?

Not only that. Out of thousands of families who lost their homes in Hurricane Katrina, the only one President Bush could identify with was the millionaire Trent Lott, who'd lost his luxury oceanfront vacation home in Pascagoula, Mississippi. With Lott by his side, Bush told reporters, "The good news is—and it's hard for some to see it now— is that out of this chaos is going to come a fantastic Gulf Coast, like it was before. Out of the rubble of Trent Lott's house—he lost his entire house—there's going to be a fantastic house. And I'm looking forward to sitting on the porch."

In the end, neither the need to rebuild New Orleans nor the need to rebuild FEMA were national priorities any longer. The House Speaker Dennis Hastert wondered out loud whether it was even worth saving a city that was "seven feet under water." By January 23, 2007, listing the nation's domestic priorities in his annual State of the Union address, President Bush didn't even mention New Orleans. He'd forgotten all about it.

In November 2007, President Bush even vetoed bipartisan legislation to rebuild the levees around New Orleans and make other necessary improvements to protect the Gulf Coast. Obviously, for him, helping residents recover from Katrina was no longer a priority. Fortunately, Congress overrode the president's veto.

Not Just Katrina

Once Republicans were done hamstringing our disaster-response agency, they moved to the next logical place to trim the fat. Their own salaries? No. Bloated highway bills or agriculture giveaways? No. Health care for returning soldiers? Of course. Must be lots of wasteful spending there, right?

The Walter Reed Army Medical Center, created in 1909, is the largest and best-known military medical center in the world. It has earned a reputation for providing the finest medical care available anywhere. It's where presidents and members of Congress go for their annual checkups. Since World War I, it's been the first stop for troops injured or wounded in combat and still serves that function today for casualties of the war in Iraq.

But that reputation was shattered in early 2007 by a series of reports in the *Washington Post* documenting shocking conditions for outpatients at Walter Reed, the disabled veterans of Iraq and Afghanistan. The articles began with a stark description of what the reporters Dana Priest and Anne Hull discovered in their four-month, on-site investigation of the base. In a February 18 article, Priest and Hull wrote:

Behind the door of Army Spec. Jeremy Duncan's room, part of the wall is torn and hangs in the air, weighted down with black mold. When the wounded combat engineer stands in his shower and looks up, he can see the bathtub on the floor above through a rotted hole. The entire building, constructed between the world wars, often smells like greasy carry-out. Signs of neglect are everywhere: mouse droppings, belly-up cockroaches, stained carpets, cheap mattresses. . . .

The common perception of Walter Reed is of a surgical hospital that shines as the crown jewel of military medicine. But 5 years of sustained combat have transformed the venerable 113-acre institution into something else entirely—a holding ground for physically and psychologically damaged outpatients. Almost 700 of them—the majority soldiers, with some Marines—have been released from hospital beds but still need treatment or are awaiting bureaucratic decisions before being discharged or returned to active duty.

News of the shoddy treatment of outpatients at Walter Reed prompted cries of outrage and unleashed a furious round of finger-pointing. Democrats in Congress blamed the Bush White House. Republicans in Congress blamed the Pentagon. But army leaders insisted that they knew nothing about problems on the base until they read about them in the *Post*—which was, in itself, a staggering admission of incompetence.

The official response sadly resembled a Keystone Cops skit more than a tightly run military. Pressured by the White House to do something quickly, the army secretary Francis Harvey fired the commander of Walter Reed, Major General George W. Weightman. Unfortunately, Harvey replaced him with the former Walter Reed commander Lieutenant General Kevin Kiley, the last man who should have been given the job. While presiding over the base from 2000 to 2004, Kiley had been informed by patients and families of problems in outpatient facilities, yet had done nothing about them. Kiley, in fact, lived across the street from the infamous Building 18, yet admitted he had never stepped inside it.

Kiley's return to duty was a brief one. The next day, an angry and embarrassed Defense Secretary Robert Gates stepped in and fired Kiley and Harvey both. "I am disappointed that some in the Army have not adequately appreciated the seriousness of the situation pertaining to outpatient care at Walter Reed," Gates told reporters.

President Bush, who traveled frequently to Walter Reed Hospital for photo-ops with returning veterans, said that he'd never been informed of outpatient problems. In the classic manner of pretending to act while doing nothing, he named a bipartisan commission to investigate the matter.

Not so fast! It soon became apparent that news of serious problems at Walter Reed—and, indeed, at veterans hospitals around the country—could not have come as a surprise to President Bush or anyone else in his administration. *Congressional Quarterly* interviewed two Republican congressmen who acknowledged that they were well aware, as early as 2004, of substandard conditions at Walter Reed while their party was in control of Congress. The Republican Bill Young of Florida, the former chairman of the House Appropriations Defense Subcommittee, said he had complained privately to the Pentagon but decided not to go public with the hospital's problems in order to avoid embarrassing the army while it was fighting wars in Iraq and Afghanistan. Tom Davis, a Republican from Virginia and the former chairman of the House Government Committee, was also frustrated by the failure of the Pentagon to do anything about conditions at Walter Reed but never pressured other committees or Republican leaders for legislation to fix the problem. Lamented Davis, "If generals don't go around and look at the barracks, how do you legislate that?"

Military leaders, in fact, had ample warning of shortcomings at Walter Reed and other military hospitals. In August 2004, investigators for the Department of Veterans Affairs interviewed outpatients and family members at Walter Reed and issued a report documenting problems with living conditions and poor access to continuing care. Veterans, said the report, are "frustrated, confused, sometimes angry" about their experiences at the hospital. Yet there was no action taken by the department or the army.

Word of problems surfaced again a year later. Indeed, the *Washington Post* wasn't first with the news in 2007. Salon.com actually broke the story of outpatient abuse with its own series of investigative reports, written by the national correspondent Mark Benjamin, beginning in February 2005. Salon reported on outpatient complaints, not only at Walter Reed, but at Ft. Stewart, Georgia; Ft. Carson, Colorado; and other military hospitals around the country. Adding insult to injury, beginning in January 2005, some six hundred outpatients held at Walter Reed for more than ninety days were forced to begin paying cash for their meals—a change of policy costing soldiers and their families hundreds of dollars a month.

The idea that wounded and disabled troops should have to pay for their own meals while recovering in a military hospital proves that the disgraceful conditions at Walter Reed are only symptoms of a much bigger problem: a nationwide, systematic breakdown of military health care. Because of new protective gear, more troops are surviving serious wounds received in combat, yet they still require months or years of rehabilitation. This means that an already overwhelmed military health-care system is forced to treat a growing number of outpatients who have serious physical and mental problems.

On top of that, the practice of charging for meals also proved that the Pentagon was trying to minimize the cost of the wars in Iraq and Afghanistan. Veterans organizations, in fact, still accuse the Pentagon of fighting the Iraq war on the cheap, no matter what the cost to soldiers. Steve Robinson, the executive director of the National Gulf War Resources Center, told Salon.com that the meal charge policy "is an example of a much larger problem relating to the overall cost of the war. It is all an indication of extreme costs they are trying to make up on the backs of these men and women."

The scandal at Walter Reed was especially embarrassing to a president and an administration that prided themselves on "supporting the troops." But, it turned out, they had brought it on themselves by trying to wage war "on the cheap," as veterans groups charged. And also, as part of their cost-cutting plans, by deciding to outsource certain operations at Walter Reed, including the maintenance of outpatient hospital facilities.

In 2003, the army had signed a five-year, $120 million contract with IAP Worldwide Services (for once, Halliburton didn't get the job!) for maintenance of Walter Reed Hospital and its grounds, including management. But bureaucratic bickering over terms delayed the contract for more than three years. Meanwhile, badly needed repairs went undone, including repairs to the notorious Building 18. IAP finally took over on February 4, 2007, just two weeks before the *Washington Post* told the world about conditions at Walter Reed.

Note that the move to cut costs and privatize operations at Walter Reed was undertaken by the Bush administration the same year the United States invaded Iraq. That decision left the world's premier military hospital in disarray and disrepair, just as the nation went to war and the number of severely wounded soldiers from Iraq and Afghanistan was rising rapidly.

In a very real sense, then, mismanagement at Walter Reed is part and parcel of overall mismanagement of the war in Iraq. That point was driven home by Michigan's Democratic senator Carl Levin, the chairman of the Senate Armed Services Committee. In March 2007, opening a hearing into problems at Walter Reed, Levin told Pentagon officials, "Today's hearing is about another example of the lack of planning for a war that was premised on the assumption that combat operations would be swift, casualties would be minimal, and that we would be welcomed as liberators, instead of being attacked by the people we liberated."

Once again, in their zeal to cut costs and shrink government down to the size where you could "drown it in a bathtub," conservatives had failed the American public.

Lesson Learned

What do the experiences of Katrina and Walter Reed tell us about conservative governance?

First, that conservatives' lack of faith in the possibilities of government can often lead to inefficiency and, worse, to catastrophic error.

Second, that conservatives' desire to shrink government across the board leads to a penny-wise, pound-foolish mentality that in turn results in all-too-avertable tragedies such as Katrina and Walter Reed.

Third, that as a result of their distaste for government, conservatives are all too willing to place incompetents and cronies in charge of crucial federal programs.

Fourth, that—from toxic tin cans to wounded soldiers' medical needs—conservatives, in the name of smaller government, invariably tend to sell off federal services to the highest bidder, leading to corruption and cronyism of the worst order.

Conservatives aren't wrong about everything. In fact, they're right in favoring smaller, more efficient government and resisting government expansion. Not even the most hard-core liberal, certainly not this liberal, would argue that bigger government is always better. But if government can't be counted on to care for our wounded combat veterans or help Americans recover from the ravages of hurricanes, floods, fires, earthquakes, or tornados, what is government for?

Where conservatives go wrong is in blindly applying their conservative principle of "smaller is better" to all government programs, with no consideration of the actual needs and demands of the moment. When you shrink and privatize too much, for the sake of smaller government and no other purpose, you end up with government breakdown and real human tragedy.

And that's what happened with Hurricane Katrina and Walter Reed. In both cases, government didn't work because conservatives didn't want government to work—and did everything possible to guarantee it would not. They succeeded, and millions of Americans suffered.

Lesson learned: Put conservatives who don't believe in government in charge of government, and disaster will be the inevitable result.

CHAPTER 7

The Party of Fiscal Responsibility

The federal government must set a timetable,
a systematic plan, to balance the budget—
and it must stick to it.
Ronald Reagan, 1976

We spent money like a drunken sailor.
Although I never knew a sailor, drunk or sober,
with the imagination of my colleagues.
John McCain, 2007

Deficits don't matter. . . . Ronald Reagan
proved that.
Dick Cheney, 2001

Republicans have lost their way.
Newt Gingrich, 2007

As we've seen, nothing makes a conservative's heart beat faster than the two words *smaller government*. It is their mantra. They chant it at, during, and in between campaign stops. They continually promise voters, "Put us in charge and we'll cut the fat. We'll make government lean, mean, and efficient."

Well, we did put them in charge. We gave them a chance to govern. And what happened? It didn't quite work out the way they promised. In fact, it came out just the opposite. Conservatives didn't deliver smaller, more efficient government. They either brought us total incompetence and blatant cronyism or the most bloated federal bureaucracy ever in our nation's history.

The record is clear. There's no denying it. Put conservatives in charge of the White House and Congress, and here's what you end up with:

- The biggest federal budgets ever
- The biggest federal government ever
- The biggest budget deficits ever
- The biggest national debt ever
- The biggest trade deficit ever
- And the biggest pork barrel ever

Hey, wait a minute! Weren't liberals supposed to be the fiscally irresponsible "big-spenders?" Wrong! Conservatives have stolen the title.

Republicans insist that they're the party to trust on national security, smaller government, and family values. Well, here are three things you should never, ever trust a Republican on: national security, smaller government, and family values.

In every category—spending, size of government, number of agencies, number of bureaucrats, total deficit, and total debt—conservatives have delivered the opposite of what they promised and the exact opposite of what conservatives have claimed to stand for.

Maybe, given the opportunity, the temptation to spend, spend, spend is just too great to resist. Or maybe conservatism just ain't what it's cracked up to be.

Conservative Economic Policy

We associate the phrases *smaller government* and *balanced budget* rhetorically with Ronald Reagan, but they didn't start with him. They have long ranked among the basic tenets of conservatism.

To go back to the beginning, the fear of an all-powerful central government haunted our Founding Fathers, with the possible exceptions of John Adams and Alexander Hamilton. As Thomas Jefferson wrote:

> When all governments, domestic and foreign, in little as in great things, shall be drawn to Washington as a center of power, it will render powerless the checks provided by one government over another and it will become just as venal and oppressive as the government from which we separated.

The vision of a smaller, federal government—more accountable to the American people and, like most U.S. families, forced to live within its means—is also reflected in Russell Kirk's ninth basic principle of conservatism: "The conservative perceives the need for prudent restraints upon power." It motivated Robert Taft and fellow conservatives of his day to oppose the New Deal as a threat to individual liberty. It inspired the politics of President Gerald Ford: "A government big enough to give you everything you want is big enough to take away everything you have." It was a key plank of the Contract with America, famously promulgated in 1994 by the aspiring Speaker Newt Gingrich, who promised to "restore fiscal responsibility to an out-of-control Congress, requiring them to live under the same budget constraints as families and businesses." And, of course, the same goals—smaller government, balanced budget—still get lip service every so often (but only for show) from George W. Bush. In fact, he only started to complain about bigger spending once Democrats took control of Congress. Before that, not a peep!

But even if Ronald Reagan didn't start or end the dialogue, he justifiably gets credit for expounding the conservative doctrine of fiscal responsibility in the political arena. In 1964, he joined Barry Goldwater in railing against an expanding federal bureaucracy. In 1976, making the first run for president on his own, Reagan preached the virtue of a balanced budget:

When Washington runs in the red, year after year, it cheapens every dollar you earn; it makes a profit on your cost-of-living wage increases by pushing you into higher tax brackets; it borrows in the capital market to cover its deficits, cutting off business and industry from that capital which is needed to fuel our economy and create jobs; it robs your savings of value; and it denies retired people the stability they need and expect for their fixed incomes.

And in 1980, one of Reagan's primary beefs against the incumbent president Jimmy Carter was his failure to control federal spending. With inflation at 13 percent and interest rates heading toward 21 percent, Reagan promised to restore the economy by reining in federal spending and getting the budget back in balance. Instead, he did just the opposite: restored federal spending and reined in any attempts to balance the budget.

Unfortunately, it was a case of "promises made, promises broken." As recounted by the Reagan budget director David Stockman in his book *The Triumph of Politics*, it wasn't long before the new president was forced to face the music. Preparing the first budget of his own presidency, for FY 1982, Reagan was told he had only two choices: raise taxes, or accept a $100 billion deficit—more than twice the Carter deficit he had promised to eliminate.

Forced to choose, Reagan folded. He'd rather whip out his credit card than raise taxes. As for a balanced budget, he sheepishly told Stockman, "I never said anything but that it was a goal."

A goal? Well, I guess it's good to have goals.

Far better to burden future taxpayers with the deficit than annoy today's taxpayers (and voters) with higher taxes, Reagan decided—and that's been the creed of conservatives ever since.

Let's take a look at four major indicators of responsible fiscal policy: federal spending, the federal deficit, the national debt, and the trade deficit. Conservatives have failed every one of them.

Federal Spending

When George W. Bush, that phony proponent of smaller government, leaves office, the United States will have been burdened with the biggest federal workforce and the biggest federal spending bill in history.

In 1888, Viscount James Bryce, the British ambassador to the United States, famously wrote of California: "It grew like a gourd in the night."

Well, the federal government didn't grow overnight. Real annual federal spending actually started to balloon under FDR, to fight World War II and later to build Lyndon Johnson's Great Society. But it really started to skyrocket in 1980 and at the beginning of Ronald Reagan's first term. Reagan, in fact, holds the dubious distinction of being the first president to send Congress a budget of more than $1 trillion. Since 1980, federal spending has almost *doubled*—not quite what you'd expect at first glance from a string of, except for Clinton, conservative presidents. In fact, Clinton's the only president since 1980 to govern in a fiscally responsible manner.

A few numbers tell the whole story.

- In 1980, Jimmy Carter's last year in office, the federal government spent $591 billion. In 1988, Ronald Reagan's last year in office, the federal budget hit $1.064 trillion—an 80 percent increase.

- In Ronald Reagan's first term, total federal spending grew 14.5 percent; under Bush 41, 7.8 percent; during Clinton's first term, 4.2 percent; and under Bush 43's first term, 19.7 percent—the fastest rate of increase in federal spending in thirty years.

- When Ronald Reagan left office, federal spending was 22 percent of GDP. When Clinton left the White House, it was down to 18.5 percent of GDP. By 2006, under George W. Bush, federal spending was back up to 20.3 percent of GDP—and it climbed even higher in 2007.

- The last budget submitted to Congress by Bill Clinton, for FY 2001, was $1.8 trillion. George W. Bush's first budget, FY 2002, grew 5.6 percent—to $1.96 trillion. His latest budget request, for FY 2008, tops out at $2.9 trillion.

As David R. Henderson, a research fellow at the conservative Hoover Institution, lamented on the blog RealClearPolitics.com: "Someone who favors relatively small government could get awfully depressed, looking at these numbers."

Indeed, federal spending is so out of control that the former Illinois senator Everett Dirksen's famous quip—"A billion here, a billion there, pretty soon, you're talking real money"—seems almost quaint. And even leading conservatives admit that their self-promotion as champions of limited government is no longer credible. The conservative congressman Mike Pence of Indiana told the 2006 convention of the Conservative Political Action Committee, "Whether it's called 'compassionate conservatism' or 'big government Republicanism,' after years of record increases in federal spending, more government is now the accepted Republican philosophy in Washington."

Inside the Beltway, we call this out-of-control federal spending "the Republican way of doing business."

Writing in the *New Republic*, the conservative commentator Robert George was even more blunt: "A government that cuts taxes and continues to spend ultimately becomes as amoral as one that raises taxes and spends."

Bigger government and more spending, of course, mean a commensurate growth in the number of federal employees. In their public statements, conservatives from Ronald Reagan on have made a sport of ridiculing federal bureaucrats. After Hurricane Katrina, for example, President Bush snorted, "Bureaucracy is not going to stand in the way of getting the job done for the people." Luckily for him, in that case, Bush had his incompetent pals to stand in the way of the bureaucracy standing in the way of getting the job done.

In their public actions, however, conservatives have proved to be the bureaucrats' best friend. Conservatives keep padding the federal payroll by hiring more and more of them. After spiking up to its highest levels under Reagan and Bush 41, the federal civilian workforce was reduced 377,000 positions by Clinton-Gore. In 2000, in fact, the United States could boast the smallest federal workforce since 1960.

George W. Bush took over in 2001, preaching smaller government but delivering just the opposite. By 2004, Bush had added some 38,300 federal employees to the payroll, and another 13,000 extra are contained in his proposed budget for FY 2008—not counting the Department of Defense!

Like any other president, Bush had a choice when face-to-face with the federal bureaucracy: slash it, or accept it and fill it with your political cronies. According to the Princeton political scientist David Lewis, political appointees in the federal government dropped from 3,423 to 2,845 during the years 1992 to 2000, under President Clinton. Bush reversed the trend, handing out jobs to 3,202 political supporters by 2004.

The number of purely political appointees is even higher today—and, more alarming, even more widespread. In testimony before the House Judiciary Committee in May 2007, the former top Alberto Gonzales aide Monica Goodling admitted that she considered active, Republican Party, Bush supporters only—not just for nomination as U.S. attorney, but for top career positions with the Justice Department. And, of course, as we learned with Katrina, the problem with having political hacks in positions of authority is that when crisis strikes, they more often than not turn out to be inexperienced, untrained, ignorant, and inept.

Now, before tackling the growing federal deficits that are the frightening by-product of increased federal spending, here is a quick repudiation of two classic examples of spin we hear from defenders of George W. Bush, in particular, to justify his eight-year spending spree.

One: "September 11 made me do it."

For a while, this was President Bush's own line of defense. He often recounted being asked by a reporter, during the 2000 campaign, whether, as president, he would ever be responsible for a deficit. "I can't imagine it," Bush supposedly replied, "but there would be one if we had a war, or a national emergency, or a recession." Then he concluded with a dramatic sigh, "Never did I dream we'd get the trifecta."

It makes a nice story. Unfortunately, as with so much from this White House, it's not true. Bush stopped telling the story when no reporter who covered Bush in 2000 could remember asking the question and the White House, despite frequent requests, could produce no evidence that the exchange actually took place.

Nevertheless, White House spin doctors perpetuated the same argument: "Yes, it's true that overall federal spending has soared under President Bush—but he had no choice because of September 11."

Coming from a White House that blames everything on 9/11, including rainy Monday mornings, lost socks, and Detroit's surprise loss to the Cardinals in the 2006 World Series, that response is hardly unexpected. It could even be considered humorous. But it's simply not true. It's important to understand that even after excluding outlays on defense and homeland security, Bush is still the biggest-spending president since Lyndon Johnson. The wars in Afghanistan and Iraq have been costly, as have protective homeland security measures and even the second-rate measures taken by Bush, but nondefense spending has gone up as well. The Cato Institute, no liberal think tank, reports that nondefense-related domestic spending has increased 36 percent since Bush took office.

Two: "Don't blame me, blame Congress."

Again, White House spin doctors try to shift the blame: We did our share. It's those free-wheeling, free-spending members of Congress who went crazy. After all, on budget matters, the president only proposes; Congress disposes.

Nonsense. While it's true that the Republican-controlled Congress played its role in expanding the federal budget and threw any previous spending discipline out the window, it's also true that George W. Bush did nothing to stop them. As the former Reagan speechwriter and conservative commentator Peggy Noonan complained in the *Wall Street Journal*, "George W. Bush is a big spender. . . . When Congress serves up a big slab of fat, crackling pork, Mr. Bush responds with one big question: 'Got any barbecue sauce?'"

For all his vaunted fiscal conservatism, Bush became the first president since John Quincy Adams never to use his veto pen to kill a spending bill. In seven years in office, he exercised his veto only twice: to limit research on embryonic stem-cell research, and to oppose a timetable for bringing U.S. troops home from Iraq. Both vetoes were policy-based. Neither had anything to do with saving money.

It wasn't until November 2007 that Bush vetoed his first spending bill. The reason he waited so long? Easy, insists the White House chief of staff Josh Bolten: "He hadn't needed to veto a bill." In other words, Bush felt no need to veto bill after bill that spent more money than he had asked Congress for. This is damning testimony for his lack of fiscal discipline.

Actually, by attempting to shift the blame for out-of-control federal spending to Congress, Bush administration officials miss the point. The culprit is neither the Republican president nor the Republican Congress alone. It's the Republican president and the Republican Congress acting in concert. The fact that federal spending soared so out of whack from 2000 to 2007 illustrates what can happen when one party controls the White House and both houses of Congress: all restraint is gone. There are no brakes on spending.

In fact, once Republicans controlled both ends of Pennsylvania Avenue, the entire political dynamic changed. As the journalist Jonathan Rauch noted in the October 2004 edition of *Atlantic Monthly*, "For Republicans, governing now meant working as a team against the Democrats. Congressional Republicans and the White House egged each other on instead of reining each other in."

For his part, President Bush kept his veto sword in its scabbard, loathe to unsheathe it against Republican-backed spending bills. For its part, the Republican Congress jettisoned the pay-as-you-go, or "PAYGO," requirement it had earlier forced on Democrats.

PAYGO simply means that members of Congress can't propose new expenditures or tax cuts without showing how these will be paid for, either through new taxes, with new sources of revenue, or by cutting some other program. The spending discipline was first adopted as part of the 1990 Budget Act and was in force throughout the Clinton presidency. At the time, conservatives in Congress bragged that this was their only way of keeping the brakes on the big-spending tendencies of a liberal, Democratic president.

Conservatives, however, sang a different tune once there was a Republican in the White House. Unable to pay for George W. Bush's trillion dollar tax cuts or his vast expansions of Medicare and the Department of Education, Republicans in Congress simply let PAYGO lapse. They changed the rules and took their foot off the brakes for George W. Bush; the results have been a flood of unwise spending and a sea of red ink.

One of the first things Democrats did upon regaining control of Congress in January 2007 was to reinstate PAYGO. But as long as George Bush is in the White House, it may be too little, too late. In terms of both spending and deficits, the horse is already out of the barn.

One thing for sure, when you're spending somebody else's money, it's hard to stop. It soon becomes addictive. And it blinds you to how much cash you're shelling out every day.

Case in point: the former House majority leader Tom DeLay, who was forced to resign in disgrace because of his unethical dealings with the crooked GOP lobbyist Jack Abramoff. Before resigning, DeLay was having so much fun spending money that he'd become as blind as a bat. The number-two Republican and top conservative in the House, DeLay declared "victory in the war on budget fat" and said there was simply no more room to cut.

In a blatant repudiation of everything conservatives supposedly stand for, DeLay insisted there was only one option left for Republicans in Congress: to keep on spending, to keep on borrowing, and to keep adding to the deficit. And that is exactly what they did. "Tax and spend" Democrats were replaced by "borrow and spend" Republicans.

Federal Deficit

What an amazing transition. In twenty-five years, conservatives have gone from hating budget deficits to loving them. They must love them. They've given us so many of them. And such big ones.

Nobody talked a better balanced-budget game than Ronald Reagan. In 1980, he told voters they should throw Jimmy Carter out of the White House because he had allowed the federal budget deficit to balloon up to $73.8 billion. By 1986, the annual deficit had soared to $221 billion. But even that was nothing compared to what lay ahead under the Bushes.

When it came to deficit spending, George H. W. Bush borrowed one of Ronald Reagan's favorite lines: "You ain't seen nothin' yet!"

Reagan set the record for the biggest budget deficit. Bush 41 quickly broke it. And despite reneging on his notorious promise—"Read my lips, no new taxes!"—Pappy Bush was still not able to balance the books. His last year in office, 1992, produced the country's worst budget deficit yet: $290 billion.

Eight years later, Junior Bush entered the Oval Office with a bad case of Pappy envy. He was determined to outdo his father in every category, and he succeeded: in cutting more taxes, spending more money, hiring more bureaucrats, starting more wars, and rolling up bigger federal deficits.

Had his father made history by going $290 billion in the red, delivering the country's biggest deficit ever? Piece of cake. Dubya set a new record of $413 billion and outdid his father four years in a row. In fact, he hasn't balanced one budget in seven years, and he won't in 2008, either.

The history of sky-high deficits reads "like father, like son."

1992—George H. W. Bush—$290 billion

2003—George W. Bush—$378 billion

2004—George W. Bush—$413 billion

2005—George W. Bush—$318 billion

2006—George W. Bush—$296 billion

2007—George W. Bush—$163 billion

George H. W. and George W.—the Bobby and Barry Bonds of deficit spending.

There was, however, one big difference between the Bushes. Bush 41 came into office saddled with a leftover Reagan deficit. Thanks to the hard work of Bill Clinton, Bush 43 assumed leadership of a government blessed with four consecutive years of surplus. Within a year, Bush had turned a $167 billion surplus into a $158 billion deficit—a stunning, downward shift of $325 billion in national wealth.

Again, the Bush White House would like to blame it all on September 11, but the facts argue otherwise. Thanks to the first round of Bush's $1.35 trillion tax cuts, signed into law on June 7, 2001, the federal government was already back in the red—long before the World Trade Center towers fell.

September 11 and the resultant wars in Afghanistan and Iraq did, of course, demand a substantial increase in spending, almost all of it deficit spending. But the Bush deficits are not due to increased spending for defense and homeland security alone. President Bush did not choose guns over butter. He opted for both. Real domestic discretionary spending, not counting defense and homeland security, rose by an average 4.8 percent over his first four years in office.

The other major contributors to the historic Bush deficits, of course, were the historic Bush tax cuts. There's simply no denying it. When there's a surplus, it's easy to pay for tax cuts as long as they don't exceed the funds available. When there's no surplus—and especially when you're in the middle of a war—the only way to pay for tax cuts is to cut spending, which George Bush refused to do, or add the cost of tax cuts to the federal deficit, which George Bush willingly did over and over again.

Bush is the first president not to ask the American people to sacrifice in order to help support a war: no rationing, no draft, no restrictions on activities or travel, no community support programs, and, of course, no new taxes. That's one of the reasons why, even though the Iraq war is unpopular, there are no protests in the street. Bush made it easy. The vast majority of Americans don't have to worry about the war. We don't even have to help pay for it. Bush simply added it to the outstanding balance on our credit card—and forced our kids to pay for it.

There's one other big difference between George W. Bush and his father on budget deficits. At least George H. W. Bush agonized over deficit spending. He even broke his "no new taxes" pledge in order to stop the bleeding of red ink. His son, by contrast, dismissed budget deficits as no big deal—and the so-called conservative Dick Cheney ended up defending them!

We know the story, thanks to the first Bush treasury secretary, Paul O'Neill. The former CEO of Alcoa turned out to be the sole truth teller in the entire Bush 43 team, during both terms. He came to the administration believing in both global warming and balanced budgets and was thus quickly booted out. But not before blowing the whistle on what went on behind closed doors.

It is thanks to O'Neill that we know that 9/11 was not, in fact, the reason for invading Iraq. It was only used, belatedly, as the excuse for invading Iraq. O'Neill was stunned to hear war with Iraq put forth as a serious possibility in the very first meeting he attended of the National Security Council, just ten days after Bush's inauguration and months before 9/11.

It is also thanks to O'Neill that we learned when Bush changed his mind about deficit spending: as soon as he walked into the Oval Office. In his memoir *The Price of Loyalty*, O'Neill relates a meeting on economic policy in the vice president's office, soon after the 2002 midterm elections, where the case was made for the second round of Bush tax cuts. Believing he was doing his job as treasury secretary, O'Neill warned that the proposed tax cuts would add to already record-high budget deficits. According to O'Neill, Vice President Cheney cut him off in mid-sentence. "Reagan proved deficits don't matter," Cheney roared. "We won the midterms. This is our due."

Welcome to the new age of conservatism. In twenty-five years, Republicans have turned traditional conservative economic policy on its head. Ronald Reagan preached that deficit spending was irresponsible and bad for the country. With equal fervor, George Bush and Dick Cheney preach that deficit spending doesn't really matter and can actually be good for the country—because it will eventually force cuts in spending.

It's a practice that David Stockman first called "starving the beast"—deliberately running up the deficit in order to provide an excuse for cutting social programs. While some liberals accused Reagan of secretly undertaking such a policy, he denied it. Today, Bush and Cheney brag about it.

What? A deficit? Don't worry about it, they insist. Nobody worries about deficits anymore. And, besides, if the deficit gets big enough, it will force decision-makers to stop spending so much money.

Of course, they're wrong on both counts. We do worry, and we should worry, about deficits, for all the same reasons articulated by Ronald Reagan. As the government goes out looking for investors to loan it money, it competes with private capital markets, which drives up interest rates. It's estimated that every 1 percent in the size of the deficit, compared to the overall economy, slaps as much as one full percentage point on the amount consumers have to pay for loans on their homes, cars, or credit cards.

Meanwhile, paying interest on those federal loans means there's less money available for building new schools, improving roads, providing health care, or achieving other important public goals. And, eventually, it's our kids who will have to pay the freight. People who roll up huge debts on their credit cards, and we all know them, inevitably end up in dire financial straits.

That's the number-one reason why deficit spending is so irresponsible. Every deficit represents an intergenerational transfer. We insist on paying lower taxes today so we can stick our children with higher taxes tomorrow. And, of course, if we saddle them with enough debt, they'll be unable to meet their own needs and unable to keep up with growing demands on Social Security and Medicare.

Bush and Cheney are also wrong in arguing that the best way, eventually, to spend less is to spend more. By the same logic, the best way to lose weight is to keep on eating because you'll eventually get so fat, you'll beg to go on a diet.

Come to think of it, a lot of famous politicians look as if they might be testing that theory, too!

On September 22, 2005, even the right-wing pundit Peggy Noonan took the Bush administration to task on this point, in the pages of the *Wall Street Journal*, no less: "Mr. Bush seems not to be noticing that once government spending reaches a new high level it is very hard to get it down, even a little, ever. So a decision to raise spending now is in effect a decision to raise spending forever."

Ronald Reagan was right. Ross Perot was right. Paul O'Neill was right. Classic conservatism is right. Deficits do matter. George W. Bush and Dick Cheney are wrong.

National Debt

At the end of the year, credit card companies don't simply erase all the unpaid debt you've racked up in twelve months. They carry it over into the next year.

It's the same with the federal budget deficit. What's left over doesn't just go poof and disappear. It's piled on to the already bloated national debt, the third major indicator of responsible fiscal policy—and the third one trashed by conservatives. Again, the so-called fiscal conservative Ronald Reagan led the way, in the wrong direction.

Reagan started out talking a good game. On February 14, 1981, the new president gave an "Economic Address" to a Joint Session of Congress, in which he made an urgent plea for reining in federal spending. After repeating his call for a balanced budget, he turned to the national debt in typically dramatic fashion:

> Our national debt is approaching $1 trillion. A few weeks ago I called such a figure, a trillion dollars, incomprehensible, and I've been trying ever since to think of a way to illustrate how big a trillion really is. And the best I could come up with is that if you had a stack of thousand-dollar bills in your hand only four inches high, you'd be a millionaire. A trillion dollars would be a stack of thousand-dollar bills 67 miles high. The interest on the public debt this year we know will be over $90 billion.

Then Reagan proceeded to go out and do the exact opposite of what he'd advocated. He built that 67-mile-high wall, and then some.

In January 1981, when Reagan took the oath of office, the national debt was indeed close to a trillion dollars—$930 billion. In his last year of office, having absorbed eight straight years of record deficits, the national debt stood at $2.6 trillion.

That stack of thousand-dollar bills, in other words, was now 168 miles high. In eight short years, Reagan had transformed the United States from the world's largest creditor nation to the world's largest debtor nation. But that was just for starters.

If you really want to get depressed, do an Internet search for the "national debt clock." It's a running total of how much we owe as a people, and how much each of us owes as an individual.

As of February 1, 2008, the national debt is $9,203,381,871,756.38.

The national debt has increased an average of $1.42 billion a day since September 2006.

The population of the United States, as of this writing, is 304,241,032.

That means that you and I each owe $30,250.30 of the national debt—in addition to whatever we personally owe on our mortgage, car loan, or credit cards.

Of course, you and I aren't going to pay it. We'll resolve the national debt the old-fashioned way, by passing it on to our kids. As President Herbert Hoover taught us: "Blessed are the young, for they shall inherit the national debt."

How could the national debt get so high? Isn't there some limit to how much debt the government can roll up? Of course, there is. The federal government has a limit, or ceiling, to its debt capacity—just as we have a limit on our credit cards. The only difference is, whenever the federal government gets close to its debt ceiling, Congress merely raises it. As it has done, over and over again, for George W. Bush.

When Bush took office in 2001, the national debt was $5.6 trillion and the debt ceiling was $6 trillion. Because Bush kept piling on more debt with his record-high budget deficits, Congress has been forced to raise the debt ceiling five times since he took office. It stands today at $9 trillion. I don't even want to know how many hundreds of miles high Ronald Reagan's stack of thousand-dollar bills is by now.

At $9 trillion, our national debt now equals more than 60 percent of the United States' GDP. Think about that. We owe more than half of what our whole economy is worth. There are at least two problems with that.

First, just like our credit cards, if you don't pay the whole bill off at the end of the month, you have to pay interest on what's outstanding. So does the federal government. To cover our debt, the federal government sells Treasury bonds, which pay an annual rate of interest to their owners.

As you can imagine, carrying a balance of $9 trillion on your credit card requires paying a ton of interest. In FY 2006, interest payments *alone* on the national debt cost us $406 billion—and that increases every year, as the national debt increases. In fact, interest payments on the national debt are now the third-largest item in the budget. Only the Defense Department and the combined income-distribution programs of Housing and Urban Development (HUD), Health and Human Services (HHS), and the Department of Agriculture get a bigger chunk of the budget.

What a waste. That's $406 billion a year that is creating no new national parks, building no new roads or bridges, setting up no new protection for our ports and rail systems, or providing no new health care for forty-five million Americans who have no health insurance at all. That $406 billion is pathetically squandered on interest, just because we lacked the discipline to pay our bills when due.

The second serious problem with our $9 trillion national debt is, Who owns it? To whom do we owe $9 trillion?

Fortunately, 40 percent of the debt is owed to the Federal Reserve Bank, another agent of the federal government. But the remaining 60 percent is privately owned by mutual funds, pension funds, insurance companies, or state and local governments.

And here's what's scary: 23 percent of our $9 trillion national debt is owned by foreign governments, mainly Japan and China. And their share of the debt has been increasing every year, which puts the United States at considerable risk. While we're buying their electronics, poisoned dog food, and lead-coated children's toys, they're buying us!

If, for whatever reason, Japan and/or China suddenly decided that the United States was no longer a good credit risk and they dumped its Treasury bills, they could put the entire U.S. economy in a tailspin overnight. Simply put, fiscal profligacy has put the United States at the mercy of Japanese and Chinese bankers. Every day, we are borrowing money from China to fund a war in Iraq.

And if you think that's bad, by one form of reckoning, it's actually a far lot worse. The former congressman Chris Chocola of Indiana argued that the federal government should adopt the same accounting standards that are used by big corporations and state and local governments. Their rules require counting expenses immediately, once a transaction occurs, even if payment will be made at a later date. By not following the same rules, the federal government is exempt from reporting shortfalls in Social Security and Medicare when calculating its bottom line.

What's that mean? Under the standard corporate system of reporting debt, the 2006 budget deficit would actually be $1.3 trillion, far more than the $248 billion reported. And the national debt would be closer to $59 trillion—or $516,348 for every U.S. household. By comparison, in 2007, the average U.S. household owed a total of $112,043 for mortgages, car loans, credit cards, and all other debt combined.

Whichever yardstick you use, whether it's $9 trillion or $59 trillion, the fact is, conservatives can no longer claim to be the protectors of the public purse. "Remember when conservatism meant fiscal responsibility?" asked the conservative commentator Andrew Sullivan.

> When you add it all up [Bush's spending], you get the simple, devastating fact that Bush, in a mere five years, has added $1.5 trillion to the national debt. The interest on that debt will soon add up to the cost of two Katrinas a year.

Trade Deficit

You hear a lot of political debate about the national debt and the budget deficit. Yet there's another deficit, lurking beneath the waters, that is equally dangerous—and equally mismanaged by latter-day conservatives. We're talking about the balance of trade.

The trade deficit is quite simply the difference in the monetary value of the goods and services the United States sells to other nations and the value of the goods and services we buy from other nations. If we sell more than we buy, we enjoy a trade surplus. If we buy more than we sell, we have a trade deficit—which is where we are now, and it's only getting worse.

Every day, cargo ships arrive from China filled with goods both cheap and expensive, and we send them back empty, except for a handful of IOUs. (Actually, we send them back full of recyclable garbage that they process for us, which isn't a prettier picture.)

Just as there's a clock for the national debt, there's also a running clock for the trade deficit. Do an Internet search for "trade ticker," if you dare.

For some unknown reason, perhaps because we can only take so much bad news at one time, the trade deficit clock is set back at the beginning of each year—and the trade deficit or surplus starts again at zero. As of February 1, 2008, the United States had a trade deficit of $61,347,361,200.82 and ticking—and that's just for the first month of 2008.

Actually, the United States hasn't seen a trade surplus since 1975. But during the last five years, under George W. Bush, we have seen one record trade deficit after another, leading up to $617 billion in the red for 2004, $726 billion in 2005, and $764 billion in 2006. And that hundreds-of-billion-dollar trade deficit, of course, is on top of the hundreds-of-billion-dollar national debt.

Some economists argue that a trade deficit is nothing to worry about. It's just one sign of a booming economy, they argue, filling the shelves of Wal-Mart with a bounty of goods at low prices—and, eventually, all that money pouring out of the United States will find its way back into our economy.

If you believe that, buy ten copies of this book and mail them to your friends, and tell them to mail ten copies to all their friends. If you do, great fortunes will find you. If you don't, a terrible fate awaits you. Or maybe not.

Understanding why a continuing trade deficit is a problem is no more difficult than imagining that you're the manager of your local convenience store. If, month after month, you're shelling out more for goods than you're taking in, you either turn it around—by cutting prices, cutting wages, or producing a better product—or, pretty soon, you're going to go broke. Same with the U.S. of A.

And if your richest supplier uses the money you give him to buy shares of your failing business? Well, that's just what conservatives call money "finding its way back" into your own pocket. Notice how well that works—until you wake up and discover you don't own the store anymore.

On this topic, the conservative commentator and former presidential candidate Pat Buchanan has it right. With his usual flair, he calls the trade deficit "a malignant tumor in the intestines of the U.S. economy."

Why? First, because, like the national debt, we owe that money to somebody. And when it comes to the trade deficit, to a greater extent every year, that somebody is the People's Republic of China. In 2006, China owned $202 billion of the United States' $764 billion deficit, giving a foreign country enormous leverage over the U.S. economy. What if China abruptly decides to unload that debt? What if other nations decide that U.S. trade is no longer a safe investment? We're in serious trouble.

The other problem with the trade deficit is its negative impact on the economy. As we buy more goods from China, we manufacture fewer goods here. As we prop up factories in Thailand, we close factories here. As U.S. money flows overseas, so do U.S. jobs.

The evidence is all around us. Direct effects of the trade deficit are failed businesses, displaced workers, lower real wages, and greater socio-economic inequality. The trade deficit hurts blue-collar Americans by pushing them out of relatively well-paying manufacturing jobs and into lower-paying service jobs. If the flood of cheap imports could be slowed or brought into balance, U.S. producers could retain workers at higher wages, giving all Americans the benefit of greater purchasing power. Explained the University of Maryland business professor Peter Morici, "Were the trade deficit cut in half, GDP would increase by nearly $300 billion, or about $2,000 for every working American."

There's one other aspect of the trade deficit that's seldom talked about: the biggest chunk of it is going for oil. As Al Gore pointed out in his masterful book *The Assault on Reason*, more than 40 percent of our total trade deficit in 2006 came from the purchase of foreign oil. The man who's done more than anyone else to wake us up to the dangers of global warming laments the fact that we are "borrowing huge amounts of money from China to buy huge amounts of oil from the Persian Gulf and to make huge amounts of pollution that destroy the planet's climate." What folly!

Critics of the United States' ever-expanding trade deficits are not limited to those who criticize the Bush administration. In January 2005, the Bush State Department itself released a report warning of the United States' negative trade dependence on China. Prepared for the U.S.-China Economic and Security Review Commission, the study concluded that from 1989 to 2003, growing trade deficits with China had cost 1.5 million U.S. jobs. And that number keeps growing. The AFL-CIO estimates that 3 million manufacturing jobs, many of them in well-paid, high-tech industries, have been shipped overseas since George W. Bush took office.

The U.S. trade deficit is one more glaring display of fiscal irresponsibility—one more serious problem negatively impacting every American famil, and one more test of good government that conservatives routinely flunk.

Pat Buchanan's the only conservative I've ever heard warn about the dangers inherent in the trade deficit. When's the last time you heard George W. Bush talk about it? The answer is, he doesn't. Probably because he's been too busy growing the federal government.

The Biggest Federal Government Ever

Bureaucrats quaked in their boots when conservatives took power. And with good reason. Conservatives, after all, had long advocated smaller government, less federal spending, fewer government agencies, and fewer government employees. Everyone knew it wouldn't take long before the axe fell.

No need to worry. The axe never did fall. It turns out that conservatives didn't mean it, after all. Not only did they not shrink the government, they ballooned it bigger than it's ever been.

Campaigning for Barry Goldwater in 1964, Ronald Reagan quipped about the seemingly inexorable growth of federal agencies: "A government bureau is the nearest thing to eternal life that we'll ever see on this earth." Nevertheless, given his own turn at the helm, Reagan steered in the opposite direction from the one he promised, bestowing a little eternal life of his own.

Despite his lip service toward smaller government, Reagan did not abolish even one government department or agency. And when he left office, there were seventy thousand more bureaucrats on the federal payroll than when he began.

But one has the feeling that Reagan accepted his inability to make government smaller with regret. By contrast, George W. Bush jumps into his ability to make government larger with glee. His legacy includes three monstrous new government programs: No Child Left Behind, the Department of Homeland Security, and Medicare Part D.

No Bureaucrat Left Behind

Laura and I really don't realize how bright our children is sometimes until we get an objective analysis.

George W. Bush

For fifty years, believing states should be free to run their own schools, conservatives ran for president vowing to eliminate the Department of Education. By the second year of his presidency, George W. Bush had doubled the department's size with the educational reform program he called "No Child Left Behind" (NCLB).

Originally hailed as a bipartisan victory for America's schoolchildren, NCLB has had mixed results, at best. Dubbed "No Child Left Untested," "No School Board Left Standing," and "No Child's Behind Left," among other nicknames, the program has been legally challenged by forty-seven out of fifty states. The Republican governor of Connecticut has sued the Department of Education over what it claims are "unfunded mandates," and many school districts have simply turned down federal funds rather than comply with NCLB's requirements.

Critics claim that No Child Left Behind places too much emphasis on test scores, forcing teachers to "teach to the tests"; it tries to force all schools into the same "cookie-cutter" program; it kills state and local initiative; and it requires states to jump through federal hoops without reimbursing them for the extra time and employees required to do so. In 2005, the White House Office of Management and Budget acknowledged that NCLB had increased state and local governments' annual paperwork by 6,680,334 hours at a cost of $141 million—all of which states and cities had to eat.

But our point here is not to assess the merits or the demerits of the program, as controversial as it may be. Our point is that what Bush's No Child Left Behind really left behind was the conservative dream of abolishing, or at least minimizing the role of, the federal Department of Education.

Through 1996, elimination of the Department of Education was a plank in the Republican Party platform. As Senator Bob Dole explained, "We're going to eliminate the Department of Education. We don't need it in the first place. I didn't vote for it in 1979." Today, the department is the biggest it's ever been since its creation in 1979, and it keeps growing. In the last five years, Education's budget has grown by a stunning 79.9 percent. When it comes to the federal role in education, it seems, small is no longer beautiful to the conservative mind.

Department of Homeland Bureaucracy

After 9/11, legislators panicked. Terrorists inspired by Osama bin Laden had managed to commandeer and fly four commercial jets through a gaping hole in our national security. Since, in legislative minds, the solution to every problem is another bill, members of Congress were desperate to write new legislation. But what?

Big-government Democrats were joined by big-government Republicans in pressing for a new government agency, ostensibly to protect the United States from future terrorist attacks. At first, President Bush resisted, insisting he had already taken care of the problem by creating the new position of security chief inside the White House, to which he named the former Pennsylvania governor Tom Ridge. Bush also strongly opposed plans by Democrats to allow homeland security employees to join a union.

Eventually, Bush caved in on the new agency but not on the union. Now, however, the tables were turned. Democrats like the Georgia senator Max Cleland, who opposed Bush's nonunion homeland security plan, were targeted as being soft on terror. Enough Democrats finally voted with Bush and the Republicans to create a new, nonunion agency.

And thus was born, on March 1, 2003, the gargantuan Department of Homeland Security, or DHS—the biggest explosion of federal government in fifty years. With 184,000 employees and a budget of more than $44 billion, DHS immediately became the third-largest government agency, surpassed only by the Department of Defense and the Department of Veterans Affairs. And it is easily the most disorganized, most inefficient, and least necessary of all.

Under one roof are now contained twenty-two previously disparate government agencies that have little to do with each other and, in some cases, little to do with terrorism. They range from the Coast Guard to the Secret Service, to the Border Patrol, to the Passport Bureau—which are now housed under the same roof as the Animal and Plant Health Inspection Service, whose job it is to protect the country from invasive insects and weeds, not terrorists.

And, of course, DHS now includes the hapless FEMA, which, as discussed in chapter 6, was stripped of its original mission of preparing for natural disasters and buried so deep in the DHS bureaucracy that it was unable to respond when Hurricane Katrina struck in August 2005.

Probably not even the DHS secretary Michael Chertoff knows who's under his command and why, or how to reach them if necessary. But the mammoth agency has quickly gained a reputation as Washington's newest and biggest cornucopia of pork. The list of cities qualifying for special antiterrorist funds has mushroomed from our seven biggest cities—and, presumably, most likely targets—to more than seventy-five today. Which means that, to protect its City Hall, Columbus, Ohio, receives funds that might otherwise be used to protect the U.S. capital.

State governments were also quick to recognize and raid the federal government's latest pork barrel. According to the agency's own inspector general, the DHS "National Asset Database" lists Indiana with 8,591 potential terrorist targets: almost 50 percent more than New York State (5,687), and more than twice as many as California (3,212). Washington State claims nearly twice as many national monuments and icons as the District of Columbia. And Montana, one of the least populous states in the nation, claims more terror targets than the big-population states of Massachusetts, North Carolina, and New Jersey.

Needless to say, not all of the potential terrorist targets proposed for DHS grants are of obvious interest to al-Qaeda. You may be surprised to learn, for example, that your homeland security tax dollars are being spent to provide chemical protection gear for such vulnerable metropolitan centers as North Pole, Alaska (population 1,750), and Outagamie County, Wisconsin (population 172,618). Not ceding any potential targets to Islamic fundamentalists, federal funds are also being used to protect Florida's Weeki Wachee Springs—a roadside resort featuring live "mermaids." We all know what a fascination terrorists have with mermaids.

While President Bush seems unaware of what a monster he's created in the DHS, those who work there are not. In a January 2007 survey of bureaucrats at thirty-six different federal agencies, DHS scored rock bottom in:

Job satisfaction—#36

Leadership and knowledge—#35

Results-oriented performance—#36

Talent management—#33

The newest, most ineffective, most disorganized, and most useless of all government agencies—this is George W. Bush's idea of smaller government.

The headquarters of the CIA is named after his father, the former CIA director George H. W. Bush. After George W. Bush leaves the White House, it would be only fitting if the DHS office building is named after him, because he is the man responsible for creating this agency.

Medicare, Lyndon Johnson Style

When George W. Bush was selected president, his advisers let reporters know that he wanted to be known as the next Ronald Reagan. What do you know? He became the next Lyndon Johnson, instead.

After Social Security, Medicare is the most important step government has ever taken to improve the lives of Americans. It was Lyndon Johnson's greatest legislative achievement, serving more than forty million senior citizens in the most efficient and cost-effective of all government programs. George W. Bush changed all that. He delivered the biggest expansion of Medicare since Johnson: prescription drug coverage, called Part D. It sounds good on its face, but Bush entrusted the management of Part D to private insurance companies. He prevented the government from negotiating for lower prices, lied about the cost of the program, and probably broke the law, in order to get his legislation passed.

Prescription drug coverage should have been part of Medicare when it was created in 1965. It wasn't included because, at the time, there weren't as many drugs available and people didn't take as many. And, besides, doctors were much more surgery-oriented. All that has changed, of course, with miracle drugs available today for people of all ages, especially seniors, and surgery considered the exception, not the rule.

So, including prescription drug coverage as part of Medicare now makes sense. The problem is, from both a conservative and a consumer point of view, George W. Bush did it the wrong way.

Part D, the biggest new government program since 1965, is the last thing conservatives expected from a so-called conservative president. Bush, in fact, knew ahead of time that conservatives wouldn't like its price tag. So he simply lied about it.

While the bill was still under consideration, the White House insisted that its price tag was $400 billion over ten years—expensive, but small enough for some conservatives in Congress to swallow. (Even so, the legislation barely passed the GOP-controlled House, 216–215.) Yet within days after the president signed the legislation in December 2003 with great fanfare in Constitution Hall, White House officials admitted that the true cost was actually $534 billion—and again, days later, said that projected total costs through 2015 could soar up to $1.2 trillion.

George Bush, in effect, snookered conservatives into another vast expansion of government by lying to Congress. In testimony before the House Ways and Means Committee, the former Medicare actuary Richard S. Foster said that he had informed Bush administration officials of the actual costs of the expanded Medicare program but was told to low-ball it or lose his job. "I felt a very strong responsibility on behalf of the public not to withhold technical information that could be useful in this debate," Foster told the committee in March 2004. "I had a difficult choice. I could ignore the orders. I knew I would get fired. . . . I considered that inappropriate and, in fact, unethical."

The White House never disputed Foster's testimony, and it was further confirmed by an e-mail to Foster from the Medicare staffer

Jeffrey Flick, which was published in the *Wall Street Journal*: "Work up the numbers and share them with Tom Scully only. NO ONE ELSE." Then Flick added in boldface: "The consequences for insubordination are extremely severe."

Order aides to lie to Congress? It's not the first time that happened in this administration, but it's still not kosher. The nonpartisan Congressional Research Service reported that by deliberately keeping Congress in the dark over the true cost of the Medicare expansion, the Bush administration may have violated five different federal laws. To date, however, the lies about Medicare, like the lies about Iraq, U.S. attorneys, undercover CIA agents, and countless other untruths put forth by this White House, will apparently go unchallenged and unpunished.

For consumers, the problem with Bush's prescription drug program is that it's a boondoggle for drug companies and private insurance companies. But what do you expect of legislation written by drug company lobbyists?

Instead of adding drug coverage to Medicare's existing benefits, the simplest and most effective way of moving forward, Bush put private insurance companies in charge, forcing seniors to wade through and choose from a swamp full of competing private plans and, in the end— surprise, surprise!—pay higher and higher prices.

Competition among private plans, rather than letting Medicare handle prescription drugs, would keep prices down, claimed the Bush White House. Not so. As reported by Families USA, the average price for the fifteen prescription drugs most commonly used by seniors increased by 9.2 percent between April 2006 and April 2007, while the consumer price index increased by only 2.4 percent. A price hike of 10 percent a year is a huge problem for people on fixed incomes—and for taxpayers, who still foot most of the Medicare bill.

Higher costs for drugs under Medicare are also assured by George Bush's biggest gift to Big Pharma: banning Medicare from negotiating with drug companies for lower prices, a practice that is used very successfully by the Veterans Administration. That's right. Under Bush's prescription drug plan, the largest purchaser of prescription drugs on the planet is prohibited from asking for a discount. Tell me that makes sense.

Thanks again to Families USA for calculating the cost of this sop to drug manufacturers. Comparing what veterans pay for the twenty most commonly used drugs with what seniors on Medicare pay for the same drugs, the median Medicare price is an astounding 58 percent higher. For the same drug! The only difference is that the VA can negotiate for lower prices, and Medicare legally cannot.

That's the unspoken underbelly of George Bush's big-government brand of conservatism. Whether it's expansion of the defense budget or Medicare, it's not just more big government—it's more big government designed to benefit private contractors. It's not government growing bigger to better serve people. It's government, made bigger, to better serve corporate America.

The Big-Government Conservative

No Child Left Behind, the Department of Homeland Security, and Medicare aren't the only examples of bigger government under George W. Bush. On top of the sixteen agencies that already handle various aspects of intelligence gathering, Bush added a new director of national intelligence, with his own built-in bureaucracy. And as if the secretary of defense, the chairman of the Joint Chiefs of Staff, and the commanders on the ground don't know enough to manage the war in Iraq, he also added a new "War Czar," operating out of the White House.

Bush also signed into law the largest transportation spending bill ever, which included Alaska's infamous $223 million "Bridge to Nowhere"—and which commentator Peggy Noonan described as a bridge connecting one island with two bears and one penguin to another island containing one bear and two penguins.

So now we know what George Bush was talking about when he called himself a "compassionate conservative." *Compassionate* means "big-spender." So much so, in fact, that the conservative commentator Fred Barnes, in his book *Rebel in Chief*, praises Bush as a totally new kind of conservative: a "big-government conservative."

Is there such an animal? Not according to Richard Viguerie, one of the founding fathers of modern conservatism. Viguerie dismisses the idea that there's any conservative virtue in big government spending as self-serving nonsense. In June 2007, he told the *New Yorker* magazine's Jeffrey Goldberg, "It's not any one thing, but when you add everything up, what you have is a massive overreach of executive powers, and massive overspending by people who claim they're conservatives."

Viguerie compares George Bush to Tom DeLay, another conservative who ended up supporting one more big-government program after another: "He's like a lot of these guys. He campaigns against the cesspool. 'I'll clean up the cesspool of government,' but after a while they all say, 'I made a mistake—it wasn't a cesspool, it was a hot tub.'"

Tom DeLay earned the nickname "Hot Tub Tom." But he's not alone. He's up to his neck in hot water with "Hot Tub Dubya."

Lesson Learned

What does the spending record of recent Republican administrations tell us about conservative governance?

Simply this: time and time again, conservatives have proved they don't know how to govern. Given the opportunity, they have either cut essential government programs to the bone, emasculating them and rendering them incapable of responding when needed, or have thrown conservative principles out the window and spent wildly and recklessly, across the board, as we saw in this chapter.

Either way, it proves that conservatives, after all the hype, are only human. Give them a credit card, and they like spending money as much as anyone else—more than a liberal, even.

But it also proves that the basic conservative governing philosophy is flawed. The smallest government is not always the best government. The cookie-cutter approach doesn't always work. Good governance requires good judgment and smart decision-making, tailoring the size of government to the real needs and demands of the time. Conservatives appear genetically incapable of this kind of analytical weighing of priorities.

If any CEO ran a major corporation the way conservatives have run the U.S. government, he or she would be fired within a year and never hired elsewhere.

Conservative politicians deserve no better treatment. They were given their chance to lead. They failed. There's too much at stake. They should not be trusted with the reins of power again.

CHAPTER 8

Less Power to Washington

I believe in states' rights and I believe in people
doing as much as they can for themselves at
the community level and at the private level.
I believe we have distorted the balance of our
government today by giving powers that
were never intended to be given in the
Constitution to that federal establishment.
Ronald Reagan, 1980

The Federal government should do only
those things specifically called for in the
Constitution. All others should remain
with the states or the people.
Bob Dole, 1995

We are committed to getting power
back to the states.
Newt Gingrich, 1995

My party is demonstrating that they are
for states' rights unless they don't like
what states are doing.
Congressman Chris Shays, 2005

It's another truism of U.S. politics: liberals believe in strong, central government; conservatives believe in limited federal government and more power to the states. Indeed, there is no issue more dear to conservatives than states' rights—and, as the Civil War proved, no issue more central to the American experience.

While the term *states' rights* does not appear in Russell Kirk's *The Politics of Prudence*, the conservative Bible, the principle is endorsed among his ten fundamental conservative principles. Number 8 reads: "Conservatives uphold voluntary community, quite as they oppose involuntary collectivism." It's up to local communities and private associations to improve the lives of citizens, Kirk argued. "When these functions pass by default or usurpation to centralized authority, then community is in serious danger."

The danger, warned Kirk, is that big government will take the place of individual, or local, decision-making. "A central administration, or a corps of select managers and civil servants, however well intentioned and well trained, cannot confer justice and prosperity and tranquility upon a mass of men and women deprived of their old responsibilities."

Richard Viguerie, the mass-mailing genius and one of the founders of modern conservatism, put it more simply. The debate over states' rights, he wrote in *Conservatives Betrayed*, is what differentiates liberals and conservatives:

> Liberals believe in turning to the government first, preferably at the highest level, regardless of constitutionality, and regardless of the fact that this empowers bureaucrats and politicians, while it weakens the power of the people. Conservatives believe that the Constitution has proved its worth, and we believe in keeping power as close to the people as possible. Such an approach is prudent from the standpoint of preserving our liberties, and efficient in terms of solving problems.

This argument is actually one of the most reasonable and compelling arguments that conservatives ever make. Yet it's always the first one they abandon whenever states dare to differ from what conservatives in Washington demand.

Take one recent and poignant example, which is usually discussed in a totally different context: the plight of Terri Schiavo.

Federal Government in the
Hospital Room

If there's anything conservatives hate more than Big Brother, it's "activist judges"—except, of course, when they're looking for activist judges to support Big Brother over the states, which was exactly the situation in the case of Terri Schiavo.

Terri Schiavo died in a hospice in Pinellas Park, Florida, on March 31, 2005. At that point, she'd been in a persistent vegetative state—unable to see, hear, talk, or respond to stimuli—for more than fifteen years. Had she by some miracle regained consciousness at the last moment, she would have been surprised to see, gathered around her deathbed in spirit, the leadership of the Republican Party—the Senate majority leader Bill Frist, the Senate whip Rick Santorum, the House majority leader Tom DeLay, and President George W. Bush—all insisting that the Congress of the United States, and not her husband, should make medical decisions for her.

It's a sad and complex story, one that you'd think would call for caution and a reliance on first principles. Republicans ended up relying on conservative political strategists, instead.

Schiavo had been in and out of hospitals, on both coasts, since she collapsed at home of cardiac arrest on the morning of February 25, 1990. After many unsuccessful attempts at rehabilitation and the findings of countless doctors that she would never recover, her legal guardian and husband, Michael, ordered that her feeding tube be removed and that no extraordinary efforts be made to keep her alive. According to Michael, he took this action in keeping with Terri's own wishes, clearly and strongly expressed in conversations they had starting early in their marriage.

Terri's parents disagreed. Convinced that their daughter would someday miraculously recover, Robert and Mary Schindler went to court to prevent the removal of Terri's feeding tube. They lost but decided to appeal. And that's where the legal battles began. By October 2003—after fourteen appeals and numerous motions, petitions, and hearings in Florida courts, and five suits in federal district courts—the courts still agreed with Michael's request to have the feeding tube removed.

By this time, however, Terri's parents had recruited Randall Terry, the media-savvy and self-promoting head of the antiabortion group Operation Rescue, to lead a crusade to keep their daughter on life-support. The fate of Terri Schiavo quickly became a national cause célèbre. And Republican politicians tripped over each other trying to "save" her—and save their Republican majorities at the same time. As a one-page memo circulated to Republican senators in Washington pointed out, whatever the correct medical diagnosis, keeping Terri Schiavo alive was "a great political issue."

First, it was the Florida governor Jeb Bush to the rescue: sponsoring and signing state legislation ordering that Terri Schiavo's feeding tube, removed by orders of a state court, be reinserted. When that legislation was ruled unconstitutional, Republican leaders in Congress stepped in. The then House majority leader Tom DeLay sponsored legislation transferring jurisdiction on this one case from state court to federal court. The Senate majority leader Bill Frist not only cosponsored the legislation, he announced from the floor of the Senate that he, as a physician, having watched a video of Terri Schiavo from hundreds of miles away, could declare her conscious, alert, and capable of a full recovery! Congress passed the Terri Schiavo legislation, known as the "Palm Sunday Compromise," and—unlike his response to Hurricane Katrina—President Bush interrupted his Texas vacation and flew back to Washington to sign the bill in the middle of the night. If only Katrina victims had claimed to be in a "vegetative" state, they might have received more presidential attention.

Plans of the Bush-DeLay-Frist posse were stymied, however, when federal judges agreed with state judges that Michael Schiavo, as her legal guardian, had legal authority to have his wife's feeding tube removed, and the Supreme Court refused to intervene.

DeLay issued a parting shot, warning judges, "The time will come for the men responsible for this to pay for their behavior." But Michael Schiavo, with the advice of Terri's doctors, was finally free to make the decision that should have been his in the first place.

Thus did Republicans make a joke out of their "firm commitment" to federalism and the separation of powers.

To their credit, not all conservatives jumped on the Schiavo steamroller. Many recognized it for what it was: a sudden, convenient, transparent abandonment of traditional conservative values for quick political gain. Treading as lightly as he could, David Davenport, of the conservative Hoover Institute, wrote, "This is a clash between the social conservatives and the process conservatives. . . . When a case like this has been heard by 19 judges in six courts and it's been appealed to the Supreme Court three times, the process has worked—even if it hasn't given the result that the social conservatives want. For Congress to step in really is a violation of federalism."

The congressman Chris Shays of Connecticut was more blunt: "My party is demonstrating that they are for states' rights unless they don't like what states are doing. This couldn't be a more classic case of a state responsibility."

But social conservatives remained blind and defiant. Appearing on FOX News shortly before Terri Schiavo's death, Newt Gingrich equated opposition to the Terri Schiavo legislation with murder: "But let me also say, every liberal I know wants every convicted death penalty murderer to have the right to appeal in the Supreme Court. And to scream 'states' rights' when the parents of an innocent person want to appeal to the Supreme Court strikes me as an amazing double standard in favor of murderers and against the innocent."

Unbelievable! Newt almost convinces you that liberals, and not conservatives, were the real hypocrites in this case. But it was conservatives, not liberals, who had preached states' rights for decades—and conservatives, not liberals, who abandoned states' rights in the Terri Schiavo case.

Tom DeLay resorted to the tactic that's always used by politicians when things blow up in their faces: blame it on the media. "I really think it is interesting that the media is defining what conservatism is," he grumbled. "The conservative doctrine here is the Constitution of the United States."

Yes, and the Constitution clearly establishes the United States as a federalist system, bound by the rule of law and limited by the separation of powers, where private, domestic matters are litigated in state courts and where Congress does not override decisions of the court simply because it doesn't like them.

Despite all the brouhaha and the conservative flip-flopping on the issue, the Terri Schiavo debate was really nothing new. It was but the latest manifestation of a question that's been argued, sometimes more publicly than others, since the earliest days of the republic.

States' Rights or Else

The debate over states' rights arguably began before there were states. It started in the colonies, moved on to Philadelphia in 1786, and has been raging ever since. It was the main item of contention among our Founding Fathers at the Constitutional Convention. It split the members of George Washington's Cabinet right down the middle. It dominated the early decisions of the Supreme Court. It sparked the Civil War. And it still lies at the heart of the debate over many of the most contentious domestic issues in Congress today, from medical marijuana to gay marriage, to global warming, to abortion.

On CNN's *Crossfire*, which I cohosted for six years with Bob Novak, Pat Buchanan, Mary Matalin, and other conservative voices, I remember the then Senate majority leader Bob Dole pulling out of his pocket a tattered copy of the Constitution, folded open to the Tenth Amendment. He carried it with him at all times. And in 1996 he made returning power to the states the heart of his challenge to President Bill Clinton.

The question of where the rights of states end and the obligations of the federal government begin is the classic American dilemma. Getting it wrong, as we sometimes have, is what derails the United States. Getting it right, which we more often do, is what keeps the United States on track. Debate over the issue divided conservatives from liberals—with conservatives favoring strong states' rights and progressives, a strong central government—until recently, when conservatives switched sides.

Round One, shaping the Articles of Confederation, was won by the states. Having won independence from a remote and repressive seat of power, the states were understandably and collectively hesitant about ceding authority to another. The articles, in fact, contained the clause "Each state retains its sovereignty, freedom and independence."

Without that declaration, of course, no banding together of the original colonies would have been possible. Yet because of it, as soon became evident, few collective goals could be achieved. Under the articles, Congress could not levy taxes directly, regulate trade, or draft troops, and nine of the thirteen states had to approve most actions. Had the Articles of Confederation not soon been supplanted by a stronger bond, George Washington's prediction would no doubt have come true: "Thirteen sovereignties, pulling against each other, and all tug-ging at the federal head, will soon bring ruin on the whole."

So Round Two went to the federal government—but barely. Delegates to the Constitutional Convention gave Congress broad pow-ers to declare war, pass navigation acts, collect taxes, and "regulate com-merce among the several states," yet there were no sanctions laid out for states that refused to comply—or states that adopted measures more strict than the federal government's. Even the critical issue of slavery posed more trouble as a states' rights issue than as a moral issue to the Founders. It came down to a debate over who would decide the terms of its existence—the states, acting individually, or Congress, acting col-lectively—and not over the merits of the practice. In the end, delegates settled on a compromise: slavery would continue on a state-by-state basis, each slave would be counted as three-fifths of a person, but the importation of new slaves would cease in 1808. That compromise merely delayed dealing with the greatest moral issue of the day. But without it, acknowledged the strong federalist Alexander Hamilton, "no union could possibly have been formed."

A similar compromise, called the "Great Compromise," resolved the thorny issue of which states had more clout: large or small, urban or rural. Assigning each state two equal votes in the Senate assured that smaller states had a strong voice. Basing representation in the House of Representatives on population gave larger states their due.

Still, the former colonies, both North and South, were nervous and suspicious of a strong central government that could take away both the rights of individuals and the rights of states. The only way the Founders were able to achieve ratification of the Constitution was to promise, ahead of time, to amend it immediately, once it was adopted. And those first ten amendments, the Bill of Rights, ended with the clas-sic affirmation of states' rights:

> The powers not delegated to the United States by the Constitution, nor prohibited by it to the states, are reserved to the states respectively, or to the people.

Of course, that wasn't the end of the battle over states' rights. It was just the beginning. One of its earliest manifestations was the debate over formation of a federal bank, pitting Alexander Hamilton, the bank's champion and George Washington's treasury secretary, against Secretary of State Thomas Jefferson. Jefferson even conspired with Congressman James Madison to impeach Hamilton over the issue but failed.

Jefferson also feared that by their efforts to shape a strong central government, Hamilton and Vice President John Adams were actually trying to reintroduce monarchy onto American soil. So he worked aggressively to undermine any strengthening of Congress or the executive branch—sometimes publicly, sometimes privately.

On March 4, 1797, John Adams took the oath of office as the second president of the United States, and the runner-up Thomas Jefferson became his reluctant and ever suspicious vice president. To Adams's ever-lasting discredit, he signed the Alien and Sedition Act in 1798. A blatantly unconstitutional suppression of free speech, it confirmed Jefferson's worst fears and drove him, in turn, to take extreme measures. Even while serving as Adams's vice president, Jefferson drafted a set of resolutions to be introduced in the Kentucky legislature. The Kentucky Resolutions, as with similar Virginia resolutions authored by James Madison, in consultation with Jefferson, declared that each state had a "natural right" to nullify federal actions it deemed unconstitutional.

Did Jefferson realize the impact of his words? Did he realize that the doctrine of "nullification" could—and would, sixty-two years later!—lead to civil war? Yes, he did.

Jefferson felt so strongly about states' rights, in fact, that he was willing to take the chance of dissolution. He was confident that other states would support Kentucky's nullification initiative, he wrote to James Madison. But, if not, he and other antifederalists remained "determined, were we to be disappointed in this, to sever ourselves from the union we so much value, rather than give up the rights of self-government."

There's no doubt where we'd be today, had Jefferson succeeded. This great nation of ours would no longer exist.

So, the debate over states' rights has serious consequences. There is no more critical political debate. At least in theory, if not always in practice, modern conservatives have continued to affirm their support for states' rights—fortunately, without being willing to go as far as Jefferson.

Conservatives and States' Rights

Both Richard Nixon and Ronald Reagan committed their presidencies to what they called "New Federalism." Attempting to reverse the trend toward a more powerful central government that began in FDR's New Deal and continued in Lyndon Johnson's Great Society, they promised to return power to the states while limiting actions of the federal government to those explicitly spelled out in the Constitution. Interestingly, at the time, many conservative states' rights advocates relied partially on a finding made by the liberal Justice Louis Brandeis in his dissent to an obscure 1932 Supreme Court decision regarding a government permit to operate an ice business in Oklahoma City: "It is one of the happy incidents of the federal system that a single courageous state may, if its citizens choose, serve as a laboratory; and try novel social and economic experiments without risk to the rest of the country."

Nixon spelled out his own state versus federal philosophy in 1972:

Do we want to turn more power over to the bureaucrats in Washington in the hope that they will do what is best for all the people? Or do we want to return more power to the people themselves. . . . I will continue to direct the flow of power away from Washington and back to the people.

Nixon's vehicle for so doing was what he called "revenue sharing": giving block grants to cities and counties to deal with such problems as the homeless, food stamps, or medical care for the indigent and letting local governments resolve matters in their own fashion, with little federal oversight.

On October 26, 1987, Ronald Reagan signed an Executive Order on Federalism, authorizing federal agencies to launch new programs "only when authority for the action may be found in a specific provision of the Constitution, there is no provision in the Constitution prohibiting Federal action, and the action does not encroach upon authority reserved to the States." At the same time, he cancelled Nixon's revenue-sharing formula because, he argued, it just encouraged states to spend more money.

When it came to states' rights, both Nixon and Reagan talked the talk. But, as we have seen, they did not exactly walk the walk. The out-come of both of their administrations was a bigger, more intrusive, more expensive federal government.

Despite Richard Nixon's talk of devolving power to the states, he created several new government agencies, including the Environmental Protection Agency, the Drug Enforcement Agency, the Occupational Safety and Health Administration, and the National Oceanic and Atmospheric Administration. He signed legislation establishing the Clean Air Act, the Clean Water Act, and the National Environmental Policy Act. And he mandated a nationwide speed limit of 55 miles per hour.

Now, I would argue that all of those Nixon accomplishments are important—laudable, in fact—but, contrary to Nixonian rhetoric, they all resulted in more power to Washington and less to the states.

And the same can be said of Reagan. His rhetoric about returning power to the states is contradicted by the facts. As we saw in chapter 7, he left behind a bigger federal government, a bigger federal workforce, a bigger federal budget, and a bigger federal budget deficit than when he took office. Not one government department or agency was elimi-nated during his presidency. Again, more power in Washington meant less power to the states.

States' Rights and Civil Rights

At this point, it's important to take time out to examine one uncomfort-able sidebar to the conservative emphasis on states' rights: its close and undeniable connection to the campaign against civil rights.

For many people in this country, especially in the South, the issue of states' rights has always had two meanings. One was the all-American message of local control: more power to the states, less power to the central government. But the other side was the sinister message of Jim Crow: let states decide how they want to handle the "problem" of "the Negro" race. The federal government had no business telling states who was allowed to worship in their churches, attend their schools, or sit at their lunch counters. "States' rule" was nothing but a euphemism for "white man's rules."

It was no accident, then, that Ronald Reagan agreed to make the first appearance of his 1980 presidential campaign in Philadelphia, Mississippi, of all places. One might think the former California governor would announce in Los Angeles or his boyhood home of Tampico, Illinois, for example. Oh, no, he deliberately went to Philadelphia, Mississippi.

Philadelphia was famous for one thing. It wasn't the capital of Mississippi or its largest city. Hardly remembered as a city of brotherly love, Philadelphia was known only as the site of the murders on June 21, 1964, of three civil rights workers: James Chaney, Andrew Goodman, and Michael Schwerner. This was one of the most shocking chapters in the civil rights movement, later memorialized in the 1988 movie *Mississippi Burning*.

Reagan knew where he was, and why. When he declared, "I believe in states' rights" in Philadelphia, Mississippi, he was speaking in a code that all good white Southern boys would understand. To the rest of the country, he might have been merely reaffirming the principles of the Tenth Amendment. To the South, he was saying, I believe in the right of states to decide for themselves on the race question—whether blacks should be allowed to vote, whether their kids should be allowed to attend public schools, or whether they would be accepted by state colleges and universities.

Nor is it a mere coincidence that Reagan was invited to launch his presidential campaign in Philadelphia, Mississippi, by the then Mississippi congressman Trent Lott. Yes, the same Trent Lott who, as a U.S. senator, met several times with the leadership of the Council of Conservative Citizens (CCC), a direct descendant of the Ku Klux Klan (KKK), and gave the keynote address at one of their conferences. And the same Trent Lott who lost his job as Senate majority leader for asserting the country would be better off had segregationist Strom Thurmond been elected president in 1948 when he ran as the candidate of the—note!—"States' Rights Democratic Party."

Nowhere is the link between states' rights and civil rights more exposed than in the platform of Thurmond's States' Rights Democratic Party. His campaign for president—conducted in 1948, before he found a home for his beliefs in the modern Republican Party—was built on three principles spelled out in the platform:

> We favor home-rule, local self-government, and a minimum interference with individual rights.

We stand for the segregation of the races and the racial integrity of each race.

We oppose the totalitarian, centralized bureaucratic government and the police nation called for by the platforms adopted by the Democratic and Republican Conventions.

This is not to say that Ronald Reagan or Trent Lott were racists. But it is to say that Reagan, Lott, and many other conservatives played the states' rights card willingly, knowing that, in the minds of many supporters, they were playing the race card, too.

Indeed, how could they not? After all, the ultimate contest over states' rights was the Civil War, which was fought over the right of states to perpetuate the "peculiar institution" of slavery. As we saw earlier, the seeds of secession were originally sown by Thomas Jefferson, in his support for nullification. That cause was taken up in the U.S. Senate by South Carolina's fiery John C. Calhoun, who led the fight for nullification over two issues the Northern states were pushing to what he perceived to be the detriment of Southern states: textile tariffs and ending slavery. Calhoun's call for states' rights—and, later, for slavery as a "positive good"—became the antebellum rallying cry of the South and led directly to war among the states, ten years after his death.

Lest there be any doubt what the "Civil War" was really all about, there are still groups today that reject that terminology. To them, the Civil War will always be known as "The War for States' Rights." And it's still being fought by those who prefer to cloak their racism in the rhetoric of states' rights rather than in the white sheets of the KKK.

Bush and States' Rights

If Nixon and Reagan, despite their state-friendly rhetoric, actually eroded states' rights, George W. Bush obliterated them.

His rhetoric toward the states was positive, too. As governor of Texas, Bush spoke often of the need to protect the independence and the authority of states. He campaigned in 2000 as the states' rights candidate, running against the big government's representative, Al Gore.

Then came Florida 2000—and states' rights went right out the window.

Look, I'm not trying to beat a dead horse. This is not the time to remount the recount. We all know that Gore won anyway, but the milk has already spilled, so to speak. Still, whatever you think of the outcome, you must admit: *George W. Bush would not be president today had not the candidate, the Republican Party, and, ultimately, the Supreme Court been willing to abandon their traditional support for states' rights—and let Washington dictate the outcome of the election.*

The conduct of elections is a local matter. The date of presidential elections is set by Congress, period. Everything else is left to the states and the local governments: what measures will be on the ballot; how many polling places will be open, how long, and where they will be located; whether voters may cast their ballot by mail; whether they can vote early; what language the ballot pamphlets are printed in; whether provisional ballots are allowed; how and where ballots are counted and the results announced—and, most important for this discussion, what happens when the results are so close that a recount seems necessary.

In 2000, the state of Florida had such rules in place, including rules for a recount. But it clearly made one hell of a mess trying to apply them.

Had this merely been a statewide election, Florida might have muddled through. But this election was about much, much more. This election would determine the next president of the United States. And there were too many forces with too much at stake to let Florida's elections officials simply take their time and do their job.

One major problem, as we all know, is that Florida's chief elections official, Secretary of State Katherine Harris, was also cochair of the Bush 2000 Florida campaign. Once the polls closed, she took off her secretary's hat, put on her Bush hat, and did everything she could to throw the election to her candidate: resisting a statewide recount, giving counties an impossible deadline, refusing to certify county returns, and issuing confusing and contradictory orders.

Again, being good at running a campaign doesn't mean you're good at governing. But using your government job to influence or win a campaign is key to the Bush governing philosophy.

Harris was not alone, though. She had accomplices in creating postelection chaos: competing daily news conferences by Jim Baker, for Bush, and Warren Christopher, for Gore; a series of unimpressive judges suddenly thrust into the national spotlight; planeloads of

Republican staffers who were flown from Capitol Hill to Florida to mau-mau local elections officials and disrupt the recount; more out-of-state attorneys assembled than at any time since the last convention of the American Trial Lawyers Association; and, sadly, a Democratic candidate who initially failed to request a statewide recount, as provided by law, and instead said he'd settle for a recount of only those few counties where he thought he could pick up the most extra votes.

It was indeed a total circus, but, eventually, it would have worked itself out. All the votes would have been counted. And the Supreme Court of Florida would have declared either Al Gore or George W. Bush the winner of Florida's electoral votes—and, therefore, the next president of the United States.

But it didn't work out that way. For the first time in history, the Supreme Court of the United States took responsibility for running elections out of the hands of the state. To Florida, the court said, in effect: "Look, you're making a mess of this. We can't wait any longer for you to get it right. You stop counting votes, and we'll declare the winner."

I'll never forget the night the Supreme Court announced its decision: December 12, 2000. On CNN, Tucker Carlson and I broadcast *The Spin Room* live from the lawn of the nation's Capitol Building, across First Street from the court. Hundreds of people huddled on the sidewalk in biting cold weather, awaiting the court's verdict. Suddenly, reporters started running out of the press room, waving copies of the decision, and lining up in front of their cameras to tell the world: the Supreme Court, not the voters, had decided that George W. Bush would be the next president of the United States.

So much for states' rights. Five brain-dead members of the Rehnquist court bought the outrageous argument put forth by the formerly state-friendly Bush campaign and the Republican Party: that it was more important, in this case, for an arm of the federal government to step in and declare a winner—after all, some people were worried about starting their Christmas shopping!—than to let a state do its job under the Constitution.

Whatever you think of the outcome, *Bush v. Gore* was an outrageous usurpation of states' rights by the federal government and a blatant overreach by the federal courts. As Justice John Paul Stevens wrote in one of four dissents to the majority decision: "Although we may never know with complete certainty the identity of the winner of this year's Presidential election, the identity of the loser is perfectly clear. It is the Nation's confidence in the judge as the impartial guardian in the rule of law."

As outrageous as it was, stealing the election in Florida was only the beginning of the trampling of states' rights by the Bush administration.

Medicinal Marijuana Goes Up in Smoke

Medicinal marijuana is another case where the conservative Rehnquist court zigged instead of zagged.

As chief justice, Rehnquist was determined to carry out the Reagan doctrine of federalism and, through a series of Supreme Court decisions, gradually restore power to the states. And, to a certain extent, he was successful. At one time, he was even credited with recruiting four other justices—Antonin Scalia, Clarence Thomas, Anthony Kennedy, and Sandra Day O'Connor—to join with him in forming his own states' rights team on the court, known among SCOTUS watchers as "The Federalist Five."

From 1995 to 2000, with the help of his four fellow federalists, Rehnquist was able to strike down twenty-two federal laws—including laws to protect schools from guns, require background checks for handgun purchases, protect female victims of violent crimes, and require states to compensate disabled victims of discrimination—based on the argument that such decisions were best made by states, not the federal government.

But Rehnquist lost the support of his federalist team when it came to medicinal marijuana. In 1996, California voters approved Proposition 215, the "Compassionate Use Act," allowing terminally ill patients, under a doctor's care, to use marijuana to alleviate their suffering. Eight other states shortly followed California's lead. Once John Ashcroft became attorney general, however, he refused to recognize the legality of Proposition 215 and sent federal agents into California to arrest two women using marijuana with a doctor's prescription.

According to Ashcroft, representing President Bush, the Controlled Substances Act of 1970 gave the federal government overriding authority to regulate marijuana use nationwide and therefore to ban its application as a medical treatment. The two women challenged his authority. California's Ninth Circuit Court ruled that the federal act was, in fact, unconstitutional as applied to medical marijuana, and the issue ended up before the Supreme Court.

Veteran court-watchers thought it would be a slam-dunk for the states. After all, voters in nine states had decided the matter. And since the marijuana was home-grown, the case had nothing to do with crossing state lines and therefore would not fit under Congress's constitutional authority to regulate interstate commerce, which was the argument most often used to justify any expansion of federal authority.

Au contraire, argued George W. Bush's Justice Department. As evidence of just how far conservatives are willing to go to throw conservatism out the window, the solicitor general Paul Clement actually cited court precedents that were originally used to justify FDR's New Deal in arguing that since there was a national market for marijuana, Congress had a right to assert jurisdiction over any individual's use of the plant.

Rehnquist, suffering from thyroid cancer, was not present for the final arguments. Had he been in court, he might have groaned out loud upon hearing Justice Scalia, once a big supporter of states' rights, justify his big flip-flop on marijuana: "Why is this not economic activity? This marijuana that's grown is like wheat. Since it's grown, it doesn't have to be bought elsewhere." No liberal could have justified federal power better.

The court's ruling on medicinal marijuana proved, once again, the inconsistency of conservatives on states' rights. They go back and forth, depending on their personal preferences, instead of on the merits of the issue. They don't like marijuana, so they willingly take drug control decisions out of state hands. But they do like guns, so they just as willingly leave gun control decisions up to the states.

As for marriage, conservatives must like the institution of marriage so much, they don't trust states to handle it.

Only One Man and One Woman
Need Apply

When I was growing up in northern Delaware, a town named Elkton, in Maryland just over the state line, had a reputation as the world's easiest place to get married—or divorced.

Elkton's reputation has long been surpassed by Las Vegas, but the point remains: it was up to states and cities to decide how much you paid for a marriage license, how long you had to wait for the ceremony, how many witnesses were required, or, the other side of the coin, how quickly you could get divorced. Across the United States, civil marriages were civil ceremonies performed according to the local civil code.

Then, early in 2004, two things happened to change everything. Massachusetts became the first state to recognize civil marriage between two men or two women. And the San Francisco mayor Gavin Newsome authorized city officials to begin performing gay marriages at City Hall.

On February 25, 2004, President Bush, facing a tough reelection challenge from John Kerry and needing an issue to appease the religious right, endorsed a constitutional amendment to ban gay marriage.

Everybody, including George W. Bush, knew the amendment was going nowhere. It failed to pass twice, in a Republican-controlled Senate. It won't even be considered in a Democratic-controlled Senate. Nevertheless, the amendment had already served its purpose. Together with eleven separate anti–gay marriage state ballot initiatives placed on the ballot by religious conservatives, it provided a "wedge issue" around which to rally conservative voters in 2004—even if, by taking power from the states, the gay marriage amendment was a most unconservative measure.

Former states' rights champion Bush defended his U-turn on gay marriage as necessary because "attempts to redefine marriage in a single state or city could have serious consequences throughout the country." Yet no one could trace either one marriage or one divorce in the forty-nine other states to a gay marriage that took place in Massachusetts.

Some leading conservatives were so embarrassed by Bush's obvious abandonment of states' rights for immediate political gain that they publicly disagreed with the president. "States have the right to make bad decisions," argued the former Georgia congressman Bob Barr. Barr also pointed out that the 1996 Defense of Marriage Act, banning federal recognition of same-sex marriage, in effect made the proposed constitutional amendment redundant.

Congressman Barr was joined in his opposition by the Arizona senator John McCain. "The constitutional amendment we're debating today strikes me as antithetical in every way to the core philosophy of Republicans," he said on the Senate floor. "The amendment usurps from the states a fundamental authority they have always possessed and imposes a federal remedy for a problem that most states do not believe confronts them." And a similar argument was made by the conservative columnist George Will in the *Washington Post*: "[I]t would be especially imprudent to end state responsibility for marriage law at a moment when we require evidence of the sort that can be generated by allowing the states to be laboratories of social policy."

But perhaps the strongest opposition to Bush's constitutional amendment came from his own vice president. Of course, it's personal with Cheney. Denying gays and lesbians the right to get married means denying his daughter Mary the right to marry her long-time partner Heather Poe. In his 2000 debate against Joe Lieberman, when forced to take sides between Bush and his daughter, Cheney chose to stand with his daughter—and, by extension, with all gay Americans.

> The fact of the matter, of course, is that same-sex relationship is regulated by the states. I think different states are likely to come to different conclusions, and that's appropriate. I don't think there should necessarily be a federal policy in this area. I try to be open-minded about it as much as I can, and tolerant of those relationships. I think we ought to do everything we can to tolerate and accommodate whatever kind of relationships people want to enter into.

What do you know? Aren't families great? The experience of a gay family member, for once, made Dick Cheney sound almost reasonable. Too bad George W. Bush's own experience with illegal drugs didn't make him sound reasonable on medical marijuana.

In the end, it was also George W. Bush who remained opposed to equal rights for gays and lesbians. And George W. Bush who was so antigay, or so politically beholden to the religious right, that he was willing to amend the Constitution in order to take away from states the power to regulate the institution of marriage. He failed to do so, but not because he didn't try.

Saving the Planet

We've talked so far of issues that rightfully belonged to the states but were seized from states and transferred to Washington by so-called states' rights conservatives.

Global warming is just the opposite. Given the nature of the problem and its solutions, it's an issue that only the federal government can deal with effectively. Yet the Bush administration has not only refused to take any action on global warming, it has blocked efforts by individual states to step into the breach with strong, albeit limited, actions of their own.

For the first six years of his presidency, George W. Bush didn't even acknowledge the existence of global warming. When a panel of scientists he appointed to conduct yet another study issued their unanimous findings that global warming was a serious threat to the planet, was caused by human activity, and demanded urgent action, he simply ignored them. When two members of his Cabinet, EPA administrator Christine Whitman and Treasury Secretary Paul O'Neill, spoke publicly of the need to take global warming seriously, he fired them. And when states tried to fill the leadership vacuum, he fought them.

Under the Clean Air Act Extension of 1970, states have the right to adopt tougher emission standards than the federal government has, as long as California, the first among the states, receives a waiver from the Environmental Protection Agency (EPA). In the past, such waivers were almost automatic. After all, who's against clean air? California had applied for, and been granted, some forty waivers under the act.

But all that changed when California—first under the Democratic governor Gray Davis, and then under the Republican governor Arnold Schwarzenegger—adopted tougher emission standards on greenhouse gases that contribute to global warming. Under the California plan, automakers would be forced to cut exhaust from cars and light trucks by 25 percent and from sport-utility vehicles by 18 percent, beginning with 2009 models. Collectively, the standards would cut greenhouse-gas emissions by 392 million metric tons by 2020—the equivalent, say state experts, of taking seventy-four million cars off the road for one year.

Following California's lead, eleven other states adopted similar proposals: Connecticut, Maine, Maryland, Massachusetts, New Jersey, New York, Oregon, Pennsylvania, Rhode Island, Vermont, and Washington. Republican and Democratic governors agreed: Global warming was too serious an issue to wait any longer. If the federal government refused to act, states must.

But that assumed the EPA would, as in the past, recognize and reward state initiatives. George W. Bush had a different plan in mind. Under White House orders, the EPA rejected all state plans under the mind-boggling rationale that it had *no legislative authority to regulate global warming*.

Even the conservative Roberts Supreme Court laughed out loud at that one. In a 5–4 decision, the court pointed out the obvious: the Clean Air Act gave the government broad authority to reduce air pollution from any source, for any reason. No new legislation was required to act on global warming.

But George Bush held still another card up his sleeve. Global warming, be damned. In effect, he directed the EPA to ignore the court's ruling, while he issued an Executive Order asking all government agencies to study (yet again!) what should be done about global warming and report back to him at the end of 2008—by which time he will packing his bags for Crawford, Texas.

The twelve states, led by the California attorney general Jerry Brown, went back to court, trying to force the EPA to let them move forward. As California's Arnold Schwarzenegger and Connecticut's Jodi Rell argued in the *Washington Post* on May 21, 2007, "It's bad enough that the federal government has yet to take the threat of global warming seriously, but it borders on malfeasance for it to block the efforts of states such as California and Connecticut that are trying to protect the public's health and welfare."

The battle over global warming is one more case where conservatives demonstrated their willingness to throw the principle of states' rights out the window whenever it doesn't fit their immediate, narrow political agenda. And the irony was not lost on government experts.

Noted James Winebrake, the chairman of the public policy department at the Rochester Institute of Technology, "Traditionally, Democrats are stronger federalists at the expense of states, and conservatives and Republicans espouse stronger states' rights. In this case, the White House is dragging its feet and you have to ask why."

Why? Because George W. Bush owes his allegiance to the energy companies that helped put him in power.

Lesson Learned

Many other violations of states' rights could be cited, but from just this quick survey, three things are obvious.

First, despite their rhetoric, conservatives don't really believe in states' rights. For them, it's simply one more political slogan that they embrace when it's convenient and abandon when it's not. On less important matters, like speed limits or the legal drinking age, they believe in state sovereignty. But on more controversial issues—abortion, gay marriage, gun control, drug use, school vouchers, global warming—conservatives want federal control.

As long—and that's the second point—as they control the federal government. You watch. As soon as Democrats again control the White House and both houses of Congress, Republicans and conservatives will revert to being the strongest proponents of states' rights across the board since Thomas Jefferson.

The third lesson learned, and the most important of all, is: as a basic governing principle, the idea of states' rights is not an ironclad rule, anyway, and it never should be.

To preach, as many conservatives still do, that every task not specifically delegated to the federal government in the Constitution therefore always and forever belongs to the states is absurd. Times change, and responsibilities change. New issues arise, thus new obligations arise. Demands on government grow, and the response of government grows.

The only true rule is there is no rule.

The test of leadership is not insisting that except where spelled out in the Constitution, states always have jurisdiction. Rather, it is determining on which issue, at which time, either the state governments acting individually or the state governments acting collectively, through Congress, can do a better job.

Like conservatives' verbal commitment to small government and fiscal responsibility, their rhetoric of states' rights is just that: rhetoric, to be ignored or flouted when it doesn't serve their political interests. Blind belief in states' rights is but one more fundamental flaw in the conservative governing philosophy.

The Failure of Conservatism

The great English philosopher G. K. Chesterton once wrote, "The Christian ideal has not been tried and found wanting, it has been found difficult and left untried."

Were he alive today, Chesterton might say just the opposite about conservatism: "The conservative ideal has not been found difficult and left untried, it has been tried and found wanting."

As we've seen over the course of this book, conservatism has failed. Yet it wasn't for lack of opportunity. For the last forty years, conservative ideas have dominated the political debate. And, for most of that time, conservatives have held the key positions of power.

Now the experiment is over. Conservatism had its moment. It was given its chance. Conservatives ruled, and they blew it. Conservatism has been tried and found wanting.

Attempting to rationalize their dismal record, conservatives offer two explanations: either that the inability of conservatives to make government work more effectively means that government is simply incapable of solving problems; or that it wasn't conservatism that failed the country, but George W. Bush who failed conservatism by abandoning its most basic principles.

Both theories are demonstrably false.

Yes, it is true that as a conservative, George W. Bush is a joke. From historic deficits to preemptive wars, he delivered the exact opposite of what conservatives had always promised.

Admittedly, I say that as a liberal. But many conservatives have come to the same conclusion. The titles of their recent books alone tell the whole story:

Bruce Bartlett—*Imposter: How George W. Bush Bankrupted America and Betrayed the Reagan Legacy*

Pat Buchanan—*Where the Right Went Wrong: How Neoconservatives Subverted the Reagan Revolution and Hijacked the Bush Presidency*

John Dean—*Conservatives without Conscience*

Victor Gold—*Invasion of the Party Snatchers: How the Holy-Rollers and the Neo-Cons Destroyed the GOP*

Richard Viguerie—*Conservatives Betrayed: How George W. Bush and Other Big Government Republicans Hijacked the Conservative Cause*

Not all conservatives agree. Some are kinder to Bush. The *Weekly Standard*'s Fred Barnes, for example, defends Bush by labeling him a new kind of conservative: a "big-government conservative." But that oxymoron doesn't go over with most movement conservatives. They aren't so easily fooled. Observed the *New York Post*'s Robert George in 2004, "Two of the core principles at the heart of modern conservatism are a belief in the virtues of smaller government and a conviction that government must be held accountable to the public. . . . In this context, Bush's first term has represented a betrayal of conservative values." His second term, of course, has been even worse.

Similarly, Buchanan and other "paleocons" (noninterventionists) blame all failures of the Bush administration on Dick Cheney, Richard Perle, Paul Wolfowitz, Bill Kristol, and other war hawks, or "neocons." Of course, ideologues will never admit that their ideas were wrong, only that mistakes were made in the way their ideas were carried out. Similarly, when things go wrong, conservatives must repudiate other conservatives in order, they believe, for conservatism to survive.

But by attempting to lay all the blame on Bush and the neocons Bush surrounded himself with, Buchanan and others miss the point. True, President Bush—who first sold himself to the nation as a "compassionate conservative" from Texas, as opposed to those cold-hearted conservatives from Washington—did indeed inflict the country with the exact opposite of everything conservatives were supposed to stand for: out-of-control spending, record deficits, bloated executive power, erosion of individual liberties, a more powerful central government, and a bellicose foreign policy.

But he was only able to do so with the help of other conservatives. For the first six years of the Bush administration, remember, conservatives were in charge—of everything! Dick Cheney and Karl Rove ruled the White House; Donald Rumsfeld and Condoleezza Rice, the Cabinet; Bill Frist and Trent Lott, the Senate; Tom DeLay and Denny Hastert, the House of Representatives; William Rehnquist, Antonin Scalia, and Clarence Thomas, the Supreme Court; Jack Abramoff, the K Street lobbyists; the Heritage Foundation, the Washington think tanks; and FOX News, the media. With George W. Bush in the cat-bird seat.

They worked together. They governed as conservatives. They set forth a conservative agenda. They promoted conservative policies. If the Bush era wasn't an era of conservative unity, we'll never see one. They embodied conservatism, and they left behind a broken government. Together, they proved that conservatism is not a viable governing philosophy.

John Dean, the former White House counsel for President Nixon, sees many similarities between the Nixon White House and the Bush 43 White House. Except, he argued, the Bush administration is even worse: "Suffice it to say that no one died, nor was anyone tortured, because of Nixon's so-called Watergate abuses of power."

Both the Bush team and the Nixon team are what Dean called "authoritarian conservatives," interested in power only for the sake of power. In *Conservatives without Conscience*, Dean identified the common personality traits of authoritarians: "enemies of freedom, anti-democratic, anti-equality, highly prejudiced, mean-spirited, power hungry, Machiavellian, and amoral." Bush, Cheney, DeLay, Lott, and other conservative leaders have governed with exactly these qualities.

So it's not just George W. Bush who failed. It's conservatism itself that failed. Because, as a governing philosophy grounded in the task of opposition, it is inadequate to the task of leadership.

Why? More than anything else, because of one fundamental flaw in its makeup. Here's the heart of the problem: when you start out believing government is the enemy, which most conservatives espouse, you can't make government work. Or, to use Ronald Reagan's famous phrase, as long as you believe government itself is the problem, government can never be part of the solution. It's a nonstarter.

Putting conservatives in charge of government is like trying to build a house with a saw and a sledgehammer. No matter how skilled the carpenter, they're just the wrong tools for the job.

Here's how Alan Wolfe, the director of the Boisi Center for Religion and American Public Life at Boston College, summed up the difference between how liberals and conservatives approach the task of governing: "Liberals, while enjoying the perquisites of office, also want to be in a position to use government to solve problems. But Conservatives have different motives for wanting power. One is to prevent liberals from doing so; if government cannot be made to disappear, at least it can be prevented from doing any good."

The conservative agenda, in other words, is not about building things up. It's about tearing things down. It's not a leadership agenda. It's an opposition agenda.

But, as we've seen throughout this book, conservatism contains another fatal flaw: its distrust of government invariably leads to an over-reliance on the private sector. This leads to conservatives serving special interests over the greater public interest. And, human nature being what it is, this in turn inevitably leads to greedy public officials who are more than willing to take advantage of private cash to fatten their own pockets. Again, it's not that Democrats would never commit the same sins. Congressman William Jefferson is living proof of that. But politicians are much more likely to reap illicit, personal financial gains when their primary mission is the care and feeding of big corporations. Witness Tom DeLay, Jack Abramoff, Denny Hastert, Duke Cunningham, Rick Renzi, John Doolittle, Steve Griles, David Safavian, Ted Stevens, and other members of Washington's "culture of corruption."

It's no accident that the three most corrupt administrations of modern times—Nixon, Reagan, and Bush 43—have all been conservative, Republican administrations. Payola goes hand in hand with conservative rule. So much so, that Professor Alan Wolfe identified it as the second most common trait of conservative governance. After their goal of preventing government from accomplishing anything, he wrote, what conservatives inevitably seek

is to build a political machine in which business and the Republican Party can exchange mutual favors; business will lavish cash on politicians (called campaign contributions) while politicians will throw the money back at business (called public policy). Conservatism will always attract its share of young idealists. And young idealists will always be disillusioned by the sheer amount of corruption that people like Gingrich and DeLay generate.

Are we to conclude, therefore, that government can't work? Absolutely not. That's what conservatives want us to believe, but it's not true.

Granted, the federal government is not the solution to all social problems. There are many tasks that families, churches, cities and states, or nongovernmental organizations can perform better. But there are also many large-scale tasks that only the federal government can handle efficiently and effectively. You'll never make government work, however, if you start out hating it, undermining it, refusing to fund it, or treating it only as a means of increasing your own personal wealth and power.

Putting it another way, the embarrassing failures of the Bush administration—Enron, Katrina, No Child Left Behind, prescription drugs, out-of-control spending—do not mean that government itself is a failure. By contrast, look at FEMA under Bill Clinton, Medicare, Social Security, or the Armed Forces: all are examples of where government performs exceptionally well in carrying out very difficult and complex assignments. Rather, those embarrassments mean that George W. Bush, in particular, didn't know how to make government work, and, again, that conservatism, in general, has failed as a system of governance.

For U.S. politics, that conclusion has profound consequences. If Bush were the only problem, the solution would be easy: replace Bush with another Republican, a "true" conservative, and this nation would be back on track. That's what the disgraced former House majority leader Tom DeLay believes to be his God-given mission.

DeLay told the *New Yorker*'s Jeffrey Goldberg, "I listen to God, and what I've heard is that I'm supposed to devote myself to rebuilding the conservative base of the Republican Party, and I think we shouldn't be underestimated." Just get back to basics, DeLay argued, and conservatism will rise again in all its glory: "I see this as a cleansing process, where you can return to your principles, which are order, justice, and freedom—the basic principles of the conservative movement. We have to redefine government based on conservative principles, we have to win the war against our culture, and we have to win the war on terror."

What DeLay doesn't understand is that the problem goes a lot deeper than that. When conservatism itself, not George W. Bush, is the real problem, the solution calls for much more drastic action. Namely, we should never again trust conservatives with the leadership of our country.

Of course, I'm not alone in that judgment. To cite one example among many, Robert Borosage, the codirector of the Campaign for America's Future, echoed my argument about the inherent inadequacy of conservatism in the August 2007 edition of the *American Prospect*:

> The problem isn't incompetence or deviation from the conservative course. The problem is actual existing conservatism itself. It celebrates military prowess when the threats to our security—stateless terrorists, catastrophic climate change, proliferation of weapons of mass destruction, the growing gap between rich and poor—have no military solution. It offers no answer to a corporate sector shredding the private social contract that guaranteed many workers health care, pensions, job security, and family wages. It opposes the very reforms vital for our economic future—the transition to clean energy and conservation, support of a world-class education system, and provision of affordable health care and retirement security.

And Borosage comes to the same conclusion about what role conservatism should play in the future: "After a quarter century of conservative dominance from Reagan to Gingrich to Bush and DeLay—the verdict is in: Conservatives cannot be trusted to guide the government they scorn. Not because they are incompetent or corrupt (although incompetence and corruption abound), but because they get the world wrong."

This is not to say there isn't any role for conservatives in government. Indeed, the right has a very important role to play. Every race horse needs a pair of reins. Every automobile needs a set of brakes. Every majority needs a minority to make sure it doesn't go too far in exercising its power. And that is the proper role of conservatives. They've proved that they don't know how to govern and must never again be trusted with power. But they do serve an important purpose as members of the minority.

Conservatives are good at criticizing policy but not at shaping policy. They are good at blocking legislation, not at passing legislation. They are good at saying no but have never learned to say yes. They are good at being against everything; they just don't know how to be for anything.

And that's the decision facing us as a nation in 2008: Will we give conservatives one more chance to tear down and destroy? Or will we entrust our federal government to those who will use it to build and improve the lives of all Americans?

The Promise of Liberalism

I believe America is ready and yearning for a new agenda. Not a dogmatic agenda, but a pragmatic one. An agenda based on a straightforward premise, the very premise on which this great nation was founded: what's best for the common good?

And that is what distinguishes the progressive agenda from the conservative agenda. For liberals, or progressives—call 'em whatever you like, but I prefer "liberal"—what counts is not strict adherence to an outdated set of principles, such as "smaller government, lower taxes," but simply what works, at this point in time, to do the most good for the most people.

It's really not rocket science. Tough government regulations to clean up the air and the water make sense, not because we like big government, but because the health and well-being of all Americans depend on a clean environment, and other people don't have the right to befoul the planet and force us to breathe or swallow their pollution.

At the same time, balancing the budget makes sense, not because we like smaller government, but because we should all live within our means, even the federal government, and we have no right to saddle our children with paying the price for our wanton spending.

Nor can we abstain from change because we're afraid of making a mistake. When liberals discovered that welfare wasn't working, they fixed it by adopting the earned income tax credit and time deadlines on moving from welfare to work. But that doesn't mean we shouldn't have tried welfare to begin with. Bold leadership means being willing to fail and then change course.

It's also time to reject the absurd notion that government is the enemy. True, government is not, and should not be counted on as, the solution to all our problems. But government is the only solution to many problems and is a necessary partner in solving even more.

Besides, how can government be the enemy? Government is not some alien body. Government is nothing but *us*, acting collectively. We are the government. And we decide, acting through our elected representatives, what direction our government takes and whom it benefits.

Conservatives have used government to benefit only the wealthiest Americans, the largest defense contractors, and the biggest polluters. On any issue, a new liberal agenda will be directed to do the greatest good for the greatest number of people. To best serve, in other words, the common good. By that test, I'm convinced that the new liberal agenda must include universal health care, protection for U.S. jobs, a living wage, strong environmental protection, strong antiterrorism measures with no erosion of our fundamental constitutional rights, and a strong defense with no preemptive wars—all within the bounds of fiscal restraint.

An agenda built on those principles will help to get the United States back on track. When the public interest once again takes precedence over special interests and when the mighty resources of our government are dedicated to helping every citizen, not just the wealthy, we can once again achieve the fullness of the American dream. For, as President Franklin Roosevelt reminded us, "The test of our progress is not whether we add more to the abundance of those who have much; it is whether we provide enough for those who have little."

That's the great opportunity facing us today: to move from a conservative agenda to a liberal agenda. To give America a whole new positive direction. To stop worrying about the past, and start building for the future. To stop figuring out how to block things, and start figuring out how to get things done.

And that's what democracy is all about. Too many Americans believe that democracy was something invented by our Founding Fathers more than two hundred years ago, stored in a pretty box called the Constitution, and stuck up on a shelf.

Nothing could be more wrong. Democracy is not static, it's fluid.

Democracy was not created once and for all; it's always in the process of re-creation. Each generation of Americans gets to create the kind of democracy it wants, based on its own set of values and priorities. And now it's our turn. In the immortal words of Thomas Paine, "We have it in our power to begin the world over again." The kind of democracy we enjoy, the kind of democracy we hand over to our kids, will be the kind of democracy we shape ourselves.

It's an awesome responsibility, but it's also how we fulfill our role as citizens of this great land. That's what President John F. Kennedy had in mind, I believe, when he gave what is the best definition of patriotism I've ever heard. President Kennedy once said, "We love our country, not so much for what it was—although we can be proud of that. We love our country, not even so much for what it is today—although we can be proud of that, too. We love our country for what it can be and, if we all work together, what someday it will be."

It is in that spirit, then, that we move forward: not lamenting how much we have lost, but celebrating how far we have come—and rejoicing in the certainty that America's best days are still ahead of us.

Bibliography

Anrig, Greg. *The Conservatives Have No Clothes: Why Right-Wing Ideas Are Failing*. Hoboken, N.J.: John Wiley & Sons, 2007.

Bartlett, Bruce. *Imposter: How George W. Bush Bankrupted America and Betrayed the Reagan Legacy*. New York: Doubleday, 2006.

Bowen, Catherine Drinker. *Miracle at Philadelphia: The Story of the Constitutional Convention*. Philadelphia: Little, Brown, 1966.

Brands, H. W. *TR: The Last Romantic*. New York: Basic Books, 1997.

Bridges, Linda, and John R. Coyne Jr. *Strictly Right: William F. Buckley Jr. and the American Conservative Movement*. Hoboken, N.J.: John Wiley & Sons, 2007.

Buchanan, Patrick J. *Where the Right Went Wrong: How Neoconservatives Subverted the Reagan Revolution and Hijacked the Bush Presidency*. New York: St. Martin's Press, 2004.

Brzezinski, Zbigniew. *Second Chance: Three Presidents and the Crisis of American Superpower*. New York: Basic Books, 2007.

Cannon, Lou. *Reagan*. New York: G. P. Putnam's Sons, 1982.

Clarke, Richard. *Against All Enemies: Inside America's War on Terror*. New York: Free Press, 2004.

Condon Jr., George E., with Marcus Stern, Jerry Kammer, and Dean Calbreath. *The Wrong Stuff: The Extraordinary Saga of Randy "Duke" Cunningham, the Most Corrupt Congressman Ever Caught*. New York: Public Affairs, 2007.

Dean, John. *Broken Government. How Republican Rule Destroyed the Legislative, Executive, and Judicial Branches*. New York: Viking, 2007.

———. *Conservatives without Conscience*. New York: Viking Penguin, 2006.

Draper, Robert. *Dead Certain: The Presidency of George W. Bush.* New York: Free Press, 2007.

Gold, Victor. *Invasion of the Party Snatchers: How the Holy-Rollers and Neo-Cons Destroyed the GOP.* Naperville, Ill.: Sourcebooks, Inc., 2007.

Gore, Al. *The Assault on Reason.* New York: The Penguin Press, 2007.

Hoff, Joan. *Nixon Reconsidered.* New York: Basic Books, 1994.

Johnson, Haynes. *Sleepwalking through History: America in the Reagan Years.* New York: W. W. Norton, 1991.

Kirk, Russell. *The Conservative Mind.* Washington, D.C.: Regnery Publishing, 1953. Citations are from the 7th revised edition, 2001.

———. *The Politics of Prudence.* Wilmington, Del.: ISI Books, 1993.

McCullough, David. *John Adams.* New York: Simon & Schuster, 2001.

———. *Truman.* New York: Simon & Schuster, 1992.

Novak, Robert. *The Prince of Darkness: 50 Years of Reporting in Washington.* New York: Crown Forum, 2007.

Perlstein, Rick. *Before the Storm: Barry Goldwater and the Unmaking of the American Consensus.* New York: Hill & Wang, 2001.

Reeves, Richard. *President Reagan: The Triumph of Imagination.* New York: Simon & Schuster, 2005.

Stockman, David A. *The Triumph of Politics: Why the Reagan Revolution Failed.* New York: Harper & Row, 1986.

Viguerie, Richard A. *Conservatives Betrayed: How George W. Bush and Other Big Government Republicans Hijacked the Conservative Cause.* Los Angeles: Bonus Books, 2006.

Wills, Garry. *A Necessary Evil: A History of American Distrust of Government.* New York: Simon & Schuster, 1999.

Woodward, Bob. *Bush at War.* New York: Simon & Schuster, 2002.

Index